Native American Herbalist's Bible

20 Books in 1

*Over 600+ Medicinal Plants & Herbal Remedies to Build Your Own
Herbal Dispensatory and Naturally Improve
Your Wellness*

Awenasa Sandoval

Table of Contents

BOOK 1: INTRODUCTION TO NATIVE AMERICAN 6

Chapter 1: History and Origins.. 7

Chapter 2: Native Americans and Their Connection with Nature ... 13

Chapter 3: The Basic Principles of Native Americans.................. 20

Chapter 4: History of Herbalism 25

Chapter 5: Traditional Medicine and Herbalism........................ 29

BOOK 2: NATIVE AMERICAN HERBAL REMEDIES 32

Chapter 1: Herbalism's Historical Overview............................. 33

Chapter 2: Herbal Treatment for Common Diseases 35

BOOK 3: NATIVE AMERICAN HERBALISM ENCYCLOPEDIA VOL 1 47

Chapter 1: The Foundations of Native American Herbalism 48

Chapter 2: The Top 200 Herbal Medicines 50

BOOK 4: NATIVE AMERICAN HERBALISM ENCYCLOPEDIA VOL 2........................ 80

Chapter 1: The Best 200 Medical Herbs To Use For Everything 81

BOOK 5: NATIVE AMERICAN ESSENTIAL OILS VOL 1 115

Chapter 1: An Overview of Essential Oils.................................116

Chapter 2: How Using Oils Can Help You Feel Better 119

Chapter 3: How to Use Essential Oils 124

Chapter 4: How to Store Essential Oils 128

BOOK 6: NATIVE AMERICAN ESSENTIAL OILS VOL 2 132

Chapter 1: List of All Crucial Essential Oils 133

BOOK 7: NATIVE AMERICAN SPIRITUALITY.........................137

Chapter 1: Native Americans' Beliefs and Practises 138

Chapter 2: Indigenous Peoples Religion and Medicine................ 144

BOOK 8: NATIVE AMERICAN NATURAL MEDICINE 150

Chapter 1: The Cherokee Legend..151

Chapter 2: Sacred Medicines for Native Americans.....................155

Chapter 3: The Main Medicinal Plants Used by Native Americans 160

BOOK 9: NATIVE AMERICAN STONES & CRYSTALS **166**
Chapter 1: Basic Information About Healing Stones and Crystals 167
Chapter 2: Common Stones and Crystals 174

BOOK 10: NATIVE AMERICAN HERBAL GARDENING **180**
Chapter 1: Primary Gardening Tools and Herbalist Equipment 181
Chapter 2: The Two Types of Beginner-Friendly Gardens 191
Chapter 3: Explains How to Prepare and Plant Your Herbs............................ 200
Chapter 4: Tips for Growing Herbs In Your Garden 205

BOOK 11: HERBAL RECIPES FOR YOUR CHILD'S HEALTH **209**
Chapter 1: Common Medicinal Herbs and Their Properties............................ 210
Chapter 3: Homemade Herbs Recipes for Kid's Health 218

BOOK 12: NATIVE AMERICANS DO IT YOURSELF **222**
Chapter 1: Infusions 223
Chapter 2: Tea 225
Chapter 3: Decoction 227
Chapter 4: Popsicles 229
Chapter 5: Baths 231
Chapter 6: Washcloths 233

BOOK 13: NATIVE AMERICAN DISPENSATORY **236**
Chapter 1: Native American Medicine 237
Chapter 2: Process of Extraction 249
Chapter 3: Different Methods for Preparing And Using Your Herbs 254
Chapter 4: The Method for Storing Your Herbs in 265

BOOK 14: NATIVE AMERICAN MEDICINAL PLANTS **269**
Chapter 1: Plants for Beauty 270
Chapter 2: Medicinal Plants 273
Chapter 4: Plants for Wealth 278
Chapter 5: Plants for Good Luck 281
Chapter 6: Plants for Protection 283

BOOK 15: HERBALISM AND NATURAL MEDICINE **286**
　Chapter 1: Introduction to Herbalism...287
　Chapter 2: History and Philosophy of Herbalism.................................289
　Chapter 3: Basics of Natural Medicine 291
　Chapter 4: Mind-Body Connection in Natural Healing 293

BOOK 16: NATIVE AMERICAN TINCTURES..**295**
　Chapter 1: Introduction to Herbal Tinctures 296
　Chapter 2: Preparation of Tinctures 298
　Chapter 3: Utilizing Tinctures for Health and Well-being 300

BOOK 17: NATIVE AMERICAN INFUSIONS **302**
　Chapter 1: Herbal Infusions: Basic Concepts....................................303
　Chapter 2: Preparation and Usage of Infusions 305
　Chapter 3: Infusions for Health and Treatment of Specific Disorders ...307

BOOK 18: NATIVE AMERICAN REMEDIES FOR COMMON AILMENTS **310**
　Chapter 1: Headaches and Migraines..311
　Chapter 2: Insomnia and Sleep Disorders 313
　Chapter 3: Digestive Disorders 315
　Chapter 4: Skin Conditions 317

BOOK 19: NATIVE AMERICAN ANTIBIOTICS...**319**
　Chapter 1: Key Concepts of Natural Antibiotics................................320
　Chapter 2: Herbs with Antibacterial Properties................................322
　Chapter 3: Using Natural Antibiotics for Infections and Diseases 324

BOOK 20: NATIVE AMERICAN MEDICINAL HERBS AND NATURAL REMEDIES...............**326**
　Chapter 1: Introduction to Medicinal Herbs 327
　Chapter 2: Preparation and Usage of Medicinal Herbs......................329
　Chapter 3: Natural Remedies for Specific Health Issues 331

CONCLUSION **334**

Book 1:
Introduction to Native American

Chapter 1:
History and Origins

One of the most intriguing and well-known minority groups in North America is the Native American population. Their culture is still very much alive today, and their history dates back thousands of years. We will look at Native Americans' ancestry and connection to the land in this part article. From the entrance of the Europeans to the present, we shall also examine some of the pivotal moments in their history. Understanding Native American culture and history is crucial to empowering oneself as a member of this minority group since knowledge truly is power.

Pre-Columbian Period

Before Columbus' voyage to America in 1492, there was a period known as the Pre-Columbian Era. Mesoamerican, South American, and North American civilizations all flourished throughout this time period. Pre-Columbian cultures were diverse and intricate, and many of their customs and beliefs have now been lost.

Before Columbus arrived, Mesoamerica was the part of the Americas with the highest population density. One of the most evolved pre-Columbian civilizations, the Maya had a sophisticated hieroglyphics system, a calendar, and a writing system known as Coptic. Another prominent Mesoamerican civilisation with a significant political and military presence was the Aztec Empire.

The Pre-Columbian Era saw the development of several diverse cultures throughout South America. One of the most powerful cultures in South America, the Inca Empire had a vast network of highways and structures. The Mayans were also very influential in South America, where they constructed some of the biggest pyramids in the world.

Pre-Columbian North America had a very sparse population, with just a few tiny towns dispersed throughout the land. Native Americans in North America were a varied group that represented a number of distinct civilizations. One indigenous group that is still present in North America today is the Navajo Nation.

Spain's conquest of America

The United States' entry brought an end to the harsh and protracted Spanish conquest of America, which had started in the late 15th century and lasted for generations. After all, the Spanish were capturing a continent that was home to several distinct civilizations. In their quest to seize power, they ran against a number of obstacles, including ferocious Native American opposition. Though there were tens of millions of fatalities, Spain eventually conquered the majority of what is now known as America.

The Native Americans Who Lived in America Before European Settlement

The Paleo-Indians are the Indigenous People who lived in North America before European colonisation. From the earliest human remains discovered in North America, which date back more than 15,000 years, to the highly mobile hunter-gatherers of the Great Lakes region, these individuals represented a wide age and cultural range. However, by 1000 BC, the majority of Native American tribes had created semi-sedentary lifestyles centred around communities, and these villages had started to grow into permanent settlements.

The Norsemen were the first Europeans to reach the United States in the ninth century. They travelled around the modern-day North American shores before arriving in Newfoundland. From there, they started exploring interior areas and encountered and traded with several Native American tribes. Off the coast of Cuba, Christopher Columbus arrived in 1492 on what he believed to be an island. Soon after, he declared Spain to be the sole owner of the Western Hemisphere.

Spain became more interested in purchasing land in North America as France's battle for control of Europe's maritime trade routes increased. Spanish adventurer Francisco Vásquez de Coronado left Mexico City in 1513 with a sizable retinue in search of wealth and native slaves. Instead, he found a large area that he dubbed New Mexico and was composed of rough mountains and wide open plains. The voyage of De Coronado continued west through Arizona and into California, where he was killed by natives close to the present-day Sacramento.

Much of what is now the southeast United States was surveyed by Hernando de Soto's second Spanish voyage in 1542. As he endeavoured to subdue the native tribes and plunder their resources, De Soto's mission was characterised by bloodshed and destruction. Juan Ponce de León annexed Florida to Spain in 1580. A detachment of Spanish troops under the command of Pedro Menéndez de Avilés travelled across Florida's east coast in 1584 in pursuit of a passage to the Pacific Ocean.

St. Augustine, the first European town in what would become Florida, was established in 1585 by Menéndez de Avilés. By 1600, France had established itself as Spain's main opponent in North America and had started to devote more funds to conquest and exploration. Hundreds of English Puritans arrived in what is now Massachusetts as a result of King James I of England's award of a charter to the Massachusetts Bay Colony in 1607.

New York City was found in 1614 by a Dutch expedition headed by Hendrick Corstiaensen while they scoured the Hudson River. The Appalachian Mountains, which would subsequently bear their name, were first explored by a party of Englishmen under the command of Captain John Smith the following year. Samuel de Champlain, a French adventurer, established Quebec City in 1618, the first European colony in what is now the United States.

A second journey into Florida undertaken by the Spanish explorer Hernando de Soto in 1620 resulted in the slavery of thousands of Native Americans. The first permanent English settlement in North America was established in 1624 by Englishman Captain John Smith at Jamestown. The present-day state of Maine was discovered by the Dutch explorers Jacob Leisler and Willem Verhulst from 1626 to 1628.

Roger Williams, an Englishman, established Providence, Rhode Island, which rejected Protestantism as the official state religion, in 1630. Samuel de Champlain, a French adventurer, established Port Royal on the Ashley River in South Carolina in 1632. Port Royal quickly developed into a significant fur trading hub. On Roanoke Island in North Carolina, Sir Walter Raleigh, an Englishman, founded the first English colony in North America in 1634. Even yet, it was abandoned in less time than two years.

Dutch explorer Adriaen Block undertook an expedition up the Hudson River in 1636–1637, which resulted in the establishment of Yonkers and Albany by Dutch inhabitants. All British subjects were to live independently, according to Massachusetts Bay Colony Governor John Winthrop, who made this declaration in 1638.

History of Native Americans from the Beginning

When the first humans arrived in North America is a matter of some debate. Nevertheless, they did so at some point during the Palaeolithic era. Early people of the continent were hunter-gatherers, according to archaeological evidence, and agriculture had only just started to be practised by 8000 BC. By 3000 BC, nomadic hunter-gatherer tribes had started to establish permanent settlements and had developed sophisticated spiritual beliefs and practises. The Atlantic shore was where the first colonies were founded. Nevertheless, when the continent was further explored, people started settling in other regions. There were several tribes spread over the United States by the year 1000 AD.

From one location to the next, the civilizations of the different tribes differed substantially, with some being far more developed than others. Even while many tribes shared similar religious practises, each tribe had its own traditions and customs. Native American oral tradition, which consists of tales and legends passed down from generation to generation, was one of the most significant components of their civilization. The tribespeople and everyone else might learn from these tales. They were curious about prevailing practises and beliefs.

Despite having different cultures and languages, all Native Americans were related historically and genetically. They had physical characteristics with people from Europe or Asia Minor, suggesting that they likely came from one or more far-off places. What brought about these folks is unknown.

At the conclusion of the Ice Age, humans crossed the Bering land bridge from Asia into Alaska. Their forefathers explored the coast of North America. By 1000 BC, they had nearly taken over the whole continent. It is unknown exactly when the Americas' first population arrived.

Due to their lengthy history of migration, which has seen people create several languages, customs, and civilizations all across the world for millennia, Americans have a rich cultural legacy. The Americas have just as many different tribal nations as Europe, Africa, and Asia.

Due to changing temperatures and expanding populations, certain Native American tribes started experimenting with new crops. Others remained in the region, grew, and excelled as farmers. As early as 5,500 BC, Mexican Indians were cultivating maize and squash. The family hunted and raised deer and bison for sustenance. To supply grass for the animals, they routinely burned off portions of the land. Many coastal tribes employed practical methods to hunt and harvest fish from boats.

After 2000 BC, a number of Native American states with numbers in the tens of thousands emerged. They established an extensive global network of commercial routes.

Columbus' voyage to the "New World" in 1492 marked the beginning of European colonisation of the Americas. Among the diseases brought by the Europeans were smallpox and measles. Native Americans became sick with these new diseases very away. The invasion destroyed several local cities.

In order to provide additional farmland and jobs for Europe's growing population, the Europeans decided to colonise America. To do this, they usually had to fight land battles with Native American groups. Various factors gave the Europeans an advantage in these conflicts. While some Native American tribes resisted colonisation, many were ultimately forced to cede their homeland.

Native Americans are now once more moving to North America and Europe in greater numbers. For Native American leaders fighting for their people, political success has significantly increased. Governments and other groups have also grown more conscious of the need to protect indigenous customs and traditions while attending to Native Americans' concerns.

In the United States, particularly during the imperial and early republican periods, Native Americans are frequently featured in history of health, sickness, and medicine. The history of Native American cultures and early European interactions frequently mentions disease epidemics, while wellness and healing are seldom given much attention.

Native American, Alaskan Native, and Hawaiian healers have employed native plants to the United States, Alaska, and Hawaii for generations to treat a variety of illnesses. There are several herbal remedies and their use in numerous cultures.

Native Americans relied largely on local flora for sustenance and healing before the advent of Europeans. The focus of contemporary initiatives to improve the diets of current generations is local flora. The Waianae and Captain Cook diets in Hawaii aim to reduce fat, calories, and additives while boosting the nutritional content of the local food supply to promote better health. Native Alaskans and members of other Indian tribes are collaborating to encourage the preservation of traditional foods. Food serves as medicine in the fullest sense of the word in this context.

Native Americans' Relationship with Nature in Chapter 2

The significance of nature to Native American culture has been well-documented throughout history and is still prevalent now. The natural environment has an impact on American Indian religion, customs, mythology, literature, food, medicine, art, and many other facets of their culture. Their way of existence is inextricably related to the environment and the land.

Once you comprehend the critical role that nature plays in Native American civilization, it is simple to see how and why nature has grown to be so important in all types of Native American culture. We've provided a succinct but thorough explanation of how indigenous peoples' conceptions of nature influence and define their worldviews. This information is a helpful and practical method to learn about and actually enjoy the amazing world of Native American art.

Chapter 2:
Native Americans and Their Connection with Nature

Nature is valued beyond everything else in American Indian culture. The idea is closely tied to the society's spiritual convictions, both of which are crucial distinguishing factors of its outlook and way of life.

Native Americans hold the view that everything on Earth, both living and nonliving, have a unique spirit that is a component of the greater soul of the cosmos. This idea is connected to Animism, a religion that emphasises the worship of an underlying spirituality.

Theories of animism include both living and nonliving things in their scope. This group contains people, living things, animals, natural elements, and geographical phenomena like rivers, mountains, and thunderstorms. Native American culture seems to love and appreciate the spirit of the land and all that it has to offer.

The Study of Cultural Evolution Is Not Based on Science

Science is often the subject that is used to explain how the universe functions and how certain realities exist, despite the fact that there are a lot of contradicting tales and discussions surrounding the Earth's beginnings. To Native Americans, a growing flower was a gift from a land endowed with its own soul, despite the fact that the mechanism of photosynthesis is today a well-known and widely accepted explanation for plant development.

Both historically and currently, many American Indians have turned to nature to make sense of things they don't completely understand. They thought that the natural elements of the

Earth were ruled by spirits. They thus started to worship the wind, creatures, nature, and even water.

All Native American cultures concur that Mother Earth is holy and that all life is sacred and emerges from the land. Every piece of work they create is infused with this idea.

Nature's Elements Are More Important

Natural characteristics are valuable and widespread in everything American Indians do and grow because they are symbolic and serve several purposes in their culture. Native Americans utilise totems to acquire strength and power, and they employ symbols in their literature and artwork to comprehend and relate to the rest of the world. If a language is represented by symbols, then nature is its vocabulary.

For instance, trees serve as a symbol of permanence and longevity in addition to being a sign of life and healing. Different kinds fill various responsibilities. The Elm tree is linked to growing knowledge and willpower, while the Cherry tree is linked to rebirth and compassion while promoting digestion. Injuries can also be treated with it.

Another illustration of how nature is closely connected to Native American beliefs and customs is the idea of an animal spirit. People commonly have a connection with a spirit animal, a mentor who profoundly affects who they are or how they live. Organisations frequently choose Spirit Creatures, the most significant and prominent animals in each tribe's territory, to serve as Tribe Totems. These creatures offer vital resources and spiritual discoveries to aid people in navigating life.

For instance, the Bat, a symbol of rebirth and death, guards the night. The Turtle, on the other hand, stands for tenacity and protects Mother Earth. The Wolf who leads with insight and a spirit of leadership is the Pathfinder. Nature is the fundamental anchor for producing all spirit and life, according to Native American culture. Native American painters stand apart from their contemporaries because of how they depict this viewpoint in their works of art. It facilitates the bigger audience for their work. The relevance of nature in American Indian culture can help viewers understand and comprehend the meaningful, unique works produced by these artists.

A pearl of equivalent collective wisdom was shared by several Native American tribes, despite their residing in various parts of what is now the United States. They acknowledged and comprehended how interdependent all natural elements are. In order to survive and maintain the health of their biological niche, people, rocks, plants, and even animals were dependent on one another.

Every action we take as individuals has an effect on the environment. This fundamental idea compared Native Americans to the animals they hunted and the berries they picked from the bush.

They were conscious of the impact of their actions. Because of this understanding, they had a degree of love and appreciation for nature that is frequently lacking in contemporary civilization.

You are still allowed to go deer hunting despite that. It indicates that they hunted there following the autumn baby season in remembrance of and reverence for the animal's contribution to their way of life.

Native Americans somewhat modified their ecological niches. To create room for farms and homes, they cleared the land. These alterations were slight, and as soon as the tribe relocated, the land immediately recovered. Although the locations have not affected the ecology, archaeological digs have uncovered traces of their towns.

When European settlers arrived in America with quite different land management practises, this method of interacting with nature created a number of problems. Early colonists like the Pilgrims saw America as a continent to conquer. They regularly expressed anxiety of this strange new planet and its inhabitants in their essays and letters.

Traditional earth management methods are being attempted to be reintroduced by Native Americans, Whites, and Americans of various cultural backgrounds. When we consider ourselves to be a component of the system, we take the surroundings into account. It's a common political response to place the blame elsewhere—on politicians, other nations, or regular people.

Blaming others isn't going to get us very far. We must all rise to the occasion and work together in order to transcend the blame game and even discover a way to cohabit with nature.

Self-Restraint

Self-control is seen in many Native American tribes in a distinctive way. The idea of self-control comes from communal living and coexisting in the natural environment, which might result in unforeseen changes. When survival in a communal culture is linked with collective power, self-control is a positive thing.

Native Americans safeguarded the lives of future generations by using natural resources sparingly. They left behind a legacy that will go on in later generations. They did not exterminate the world for their own benefit.

The Iroquois Confederacy's "Seventh Generation doctrine" "mandates that tribe decision-makers examine the ramifications of their acts and decisions for descendants seven generations into the future."

The Haudenosaunee Confederacy has been governed since 1142 A.D. Nevertheless, Benjamin Franklin adored it and based many of the Constitution's concepts on it. This network exists. Recognise the connections between animals, people, and the environment and how these impact both our lives and the lives of present and future generations.

Alterations To Climate

Everyone on planet seems to be impacted by climate change, which seems to be a major problem. To overcome these difficulties, many American communities are turning to Native American wisdom.

As the Houma Nation discovered, climate change has completely destroyed the coastal regions of Louisiana's Gulf Coast. Erosion, damage from the oil industry, and the deliberate destruction of an ecosystem are all examples of intentional ecosystem degradation. They have been surviving for decades by fishing, harvesting prawns, and engaging in other subsistence activities in the marshes and along the beach.

Massive erosion has taken place along the Louisiana coast as a result of urbanisation and climate change. Islands disappeared, the terrain swiftly altered, and pollution destroyed fish and crabs. Since their way of life has been destroyed, the Houma will be unable to transmit it to subsequent generations.

In coastal marshlands, several fish and crab species reproduce. Native coastal cultures have traditionally protected these ecosystems by planting trees and marsh meadows.

This natural cycle allowed (young fish) fry to flourish. Several times, commercial fisheries and oil firms have constructed canals across these locations, ruining this special stream and drastically reducing fish reproduction.

Agriculture

Not everyone believes that Native Americans were the first farmers. On the Great Plains, a stereotype shows the courageous riding a horse and living in a tent.

But contrary to common opinion, farmers were the first to contact the Native Americans. The pilgrims learned agricultural methods at Tisquantum. They possessed a variety of agricultural talents, as a result, we know.

To provide food for huge populations, several nations have created sustainable agricultural systems. The Cherokee grew and farmed at least 15 different types of maize before Europeans arrived.

Food production is influenced by spirituality as well. Maize, squash, and beans were the Three Sisters' main crops for the Iroquis. These three crops are grown together in our gardens in a complimentary but useful way.

Food production is influenced by spirituality as well. Maize, beans, and squash were the Three Sisters' main crops for the Iroquis. These three crops are grown together in our gardens in a complimentary but useful way.

The Three Sisters have traditionally stood in for the souls of young women, often known as "Our Life." In order to show gratitude and appreciation for the crops, offerings and prayers of thanksgiving were presented to the Three Sisters.

An key element of long-term sustainability is this comprehension. In most contemporary societies, it is absent. The Pilgrims learned several organic farming techniques from the Wampanoag, a tribe that is renowned for keeping the Pilgrims alive during the first year. They looked to nature for support.

The Wampanoag supplemented their diet with wood ash and fish leftovers since plants, like animals, require nourishment. These organic farming practises nourished the earth as opposed to depleting it.

Permaculture: Regenerative Agriculture

Farming methods that place an emphasis on natural and holistic methods include permaculture and regenerative agriculture. The majority of Native Americans who farm in the United States are women. Actually, Native Americans and tribal groups hold fifty percent of Arizona's agricultural land.

The dryland agriculture of the Hopi is widely recognised. The dry environment of the Southwest is ideal for this traditional agricultural technique. Today's Hopi farmers use less irrigation and sow their crops deeper than was previously advised.

The Button Family of the Akimel O'odham (River People, Pima) of the Indian Gila River Community is the owner of Ramona Farms, one of Arizona's largest Native-owned farms (commercial). Along with raising commercial crops like lucerne and cotton, they also brought back several ancient heritage plants once grown by tribes in the southwest.

They are growing the ball, a tepary bean that does well in dry environments. Working with your environment, land, and cultural legacy is demonstrated here once more.

Foraging

Wild plant harvesting is a good method to enhance our food supply and re-establish a connection with nature. We may appreciate everything that nature has to offer and the effort that goes into producing meals for the entire group when we go in search of wild foods.

Foraging does not decrease the crop, as the indigenous peoples taught us. We only take about a third of a crop, allowing the remainder to continue to develop and reproduce. This guarantees that there will be sufficient for present-day populations as well as the upcoming foraging trip.

Both Native Americans and early American colonists valued foraging as a skill. It provided treatment in addition to components for food and flavouring. Iroquis records show that more than 80 wild edibles were collected.

Fishing And Hunting

Hunting and fishing were popular ways to increase the protein in one's diet. All of the animal parts that had been collected had to be used. Anything could not be thrown away.

Native American tribes frequently observed harvest festivals to honour hunting and food production.

The local hunters killed three deer. The remainder of the animal was left to decay after the rack and haunches were removed. I was shocked by the waste and callous disregard for something so helpless as a white-tailed deer that had sacrificed its life.

Spirituality and Religion

Native Americans have discovered how to live in harmony with nature rather than fighting it. Their culture reflected this as well. Native American religions asserted that its followers had a spiritual bond with their Creator(s).

Native Americans have understood that their acts on Earth had an influence on future generations, as we learnt from the Iroquois Confederacy. We must respect that bond since their ancestors only relied on the riches of the land. Like their ancestors, they want to provide their kids a secure future.

Chapter 3:
The Basic Principles of Native Americans

Native Americans have a vibrant, diversified, and deeply ingrained culture. Even if they take what appears to be a simple habit seriously, it may be extremely meaningful to them. In this part, we'll examine some of the fundamental principles held by Native Americans and consider how they might aid in the development of a successful marketing strategy. These qualities will unquestionably have a beneficial impact on your marketing, from ideas like respect and reciprocity to creativity and intuition.

Honesty and Integrity

Native Americans have a long history of upholding steadfast moral principles. These principles are crucial because they enable us to remain authentic and sustain our interpersonal connections.

Living true to our obligations, whether they are made to others or to ourselves, is the definition of integrity. Truth-telling is always honourable, even when it might offend someone. We think the greatest approach to get along with people and maintain strong relationships is to be honest.

These principles are crucial because they enable us to remain authentic and sustain our interpersonal connections. They aid us in exerting ourselves in all we undertake. Assume we can be truthful with one another and ourselves. Then we won't have to worry about what other people think of us as we can concentrate on our objectives.

Putting Value In Work Before Money

The most important thing in life is not money. labour is. Native Americans are so successful because they have always put a high priority on hard labour. Here are the five core principles that Native Americans adhere to and use to govern their behaviour:

Native Americans are respectful of people and their property. They never misuse their position of power or influence or take unfair advantage of others. They are aware that peaceful coexistence is possible if people respect one another.

2) Personal accountability: Native Americans are accountable for their own choices and the results of those choices. They are aware that doing good actions will result in good things, and doing evil deeds will result in bad things.

3) Collaboration: Native Americans work together to accomplish shared objectives. They are aware that teamwork is both more efficient and enjoyable than working alone.

4) Self-reliance: Native Americans depend on themselves for assistance or support rather than on others. If something needs to be done, they find a method to do it without help from others.

5) Fortitude: Despite how hard a task may first appear to be, Native Americans are tenacious, persistent individuals who never give up on their aims.

Recognise The Position of Women in the Society

How vital women's roles are in Native American civilization cannot be answered in a single way. There are a few things, nevertheless, about which there is assurance. First, for millennia, Native American women have been integral to maintaining and defining the culture. Second, it's crucial to keep in mind how frequently males and society have marginalised and even repressed Native American women, which has made them more dedicated to preserving their cultural history than many other groups. Third, it's important to recognise the distinctive viewpoint that Native American women have to contribute when examining the problems that now confront their community.

Strong ties within families and in society

Families of Native Americans are deeply rooted in their culture and its ideals. Native American culture is built on the family, which also has a significant social significance. Families are in charge of rearing their kids, educating them about their customs and culture, and imparting the values that are significant to them.

It is also the duty of family members to sustain the cultural norms of their tribe. They take part in rites and ceremonies, as well as give the community labour and financial assistance. Many tribes have chiefs or elders in charge of maintaining the tribe's traditions and customs.

Relationships with other families are important to Native American households. Together, they socialise frequently, exchanging tales and recipes. Additionally, they support one another when necessary, such as when a member of the family is ill or needs aid with a challenging work.

Respect for one another on a mutual basis

Native Americans respect one another and see themselves as belonging to the same group. Respect is based not just on blood relationships but also on shared customs and ideals. Native Americans have the view that it is everyone's duty to protect the traditions and morals of their tribe.

Tribal elders are crucial in encouraging Native Americans to respect one another. Elders are revered for their wisdom and experience, and they are frequently seen as sources of direction and insight. When disputes emerge, elders assist in their peaceful and democratic resolution.

Native Americans consider themselves to be custodians of the environment. They cooperate to save sacred sites from development and take care not to harm or deplete the environment. Ceremonies honouring the Earth's spirit creatures, who are regarded as essential players in the preservation of the ecosystem, are held in towns around the nation.

Living in peace with nature is crucial, according to Native Americans. Using natural resources to make arts and crafts, this ideology has inspired several tribes to establish ecological agriculture, eco-tourism, solar energy production, and recycling initiatives.

Respect Nature's Natural Laws

Native Americans follow a few customs that have been passed down from generation to generation. Honouring the environment includes respecting the land, the creatures, and the spirits.

Respecting the Land

We are raised to appreciate our country from the moment of our birth. We are not permitted to harm it or take anything that is not rightfully ours. Breaking these principles might have a severe impact on both us and our ancestors, according to Native Americans, who believe that everything on earth is interconnected.

Native American culture also places a strong emphasis on animals. We treat them with the same respect that we would want to be afforded in return because we view them as being representations of the Earth itself. We are considerate of their personal space, food sources, and security.

Buddhism And Religion

Native Americans have the belief that this earth and the supernatural realm are intertwined. Every living thing has a spirit; through ritual and prayer, we may connect with these spirits and learn from them. We name this world "Wakan Tanka," which means "Great Spirit." We may better comprehend our role in the world and how to take care of our environment and one another by making this link, which is crucial.

Observe Mother Earth

Native Americans from long ago believed that Mother Earth had a soul and a voice. She was adored by them as the source of all life and the bodily manifestation of all that was sacred.

The idea of tapu, which includes our spiritual ties to nature and our need to preserve it, underpins Native Americans' respect for Mother Earth. Karakia (prayer), waiata (songs), manuhiri (landforms), and strength (bodies of water) are the four basic themes that make up tapu.

Karakia alludes to the way we express our gratitude to the Creator via prayer. To protect Mother Earth, we must never forget that we are a part of everything. Our oral history and song, known as waiata, facilitate communication with the spirits of the natural world. We refer to place names, famous landmarks, and other tangible symbols of our culture and tradition as manuhiri. PouWERi is the term for the rivers, lakes, and other bodies of water where we congregate for worship, rituals, and hunt/gather activities.

Generosity

The Native American people have based their culture and civilization on a wide range of various and unique foundations. They all play a crucial part in their lives and vary from charity to reverence for the earth.

Generosity is one of the most crucial pillars on which Native American civilization has been built. The Native Americans have always been helpful, whether it is by giving to those in need or by sharing their meals with the hungry. This kindness extends to the community as well as relationships between people. For instance, during a natural disaster like a storm or flood, communities band together to help and support one another.

Respect for the land is another crucial pillar on which Native American civilization has been built. Native Americans place a high value on honouring and caring for the land, from safeguarding holy places to protecting the environment. They may stay in this nation long after others have departed because of this regard.

Chapter 4:
History of Herbalism

One of the oldest and most important branches of medicine is herbal medicine. For thousands of years, it has been used to treat a variety of medical issues. We'll go into great detail on the history of herbalism and its use in contemporary medicine in this section post. We'll look at the components that make herbal medicine such a powerful kind of treatment, as well as its advantages and risks.

Herbalism: What Is It?

Herbalism is the practise of using plants as medicines and cures. Since ancient times, people have employed plants for therapeutic purposes, and there are several varieties of herbal treatments. There is still much to learn about the difficult subject of herbalism.

Dietary supplements are one sort of herbal medicine that is often utilised nowadays. Dietary supplements are goods designed to improve health by adding nutrients traditionally thought to be good for people to the diet. Dietary supplements come in a wide range of varieties, such as vitamins, minerals, herbs, and antioxidants.

There is proof that some conventional herbal treatments may be beneficial for some ailments. To yet, however, there is little scientific proof to back up the use of conventional herbal therapies as treatments for serious conditions like cancer or Alzheimer's.

Where Was the Origin of Herbalism?

One of the oldest sciences on the planet is herbalism. It was utilised by ancient humans to heal themselves and dates back to a time before recorded language. Herbalism began with plants and has expanded through time to incorporate other facets of alternative medicine, such as Ayurveda.

Plants were the foundation of herbalism, and they remain its main emphasis today. However, herbal therapy has expanded throughout time to incorporate other facets of alternative treatment, such as Ayurveda. Traditional Indian medicine known as ayurveda places a strong emphasis on treating patients with herbs and other all-natural treatments.

Using plants as food in the Stone Age

The use of herbs to treat mental and emotional disorders dates back to ancient times. Herbal medicine was used by humans in the stone age to cure a variety of illnesses.

In the Stone Age, plants were the primary source of medicine for herbalists. They would recognise the traits of the herb and employ them to treat particular afflictions. Angelica, dandelion, elderberry, lavender, nettle, rosemary, sage, and verbena were some of these plants.

Plant extracts were also used by prehistoric herbalists to treat wounds. The extract would be combined with hot water and applied to the wound. The herb would aid in clearing out any infection and bringing down swelling.

Herbalism in the Past

Herbal medicine has been practised for ages, and several plants have been employed for a variety of uses. Wildcrafted botanicals, tinctures, tea, and treatments are some of the most popular herbal products. Herbal medicine can be used as an alternative to conventional medicine and to treat a wide range of medical disorders.

Herbaceous plants have been present for 125 million years, and herbalism has a long history with humans and other human-like creatures. As a result, the earliest humanoids did not emerge until around 5 million years ago. Up until around 12,000 years ago, all humans were hunter-gatherers; this would make it the longest era of human civilization. The goal of this extensive and successful clinical experiment is to identify the medicinal and other powerful qualities of plants.

During this time, the best foods, weapons, fuels, medicines, dyes, toxins, fabrics, and spiritual/hallucinogenic experiences were produced by plants. They all had an effect on people's bodies, brains, and societies. A far more rigorous approach to herbal medicines was made possible by the advent of agriculture (around 10,000 years ago) and the development of more substantial societies in later human history. Only a few fragments of knowledge exist about preliterate herbal remedies, despite the fact that herbal therapy has been used for more than 5,000 years.

The Palaeolithic period, some 60,000 years ago, is when medicinal plant usage first emerged, according to archaeological data.

On a floral garden with plants like Grape Hyacinth, Marshmallow, Henbane, Thistle, Yarrow, Ephedra, and others, a man was interred close to Shanidar, Iraq.

Additionally, research on the dental plaques of Neanderthals has shown that they consumed poplar, yarrow, and chamomile plants. Ancient herbal knowledge may be seen in the finding of Otzi, a 5,300-year-old iceman from the Later Neolithic-Early Period. He was found with a rucksack containing food, tools, and healing herbs, and was practically bald.

Otzi was carrying dried Sloe Berries from European Blackthorn, which have been shown to have medicinal properties including those of a carminative, immune system booster, anti-microbial, high in vitamin C, anti-inflammatory, and anti-inflammatory Birch Polypore, a fungus with antiviral, vermifuge, and antibacterial properties. Both Whipworm, a parasitic nematode, and Lyme disease are thought to be curable. Otzi had firsthand knowledge of the Sloe Berries' therapeutic benefits because they had already been dried out from the previous autumn, showing that they had been used for a specific reason.

Contemporary herbalism

Herbalism has a long history that predates written history. One of the oldest cultures whose use of herbs for healing is recorded was the ancient Egyptians. More than 2,500 years ago, Chinese herbalists created a medical system centred on herbal remedies. Herbalism was employed in the Middle Ages to cure a variety of diseases. Herbalism is being utilised today for both therapeutic and recreational purposes.

American Indian herbalism

Herbal medicine has been used by Native Americans for generations and is still used today. Native Americans in North America have used plants as medicine for centuries. They had passed on their understanding of these plants from father to son.

Native Americans frequently employ sage, cedar, calamus root, dandelion, chicory root, wild mint, and Black Cohosh among other plants. These plants were used to cure a variety of conditions, including as toothaches, headaches, cold and flu symptoms, and pain alleviation.

Additionally, several tribes employed herbal treatments to boost vitality and encourage conception. Additionally, people employed herbal medicines to treat injuries and stave off illness. Many Native Americans still employ herbal medicine today to address a range of health issues.

Chapter 5:
Traditional Medicine and Herbalism

Native Americans carefully chose plants that could be used without risking their health and that would benefit their communities. Native Americans used a variety of medicinal herbs for healing. As a kind of first-aid therapy, some plants and roots, for instance, were pulverised or consumed before being applied to wounds. Others were simmered in herbal decoctions to treat fevers and bacterial illnesses; these medicinal concoctions might also contain additional anti-microbial herbs or poisonous plants.

Animals and minerals were also employed as medicine to cure common illnesses, so it wasn't just plants that were used. Many people used a geode containing different forms of cinnabar (mercury sulphide) to heal rashes, cuts, or other skin conditions. Additionally, they would take different stones as liquids or tablets to stimulate their stomachs and help them release intestinal gases. There are several documented instances of rocks and other minerals being used as medicine throughout history.

Finding the plants that would be most helpful to the community required a lot of work, especially because many of them may be harmful if not handled properly. For medicinal purposes, several native plants were turned into a fine powder or decoction. Its powder or decoction would be combined with water and drunk to treat specific ailments, including as fever, digestive problems, and parasites. The majority of the decoctions were prepared using the plant's roots, bark, leaves, or seeds; some species also utilised stones. One plant may be used to make the medicines, or a mixture of multiple plants may be used. Each plant's treatment occasionally included alcohol to make it easier to swallow when ingested.

Herbs were used in rituals and daily life to preserve health and stave off disease. For instance, the Blackfeet tribe's traditional curriculum gave its children the knowledge and skills necessary to become expert hunters. The little ones were shown how to gather and prepare a variety of medical plants. Additionally, they picked up cleaning and processing techniques for food plants. Herbs were frequently used to keep people healthy and stave off disease.

People who are searching for native plants must respect the land and be careful about the species they choose. Since many of these places are so important to Native Americans' culture, they are now mostly protected by federal law. Native plants are protected by the Endangered Species Act and the American Indian Religious Freedom Act. For instance, Congress approved the Native Grasslands Protection Act, which safeguards threatened grasslands in six Western states, including Idaho and Montana.

It's important to remember that many of these plants, especially those in high-altitude regions of Oregon and California, can only be found in or near rocks or cliffs. These locations are teeming with wild medicinal plants, but if you don't seek for them, you can miss them because they're tucked away in a rock fissure or have fallen down a cliff. It is simple to become lost in these dangerous locations due to the loose soil and rocky terrain. In certain locations, gathering wild plants is not advised.

Many of the natural remedies used by Native Americans are still in use today, demonstrating the Native American connection to medicinal plants. Native Americans have mastered the utilisation of untamed natural resources for healing and maintaining health. There has been no alleged loss of therapeutic understanding as a result of the transmission of this knowledge and tradition from one generation to the next. By showing people how to utilise the plants, we might be able to maintain Native Americans' traditional medical practises.

Herb collecting is now often referred to as "picking," although it has historically gone by many other names, including "gathering," "gatherin'," "picking," and even "pickin'."

Every culture has its own customary techniques for preparing food and medicinal plants. A prime example is Native American culture.

Advantages and Uses of Native American Herbal Medicine

The use of plants in herbal medicine is used to cure and even prevent a wide range of illnesses. We all know that many early Native American nations relied on herbal medicine to keep their populations healthy. Despite the development of modern science, herbal medicine is still used in more than half of the world because it is effective.

- Affordability: Despite the rapid improvement in human health brought about by modern medicine, many individuals currently cannot afford basic necessities due to rising costs and more convoluted and difficult access to medical treatment for some than for others.

- Herbal medicine, on the other hand, works just as well and is far less expensive. The fact that herbal medication functions well without side effects is another benefit.

- Various forms are available: Many people find it difficult to take any type of medication, whether it be herbal or pharmaceutical, and many people who find one form of the medication difficult to take will take it in a different form. The most convenient way to receive your medicine is to buy herbal remedies from one of the many herbal stores, pharmacies, or even online. We advise customers to make sure they always get their herbs from reliable sources.

- Treatment efficacy: Numerous studies have been conducted on various herbal treatments, confirming their effectiveness and ensuring their safety for use.

- Immunological-boosting qualities: Herbal medicine supports the body and helps to maintain those physiological processes rather than interfering with them. It does this by strengthening immunological functions. The component of everyone is enhanced to the point where it suddenly feels lighter and is capable of performing at its highest level.

- Native Americans were among the first to use herbal medicine, and they had a close enough bond with nature to understand the advantages of particular plant remedies. As a result of this relationship's widespread use today, many individuals find it valuable.

Book 2:
Native American Herbal Remedies

Chapter 1:
Herbalism's
Historical Overview

Herbal medicine has a long and diverse history. To put all the significant herbalists who paved the way on one chronology would almost be impossible!

While it is challenging to summarise centuries of herbal history in one place, a brief historical timeline paints a clear yet vital picture of how modern herbalism came to be.

- 2800BC- Shen Nung's earliest known herbal remedy is the "Pen Ts ao."
- Around 400 BC, Hippocrates developed the concepts of diet, exercise, and happiness. It was written in Greece somewhere about 1000 BC.
- The earliest Greek herbal with drawings originally published in c100BC.
- Around the year 50 AD, commerce in plants and herbal medicines spread across the Roman Empire.
- Around 200 AD, the herbalist Galen created a system for categorising diseases and their corresponding therapies.
- Around 500 AD, Myddfai's physicians adopted Hippocrates' theories. Every monastery featured an infirmary and a physic garden where monks tested out natural cures about the year 800.
- Around 800 AD, the physician Avicenna composed The Canon of Medicines. Arab culture has always had a strong effect on medicine and healing.

- In the 1200s AD, herbalists, not apothecaries who employed arsenic and mercury and bled, cleansed, and prescribed it, were effective in stopping the plague.

His Holiness Henry VIII promoted the use of herbal treatments in the 1500s AD. Several Acts of Parliament have regulated medical practises, including protection for "simple herbalists."

Herbs are accessible to the poor in the 1600s AD, but 'drugs,' made from rare plants, animals, or minerals, are only for the affluent. 'The English Physician,' a classic herbal by Nicholas Culpeper, condensed the description of herbal medicine use.

Herbal medicines started to be displaced by mineral-based pharmaceutical cures in the 1800s AD. Widespread availability of over-the-counter forms of strong drugs like laudanum and mercury led to tales of their negative effects emerging. Due to the pharmaceutical industry's rapid expansion, herbal treatment has lost popularity and is now considered "outdated."

- 1900s AD- A substantial boost in worldwide pharmaceutical manufacturing followed the discovery of penicillin and the expansion of the pharmaceutical sector following World War I. Only a small number of herbalists currently practise this ages-old craft. Herbalists no longer have the authority to write prescriptions for patients under the Pharmacy and Medications Act of 1941. The public's fury prevented the Act from being put into effect.
- 2000AD- As of right now, European legislation requires that all herbal medicines undergo the same testing as traditional pharmaceuticals. After that, natural remedies would be accepted for sale. The UK government is now evaluating this law's potential effects and public opinion.

Chapter 2:
Herbal Treatment for Common Diseases

When people think about herbs, they typically think of age-old cures like lavender oil for relaxation or peppermint tea for headaches. However, there is a vast array of herbs that may be utilised to cure many ailments and disorders. Some of the most popular herbs used to treat sickness and illness will be discussed in this section. You may more accurately determine which herbs might be helpful for addressing your health concerns by knowing about them and their qualities.

Internal Pain

Abdominal discomfort can be caused by a number of things. The most typical one is GERD, or indigestion brought on by excessive stomach acid production. Tumours, ulcers, and gallstones are among more reasons. Herbs can be used to treat a wide range of conditions, including:

-Indigestion: Try gargling with salt water or taking an over-the-counter antacid like Prilosec OTC (omeprazole) or Pepcid AC (famotidine). If none of these help, try drinking a cup of warm water with a spoonful of ginger before meals.

-GERD: Treating GERD entails preventing acid reflux, which can be accomplished by making dietary and lifestyle changes, such as giving up alcohol and spreading out your meals throughout the day rather to eating one big meal. If everything else fails, you might need to take medicine to treat your symptoms.

-Gallstones: Take fibre supplements such as choline bitartrate (Centrum) or psyllium husk powder (Metamucil). Sometimes a stone can be surgically removed.

-Ulcers: Infections or allergies that enter the gastrointestinal tract frequently result in ulcers. Surgery may be required as part of the treatment plan, along with antibiotics and analgesics to lessen inflammation and discomfort.

-Tumours: The GI tract is the site of more than 80% of malignant tumour onset.

Aches

Herbs may be used to cure a wide variety of ailments and disorders. Here is a list of some of the most typical ones: bronchitis, asthma, colds, flu, and sore throats. In addition to these ailments, herbs can also be used to treat skin disorders, menstrual cramps, and digestive difficulties.

ADHD

Focusing difficulties, hyperactivity, and impulsivity are hallmarks of attention-deficit hyperactivity disorder (ADHD), a mental health disease. While there isn't a single component that causes ADHD, it is thought to be a result of a hereditary and environmental cocktail. Normal onset of symptoms occurs between the ages of 6 and 12, however they might last into adulthood. ADHD cannot presently be cured, although it may be treated with medication, counselling, and behaviour therapy. As many plants have anti-hyperactivity qualities, herbal medicines can also help cure the symptoms of ADHD.

1. Ginkgo biloba extract: Alzheimer's disease and other cognitive problems have historically been treated in China using ginkgo biloba, an extract from the ginkgo tree. Because ginkgo biloba possesses anti-hyperactivity qualities, researchers think it may potentially be useful in treating ADHD. According to one study, ginkgo biloba helped persons with ADHD become less impulsive and more focused.

2. Another plant that is frequently used to treat illnesses like anxiety disorders is passionflower extract. According to certain research, passionflower may also successfully cure ADHD symptoms including impulsivity and hyperactivity. When compared to those

who received a placebo, research participants who took passionflower extract saw substantial gains in their ability to focus and resist distraction.

Alzheimer's condition

Alzheimer's disease is a neurological condition that progressively impairs memory and reasoning. Although there is presently no cure, herbal therapies are being researched as potential treatments.

According to one study, ginkgo biloba can help Alzheimer's sufferers remember things better. Ginkgo leaves contain chemicals that could shield the brain from disease-related harm. Another study discovered that the herb rosemary helped lessen Alzheimer's symptoms in rats. In humans, rosemary has been shown to aid with memory and cognitive function.

Co-enzyme Q10, omega-3 fatty acids, and chamomile tea are among other herbs that have been investigated for possible benefits on Alzheimer's.

Anemia

Haemoglobin shortage is known as anaemia. Numerous issues, such as an iron shortage, an illness, or pharmaceutical side effects, might contribute to this. Many plants can be used to cure anaemia.

Berberine, ephedrine, garlic, ginger, licorice, and vitamin C are among the herbs that have historically been used to cure anaemia. Black cohosh and crimson yeast rice are two more recent choices.

It's crucial to discuss which herbs could be best for you with a healthcare professional. Talk about any additional anemia-related symptoms you may be having.

Anxiety

Each person has a unique experience with the many sorts of anxiety. Some people struggle with generalised anxiety disorder, which is characterised by excessive concern about a wide range of issues. Others have panic disorder, which is characterised by frequent, extremely frightening attacks that can continue for several minutes or even hours. Others, however, suffer from social anxiety disorder, which is characterised by a dread of ridicule or disapproval from others.

Herbal medicine is frequently highly successful in treating anxiety. Here are some of the most common herbs used to treat anxiety: valerian (Valeriana officinalis), hops (Humulus lupulus), kava (Piper methysticum), lavender (Lavandula angustifolia), lemon balm (Melissa officinalis), chamomile (Matricaria chamomilla), passionflower (Passiflora incarnata) and St. John's wort (Hypericum perforatum).

Appendicitis

If untreated, appendicitis is a dangerous medical illness that can be fatal. Appendages, which are tiny, mobile portions of the large intestine, can get obstructed owing to infection, which is the typical cause of appendicitis. The appendix may become encircled by fluid and inflamed (red, hot, and painful).

Appendicitis without treatment can result in peritonitis, a major lesion to the lining of the abdominal cavity, which can be fatal. Surgery to remove the appendix is frequently used as a kind of treatment for appendicitis. Many herbs efficiently cure appendicitis, and they have been used for ages to treat a variety of diseases and wounds. These plants include opium poppies oil, dandelion root, burdock root, goldenseal root, chickweed, red clover flowers, horsetail tea, and white willow bark extract. Let's say you have symptoms or indicators of appendicitis. It is crucial to get medical assistance from a specialist as soon as you can in that situation.

Waking up wet in bed

Herbs may be used to cure a wide range of ailments and disorders. Bedwetting is one of these ailments.

A medical disorder known as bedwetting causes nighttime urinating that is excessive. Numerous factors, such as stress, worry, or a nervous disposition, might contribute to this.

Bedwetting can result in issues including bladder infections, urinary tract issues, and even kidney stones if it is not managed. By assisting in lowering the tension and worry that may be contributing to the issue, herbs can help treat bedwetting. Herbs can also aid with bedwetting symptoms including soreness or discomfort in the bladder.

Bloating

Herbs may be used to cure a wide range of ailments and disorders. The following are some of the most typical:

1. One of the most frequent causes of stomach discomfort is acid reflux, which may be managed with herbs like peppermint or ginger.

2. Bronchitis: A respiratory infection that often affects the lungs, bronchitis can be brought on by a cold or the flu. Bronchitis can be treated with over-the-counter cough medications and natural therapies like echinacea.

3. Constipation: Dandelion, fennel, ginger, and other potent herbs may all be used to treat constipation, which affects many individuals at some time in their life.

4. Cystic acne: An excess of sebum, a natural oil, is what causes this form of acne. Herbs like rosemary, thyme, and sage have substances that stop the formation of sebum, making them great cystic acne remedies.

Blown-up bones

There are several herbal remedies available to mend shattered bones. Herbs can be applied topically and consumed. The herb is administered topically when an injury is present. The quickest time after the bone has been cracked is when this treatment is most effective. Herbs can be taken internally both before and after a bone is broken. Numerous herbs have been shown to help in the recovery of bone fractures and various wounds. Some of the most popular plants used for this purpose are listed below:

One of the most well-liked herbs for treating bone fractures is turmeric (Curcuma longa). A yellow spice called turmeric is native to Pakistan and India. Because of its anti-inflammatory characteristics, it has been used as a herbal treatment for ages. Turmeric has been demonstrated to lessen inflammation and hasten the healing process when administered topically. Additionally, it has been demonstrated to encourage new cell formation and improve connective tissue strength.

Garlic (Allium sativum), a common herb for treating bone fractures, is another. The first written accounts of garlic as a medicinal herb that might aid in the treatment of wounds and general health can be found in ancient Greek literature. One of the first medications used by humans is garlic. It has been used historically as a home remedy for a variety of diseases. Applying garlic extract topically can hasten the healing process while preserving garlic's excellent anti-inflammatory qualities.

Boils

A pustular boil is the most typical type of boil among the numerous others. Bacteria that produce pustular boils thrive in warm, damp environments. The face or neck are frequent locations for this kind of boil.

Finding the aetiology is the first step in treating a pustular boil. If you are aware that Staphylococcus aureus is to blame, you may clean up your surroundings and take antibiotics to treat the boil. Your doctor would probably recommend an antibiotic depending on the type and location of the boil if you don't know what caused it.

You must monitor the boil for evidence of healing after determining the source and treating it. If a boil is not treated right away, it may explode and spread an infection. Therefore, if you have a pustular boil and notice any infection-related symptoms like redness, discharge, or pus, you should always seek medical assistance.

Bruises

Bruises can result from a number of different things, including falls or being struck by an item. They could take a while to heal and might be quite painful. The best technique to treat bruises can vary depending on their nature and the underlying reason.

It's crucial to immobilise the region with a bandage or splint if the bruise was brought on by falling. If the injury was caused by being struck by something, it is critical to seek emergency medical attention. Bruises come in a variety of sizes and hues, but all require medical attention to heal correctly.

Burns

Over 600,000 instances of burns are treated in hospitals each year in the United States, making it one of the most frequent injuries. There are many distinct types of burns, and every one needs a particular course of treatment. Some of the most typical burn kinds are listed here, along with the appropriate treatments:

The only therapy for first-degree burns, which are the least dangerous kind of burns, is to repeatedly spray the burned area with cold water throughout the day.

First aid procedures for second-degree burns include chilling the burnt area with cold water or ice, applying pressure to minimise swelling, and removing any dirt, debris, or clothes that may be concealing the burn. Second-degree burns result in a partial loss of skin tissue.

Total skin tissue loss occurs with third-degree burns, necessitating medical care, including intravenous fluid treatment and antibiotics to avoid infection. Additionally, many third-degree burns leave behind lasting scars.

Deep gashes or open lesions that may need surgical repair characterise fourth-degree burns. These burns are extremely dangerous and can cause significant harm.

Cold, common

Herbs can be used to treat the common cold, a viral illness of the respiratory system. Many people find herbal medicines to be more pleasant than conventional treatments since they are both safe and effective. Echinacea, garlic, goldenseal, and ginger are some of the most popular herbs used to cure colds.

Constipation

Herbs are a prevalent condition that may be used to cure constipation. Ginger, dandelion root, and licorice are just a few plants that help those who are constipated. These herbs encourage digestion, which facilitates easier elimination of waste products from the body. Lavender, fennel, and catnip are further herbs that ease constipation. Some individuals get relief from constipation by using natural laxatives like buchu or senna.

Dementia

Significant memory loss and trouble completing demanding activities are symptoms of dementia. Dementia has several origins, with Alzheimer's disease being the most prevalent type. Head trauma, brain tumours, and stroke are further reasons. Although dementia cannot be cured, there are several therapies that can help sufferers lead better lives.

Cognitive rehabilitation therapy is one method of dementia treatment. Patients who get this therapy are able to develop new abilities and operate better overall. Medication therapy is a different kind of medical care. There are several drugs available to treat dementia; each one may have various advantages and disadvantages. Any proposed therapy should be discussed with a doctor before beginning.

For those with dementia, cognitive rehabilitation treatment can be highly beneficial. It teaches them new skills like cooking or cleaning, which can make it easier for them to live independently and relieve carer pressure. To support persons with dementia in continuing to work or engage in other enjoyable activities, occupational treatments can be used in conjunction with cognitive rehabilitation therapy.

Although dementia cannot be cured, there are several therapies that can help sufferers lead better lives. One such therapy that has demonstrated promising outcomes in symptom reduction and overall function improvement is cognitive rehabilitation therapy.

Diarrhea

Diarrhoea is a frequent issue that may be treated in a variety of ways. Consuming salty meals to quench the body's thirst and drinking lots of water are two of the easiest treatments for diarrhoea. Additionally, some advise using over-the-counter diarrhoea medications such Pepto-Bismol or Bisacodone. Your doctor could suggest a particular antibiotic or antidiarrheal drug if these treatments don't help. Using natural medicines to relieve the symptoms is another option. Aloe vera gel, ginger, hops, peppermint oil, and turmeric are a few well-known herbs for the treatment of diarrhoea. Before using any herb as a therapy for diarrhoea, speak with your doctor first because some of them might not be suitable for young children or pregnant women.

Hair Fall

There are several treatments for hair loss, which is an issue that many people face. Hair loss can be brought on by a variety of factors, such as disease, stress, and heredity. Medication, surgery, hair restoration, and natural therapies are available as treatment alternatives.

Migraine

In the United States, nearly 30 million people suffer from the dreadful condition known as migraine. This particular sort of headache usually affects just one side of the head and lasts for four to 72 hours. Migraines differ from other headache kinds in that they often worsen with exposure to light or noise and have a pulsing aspect.

A mix of hereditary and environmental factors contribute to migraines. According to research, women are more prone than males to get migraines, and they often happen around particular times of the menstrual cycle. There is no one known reason for all migraine occurrences, though.

There is presently no known cure for migraines, however there are several therapies that can lessen symptoms. Some popular treatments include over-the-counter analgesics like ibuprofen or naproxen, prescription drugs like ergotamines or triptans like Elavil, and herbal medicines like ginger or turmeric. It could also be essential to make certain lifestyle adjustments, such avoiding stressful circumstances or abstaining from alcohol entirely.

Herpes

Herbs may be used to cure a wide range of ailments and disorders. For instance, herbal medicines can be used to treat the virus known as herpes. Herbal treatments are effective because they target the infection's primary cause rather than merely its symptoms. Herpes may be treated with a variety of herbal treatments; the key is to select the one that works best for you. Ginger, garlic, and cayenne pepper are a few of the most often used herbal treatments for herpes.

Impotence

There are several conventional and non-conventional treatments for erectile dysfunction (ED). Herbalism is one kind of alternative medicine. Several plants, some of which are fairly strong, have historically been used to treat ED. The following three plants can raise your libido:

An plant called gentian has long been used to increase libido. It functions by boosting blood flow to the genitalia, which can enhance arousal and performance during sexual activity.

Another herb that works well to treat ED is l-arginine. It improves blood flow and makes the penile more firm.

And last, Rhodiola Rosea is a well-known plant for enhancing immune function and general energy levels. Additionally, it has been demonstrated to assist in the treatment of ED.

Renal stones

Up to 10% of the population suffers from kidney stones, which is a widespread condition. Small stones may develop when urine gets too concentrated. Additionally, obstructions in the urinary tract, such as stones in the bladder or kidney, might result in the formation of stones. Kidney stones can become trapped, causing discomfort and a challenge urinating. Kidney stones cannot be cured, however there are several therapies that can aid with symptom relief.

Many people get relief from kidney stones by consuming a high-fiber diet and drinking lots of water. Additionally, some patients employ natural therapies like kidney stone vitamins or tablets. Some of these treatments might include diuretics like cranberry juice or iced tea, oxalate-fighting herbs like turmeric or dandelion root, and minerals like potassium citrate. Surgery could be required to remove a stone that is obstructing the urine's flow or to remove smaller stones that are resistant to other methods of removal.

Malaria

Plasmodium falciparum and P. vivax, two protozoan parasites, are responsible for the potentially fatal and serious sickness known as malaria. The parasite can cause fever, chills, sweating, muscular discomfort, and exhaustion and can enter your body through the mouth, nose, or skin. In extreme situations, malaria can cause coma, convulsions, and even death. Malaria cannot be cured, but it may be treated with antimalarial pills that destroy the parasites within your body, anti-mosquito netting, and medications to lower fever and inflammation. In early trials, it has been found that several herbs can help prevent malaria infection; however, further study is required before these herbal therapies can be advised as routine treatments for this illness.

Period Cramps

Herbs can frequently be used to relieve the cramps that many women suffer during their period. Numerous herbs that are used to relieve menstrual cramps also ease arthritic and migraine pain. Ginger, borage oil, chamomile, lavender oil, and peppermint oil are common plants used to relieve period cramps.

Morning Malaise

Up to 20% of pregnant women have morning sickness, which is a common symptom. Morning sickness can linger for a few days to over a week and can be mild, moderate, or severe. Morning sickness can have a variety of causes. Nevertheless, it could be brought on by alterations in the environment (like travelling), diet (particularly bland food), hormones, diseases, or stress.

Although there is no known therapy for morning sickness, there are various options that can help ease symptoms. Prescription drugs like domperidone or ondansetron as well as over-the-counter medicines like ibuprofen or acetaminophen are often used as treatments. Other therapies include acupuncture, resting, changing one's diet to include bland foods, and drinking lots of water. The need for hospitalisation may arise if the symptoms are severe.

Nausea

A common symptom of a number of diseases and disorders is nausea. Even though there are many treatments, many of them work well when combined with other therapies. The most often treated nauseous conditions include morning sickness, malignancy, pregnancy, and gastroenteritis.

Herbs come in a wide variety and can be used to relieve nausea. Ginger root, lavender, mint, and other herbs can help lessen nausea sensations. Other herbs, such licorice and turmeric, can help lessen vomiting or irritation. Online or at health food stores, you may find a variety of herbal cures. You should see a healthcare provider to determine the best alternative before using a natural cure to relieve nausea.

Book 3:
Native American Herbalism Encyclopedia Vol 1

Chapter 1:
The Foundations of Native American Herbalism

Cherokee medicine, like that of many other Native American tribes, was handed down through the centuries to "selected" healers. Traditional Cherokees consulted medical professionals for guidance on a variety of topics, ranging from medical worries to interpersonal disputes and emotional challenges. Other Native American societies employed similar treatments for colds, pains, and other mild illnesses.

The medical circle

Boneset tea and wild cherry bark were popular remedies among Cherokee and other Native American tribes for coughs, sore throats, and diarrhoea. Traditionally, a tea made from the roots of blue cohosh was used to lessen labour pain and speed up delivery. Devil's club and wild carrot blossoms may be helpful for those with diabetes. Feverwort, Dogwood, and Willow bark teas have been shown to help ease the symptoms of the common cold.

Hops, wild black cherry, and wild lettuce have all been utilised in the past to make sedatives for major surgeries. For instance, penicillin was first used as a Native American remedy before entering contemporary medicine.

Medicine's Inner Circle

Take a bite off of this root. 2000 BC.

That is a pagan root from the year 1000. Here, say this prayer.

That prayer was created around the year 1500. Take a sip of this concoction.

Snake oil is the name of the drug in the year 1940 AD. Take and swallow this pill.

That medication isn't working, it's 1985 AD. From here, take this antibiotic.

2007 A.D. – That antibiotic has lost its potency. Eat this root by taking it!

Native American Medicine Wheel with 4 Directions

Native Americans have a close relationship with nature, which they rely on to establish and preserve harmony, health, and wellbeing. A reference to "Mother Earth" is made, and numerous rituals and customs have embraced her importance. One illustration is the medicine wheel, which symbolises the circle of life and completion in a metaphorical sense.

There are several sizes and forms available for the Medicine Wheel. It could be a tangible object, a work of art, or a ground-level concrete construction. Numerous Medicine Wheels have been built by indigenous tribes in North America throughout the years.

The Medicine Wheel and Native American rituals have a circular format that is frequently clockwise or "sun wise." This makes it simpler to synchronise with natural forces like gravity and the rising and setting of the sun.

Chapter 2:
The Top 200 Herbal Medicines

Agave

The succulent plant species agave is indigenous to the United States. More than 100 distinct agave species exist, with sizes ranging from tiny plants that may be hidden away in a corner to huge plants that can grow up to 10 feet tall. Agaves are utilised for their fruit, flowers, and succulent leaves. Reducing stress, enhancing blood circulation, combating inflammation, and supplying antioxidants are a few advantages of agave use.

Alder

The alder tree is widespread over most of the United States. The sturdy alder tree, a native of North America, can flourish in both dry and wet climates. The leaves of the alder are alternating with serrated edges, and the bark is rough and scaly. The fruit is an acorn, while the blooms are tiny and green. Acorns of different varieties are produced by male and female trees.

Syrup, beer, vinegar, soap, glue, paper, plastics, colours, and other items may all be made from alder tree sap. Alder wood may also be used to make furniture, building materials, and other things. Additionally, the bark's usage as an astringent or a remedy for cold and flu symptoms is possible. If taken in significant numbers, substances found in alder plant roots can be harmful. But the roots may also be utilised to cure a variety of illnesses.

Alder

The variety of native American herbs exceeds 1,500. Indigenous people have utilised many of these plants for generations for a variety of purposes, including healing, promoting fertility, and protecting against pests and illness.

Native American plants that are particularly well-liked include:

Alders, or Alnus rubra, are widespread trees across most of North America. To cure colds and other respiratory conditions, a tea made from the bark is made. Additionally, the leaves and branches can be used as treatments for skin diseases, arthritis, and other ailments. In the past, furniture and tools were made from alder wood. Wine and honey are made from the blossoms.

'Ole Vera'A succulent plant with African roots is aloe vera. It has thick, emerald-green leaves with white stripes that may reach a height of four feet. Bees pollinate the plant's yellow blossoms, which it produces. Aloe Vera has long been used medicinally, and it is currently being researched for potential health advantages.Aloe Vera may provide a number of advantages, including as lowering inflammation, easing pain and swelling, and enhancing skin health. It has antibacterial qualities and works well as a natural detoxifier. Aloe Vera is used by some people to treat eczema, psoriasis, varicose veins, acne, and other skin disorders.

Amaranth

Ancient, gluten-free grain known as amaranth is very nutrient-dense. It's a fantastic source of fibre, antioxidants, vitamins, and minerals. The following are a few advantages of eating amaranth:

1. It contains a lot of fibre: More fibre per cup of cooked amaranth than any other grain, at 10 grammes! This may prolong your sensation of fullness and encourage regularity.

2. It's nutrient-rich: Amaranth is a strong source of vitamin B6, which is crucial for red blood cells, and vitamin C, which aids in infection resistance. Copper, magnesium, potassium, and phosphorus are also present.

3. Amaranth is a good weight reduction alternative since it has a low glycemic index and is low in calories, which prevents blood sugar increases after meals. This makes it a fantastic option if you want to either lose weight or keep it off.

4. It possesses anti-oxidant qualities: Amaranth contains a lot of antioxidants, including lutein and zeaxanthin, two carotenoids that have been related to the reduction of cancer risk.

Amaranth

An old grain called amaranth is renowned for its medicinal properties. Wild populations of this grass-like plant may be found all throughout North America. The following are the top three advantages that amaranth may offer:

1. Amaranth is a fantastic source of iron, which is necessary for producing healthy red blood cells.

2. Amaranth is a good source of vitamin B6, which supports the health of your neurological system and brain.

3. Fibre from amaranth can aid in improved digestion, lower the risk of obesity, and lower the risk of heart disease.

Licorice from America

North America is home to the plant known as native American licorice. This plant is used to cure a variety of illnesses, including as diarrhoea and respiratory ailments. Licorice is also proven to increase energy and heart health.

Additional advantages of licorice include lowering inflammation, enhancing joint health, and lowering stress and anxiety. It is also thought to possess anti-cancer qualities.

Christmas Mistletoe

The tough, quick-growing vine known as American mistletoe (Viscum album) can grow as high as 10 feet. The shrub bears tasty red berries and white blooms. The root and leaves offer therapeutic qualities that make it useful for treating wounds, bruises, and coughs.

Mistletoe is also a component of herbal medicines for illnesses including bronchitis, nervousness, and low blood pressure.

Angelica

For generations, several indigenous American plants have been utilised to cure a wide range of illnesses. Angelica, ginger root, lavender, and garlic are a few of the most well-known and well-liked.

The plant angelica has various health advantages. For instance, angelica is said to assist in enhancing heart health by lowering inflammation and assisting in blood purification. Angelica is also beneficial in the treatment of hypertension and other cardiovascular diseases. Angelica can also aid with digestion by fostering good bacteria colonies in the stomach.

Another herb with many health advantages is ginger. Ginger has a reputation for being a powerful painkiller and an anti-inflammatory. In addition, ginger can boost the immune system, aid with circulation, and joint health. Ginger not only has health advantages, but it also tastes great!

Alopecia Sage

Salvia pratensis, sometimes known as antelope sage, is a perennial shrub that can reach heights of two to four feet. The branches are thick, the leaves are positioned in opposition to one another. The bell-shaped blooms are blue or purple in colour.

The anti-inflammatory, pain-relieving, healing, and stress-relieving properties of antelope sage are just a few of its numerous advantages. In order to treat respiratory conditions including bronchitis and asthma, it also functions as an anti-inflammatory drug.

Arnica

The Alps are home to the flower arnica. Arnica includes a number of different substances, including the analgesic and anti-inflammatory arnica Montana lactone. Arnica may be applied topically to heal wounds and other skin ailments and also has vasoconstrictor effects.

Withania somnifera, sometimes referred to as Indian ginseng, is a plant that is indigenous to India and Nepal. It has been used for ages as a traditional herbal remedy in the area. For its potential to enhance cognitive performance, lessen stress and anxiety, and enhance sleep quality, ashwagandha has been investigated.

Aspen

This sturdy tree swiftly reaches heights of 12 to 20 feet, has thin leaves, and blooms in late spring with fragrant white or pink flowers. With tiny, thorny needles, the bark is rough and reddish-brown in colour. The sap is processed into throat lozenges and used to heal wounds and other skin issues. Additionally, arrows, tools, and furniture are all made of wood.

Astragalus The Fabaceae family of flowering plants includes the genus Astragalus. About 20 species exist, all of which are indigenous to North America. Native American tribes employ several of the species as part of their traditional medicine.

Some of the genus' members are utilised as supplements or components in conventional medicines. In particular, astragalus membranaceus is renowned for enhancing blood flow and minimising inflammation. Another species in the genus, Astragalus sinicus, has long been used to treat cardiovascular diseases and other illnesses that impact the circulatory system. Some plants in the genus include edible roots and stems that may be used to prepare meals or tea.

Attractylodes

Within the lily family, there are roughly 20 blooming plants of the Attractylodes genus. They naturally grow in wet places like stream banks and seeps in North America. Native Americans utilise several of the species for medicinal purposes. Some species are used to cure stomachaches, respiratory infections, sore throats, and colds. The raw or cooked leaves and stems of several species are also consumed.

Boswell Fir

A native tree to North America, the balsam fir may reach heights of 40 feet. It features fragrant, cone-shaped blooms and triangular leaves. Balsam oil, which is used to treat skin disorders and as a fragrance ingredient, may be made from balsam fir sap. The balsam fir tree is also well-known for its therapeutic benefits, which include the treatment of respiratory issues, inflammation, and discomfort.

Banana Root

A perennial plant, balsamroot usually reaches a height of 1-2 feet. The serrated margins of the lance-shaped leaves. At the stem's summit, there are clusters of tiny, green blooms. Copal resin, which is found in the root and used to cure and promote healing of skin diseases. Native Americans have utilised balsamroot for a number of diseases as a natural treatment for millennia. Additionally, it has anti-inflammatory qualities that make it useful for treating arthritis and other types of pain. Balsam root is also a powerful anti-stress and anti-anxiety medication.

Barberry

The North American native species of the barberry family is the barberry (Berberis aquifolium). These bushes often have little, spiky leaves and a height of up to 3 feet. The fruit is a purple drupe, while the blooms are white and bell-shaped. Native Americans have long utilised the bush for medicinal purposes.

Using barberry can help with cleansing, wound healing, circulation improvement, and inflammation reduction. This herb is a beneficial supplement to any health programme because to its antiviral and antibacterial characteristics.

Bearberry

Numerous fantastic native American plants offer numerous advantages, from curing small diseases to promoting general wellbeing. The top five bearberry plants for your medicinal garden are listed below:

(Campsis radicans) Blue Cohosh

Hot flashes and dry vaginal passages are two menopausal symptoms that this plant has historically been used to alleviate. Additionally, it lessens cramping and blood flow during menstruation.

Arctostaphylos uva-ursi, or bearberry

Black bearberry, one of the most well-liked bearberries, is a fantastic option for individuals seeking an anti-inflammatory and antioxidant plant. It can be helpful in controlling other menopausal symptoms including hot flashes and vaginal dryness as well as skin issues like dermatitis.

Insect pollen

One of the most well-liked natural supplements on the market is bee pollen. Bee pollen has been used for millennia by Native Americans to enhance their health and wellbeing. A top-notch source of protein, fibre, vitamins, minerals, and antioxidants is bee pollen. Improved immunity, greater sleep, and less inflammation are a few advantages of bee pollen.

Beech The sturdy beech tree may flourish in a range of conditions. Bees may find food and nesting places on beech trees, which are advantageous for beekeeping. Beer, wine, and spirits are produced from the beech tree's leaves and twigs. The beech tree's wood is also employed to create cabinets, furniture, and other things.

Beeswax

Natural wax produced by honey bees is called beeswax. It can be applied to polish furniture or as cosmetics. Additionally, certain pharmacological medicines include beeswax.

chokecherry black

Small and deciduous, the black chokecherry (Prunus serotina) can reach a height of 25 feet. The bark is silky with black flecks, and the fruit is a deep purple cherry. The blooms are white with pink petals, the leaves are elliptical, and the margins are crenate (serrated).

The black chokecherry grows naturally in low-lying places close to water in the eastern United States. It may grow in either full sun or shade and enjoys damp, acidic soil. The tree can tolerate drought, but it thrives when watered often while it is actively growing.

The medical benefits of black chokecherry, which include anti-inflammatory, antiviral, and antioxidant qualities, are well known. It has historically been used to treat ailments like fever, gout, and rheumatoid arthritis. Wildlife species like deer and turkey also use the tree as a food source.

Black Cohosh Black Cohosh is a North American herb that has been used for many years to cure a variety of illnesses. Typically, the plant may be found in wet locations close to bodies of water. As a female contraceptive, it has historically been used to ease menopausal symptoms. In addition, black cohosh relieves menstrual cramps, anxiety, sadness, hot flashes, and sexual dysfunction. Several Usages of Black Cohosh

1) Female Contraceptive: Due to the plant's ability to suppress ovulation, black cohosh has long been used as a female contraceptive.
2) Menopause Relief: Black cohosh is also frequently used to treat the symptoms of menopause, including hot flashes, nocturnal sweats, mood swings, and exhaustion. Black Cohosh performed better in investigations than other conventional therapies like hormone replacement therapy (HRT) or antidepressants.
3) Anxiety & Depression: Numerous studies have demonstrated that black cohosh can assist those who suffer from anxiety and depression by reducing their symptoms.
4) Black Cohosh has also been shown to reduce the symptoms of hot flashes.

Popular native American plant known as black gum ephedra has been used for generations as a stimulant and treatment for asthma and other respiratory conditions. The blood is purified and toxins are eliminated from the body by cranberry root. The dandelion root, on the other hand, functions as a natural anti-inflammatory. Both the well-known spices ginger and garlic have therapeutic qualities. The herb yarrow is also useful for alleviating menstrual cramps, anxiety, and sadness.

White Haw

Native Americans depend on the plant black haw for survival. It has been used for many years to treat a number of diseases. The plant is a wonderful complement to any healthcare routine since it also has antibacterial and antiviral capabilities. Five advantages of utilising black haw are as follows:

1. It aids in infection prevention.

1) It reduces inflammation, 2.

2. It could enhance circulation.

3. It can lessen swelling and soreness.

4. It possesses antioxidant and anti-inflammatory effects that help delay ageing and improve general health.

BlackBerry Black

A tough shrub, the black raspberry may reach heights of 4 feet and a width of 2 feet. The blooms are pink, and the leaves are ovate-shaped. When mature, the fruit is black and has two seeds. The black raspberry has medicinal qualities and is used to cure a number of conditions, including kidney stones, arthritis, bronchitis, colds, gastritis, heartburn, headache, and indigestion. In addition, the leaves can be used to make tea to treat conditions like stress or sleeplessness.

Bloodroot

In the eastern and central regions of the US, bloodroot is a wildflower. The root is used to cure a variety of medical conditions, including as pain, digestive disorders, and skin infections. Bloodroot is also utilised to enhance mental capacity, including memory.

Bloodroot

North America is home to the perennial plant known as bloodroot. Native Americans have utilised this plant for many years to cure a range of illnesses. Bloodroot is a well-liked option for treating pain and inflammation since it includes anti-inflammatory and antioxidant components. Bloodroot has a number of advantages, including easing mood swings, lowering stress levels, and decreasing joint inflammation.

Red Cohosh

A perennial plant, blue cohosh can reach a height of one foot. The ovate, lance-shaped, and blue-green leaves are in form. The blooms are tiny, purple, and white. The root is fibrous and meaty. Native Americans have been using blue cohosh as a kind of traditional medicine for many years. It is said to contain qualities that aid in enhancing sexual function, reducing discomfort, and boosting circulation. The use of blue cohosh can enhance fertility, ease menstrual cramps, and improve mood.

False indigo blue

Wildflowers of the blue false indigo kind are indigenous to North America. Native Americans have long utilised this plant for medicinal purposes. People can utilise blue false indigo nowadays for a number of advantages.

It is well known that blue false indigo can aid with circulation and inflammation management. Colds, the flu, and other respiratory illnesses can also be treated with it. False blue indigo also helps to smooth out wrinkles and enhance complexion.

Spruce Blue

Numerous health issues, including as inflammation, the flu, and asthma, are treated by this plant. It strengthens the immune system and eases tension and headaches. Additionally, it can lessen depressive and anxiety symptoms.

Blueberry

All ages can benefit from the numerous advantages of Native American plants. They have a lot of anti-inflammatory characteristics, which can reduce the symptoms of arthritis and chronic pain. Elderberry, Oregon grape, and wild berry are some of the top blueberry herbs.

These plants all have advantages to your health in particular ways. Elderberry is a natural pain reliever that can assist with back and arthritic pain. Antioxidants, which help shield your cells from harm and perhaps enhance your general health, are abundant in oregon grapes. An excellent source of vitamins, minerals, and anthocyanins, which all promote good health, is the wildberry.

Eupatorium perfoliatum, a perennial plant known as "boneset," is found in damp regions of the eastern United States. The leaves and root can both be utilised medicinally, with the root being the more often used component. For generations, boneset has been used to treat bronchitis, anxiety, chest discomfort, and other respiratory conditions. The stems, bark from the roots, leaves, and flowers are all said to have therapeutic qualities.

A boneset can decrease swelling and heat, boost a healthy immune system, and help with digestion, among other advantages. It has also been demonstrated to lessen stress and elevate mood. Additionally, some studies suggest that bonesets are a useful treatment for neurological diseases including epilepsy.

About 40 trees and shrubs make up the genus Boswellia, which belongs to the Fabaceae family of peas. The deserts and semi-arid regions of North Africa, the Middle East, India, and Australia are home to the indigenous flora. The medicinal benefits of Boswellia oil (Boswellia serrata) are brought on by its active components.

Cold pressing is used to get the oil from the fruit or resin of Boswellia serrata plants. Alpha-boswellic acid, which has anti-inflammatory effects, makes up to 80% of it. Boswellia oil is used in traditional medicine to treat a wide range of issues, including inflammation, eczema, psoriasis, pain from arthritis and other medical diseases, and breathing issues including asthma. Additionally, some studies have indicated that it helps lower cholesterol and guard against heart disease.

Bok weed Snakeweed

The perennial herb known as broom snakeweed (Glechoma hederacea) can reach a height of around one metre. Its little, delicate blooms are produced together with smooth, somewhat wiry foliage. The plant is indigenous to the eastern United States and thrives in wet environments including bogs, swamps, and stream banks.

Numerous glycosides found in the root of broom snakeweed have long been utilised as medicines by Native Americans. These include squalenone, squalane, berberine, and barbaloin. These glycosides can be used to treat diseases including arthritis, asthma, and Crohn's disease since some of them have anti-inflammatory effects.

Broom snakeweed also enhances blood circulation and lessens inflammation brought on by illnesses or accidents. In addition, the plant contains natural antioxidants that can help shield the body from the harm that free radicals can do.

Brush Buck

Native to North America's Rocky Mountains, buckbrush is a perennial plant. The herb is frequently used to reduce stress and encourage relaxation. It has long been used as a home cure for sadness, anxiety, and headaches. Additionally, buckbrush possesses antifungal and antibacterial characteristics that can be used to treat infections.

Buckthorn

A shrub or small tree, buckthorn (Rhamnus cathartica) can reach heights of up to 6 feet. The opposing, elliptical leaves are between two and four inches long and one inch broad. The fruit is a dry capsule, and the blooms are a reddish-purple colour.

The bark is reddish-brown, scaly, and smooth. The twigs have delicate hairs covering them. The fruit is a sour berry that includes the chemical oxalic acid, which can irritate skin.

Buckthorn has been utilised for generations as a source of medicinal leaves and bark. Native Americans utilised buckthorn to cure a variety of conditions, including sores, inflammation, the flu, colds, diarrhoea, indigestion, and stomachaches. Buckthorn is useful for treating a variety of conditions, including psoriasis, lowering pain and fever, halting bleeding, enhancing circulation, strengthening the immune system, and combating infection.

Burdock Berry

(Elymus canadensis) Buffalo Berry

Much of North America is home to the perennial plant known as the buffalo berry. The leaves and blooms are edible, while the roots and stems are used to manufacture medicine. For hundreds of years, the buffalo berry has been used to cure a wide range of illnesses, including diabetes, cancer, heart troubles, lung disorders, and more. The following are a few advantages of utilising buffalo berries:

1. It facilitates blood sugar regulation.

2. It lessens inflammation.

3. It might benefit heart health.

4. It might benefit respiratory health.

5. It is an antioxidant and can fend off harm from free radicals.

Burdock

Herbaceous burdock may be found over most of North America. Native Americans have utilised it for medical purposes for ages. Burdock has a wealth of minerals and has several health advantages. Here are the top five:

1. Burdock is an excellent source of antioxidants and dietary fibre. According to a research published in the "Journal of Medicinal Food," burdock extract has antioxidant activity that is equivalent to certain well-known antioxidants like vitamin E and resveratrol. This helps shield cells from free radical damage, which can aggravate a number of illnesses including cancer.

2. Burdock has a lot of calcium. More than twice as much calcium as one cup (60 grammes) of milk may be found in one cup (120 grammes) of cooked burdock! This is due to the substantial levels of oxalic acid and phytate found in burdock, which bind up minerals like calcium and prevent their absorption by the body. However, dissolving these inhibitors by boiling or steaming the burdock before eating will increase calcium absorption.

3. Vitamins A and C are abundant in burdock. Cooked burdock includes 5 percent DV (daily value) of vitamin C and 16 percent DV (daily value) of vitamin A, two important nutrients.

Root, Calamus

Tribal healers have traditionally employed Native American plants to support health and wellbeing. One such plant, valued for its therapeutic powers, is calamus root. The following are some advantages of calamus root use:

1. Calamus Root Can Lower Stress and Anxiety Levels

Calamus root has a strong anti-anxiety and anti-stress impact. This is partially attributable to its capacity to balance emotions and reduce symptoms including restlessness, irritability, sleeplessness, and tension headaches.

2. The Use of Calamus Root for Detoxification

The potential of calamus root to facilitate detoxification is one of the key advantages of utilising it. It improves the functions of the kidneys, liver, intestines, lungs, and skin in the body's natural elimination processes. This can improve general health and wellbeing by removing harmful pollutants from the body.

3. Using Calamus Root to Improve Digestion

The capacity of calamus root to enhance digestion is another advantage. It promotes overall digestive health and well-being by aiding in the breakdown of food so that it may be absorbed into the circulation more readily.

Golden Poppies

Native to North America, California poppy (Eschscholzia californica) has long been used as a medicine. It functions as an anti-inflammatory, antioxidant, and anti-anxiety agent. Additionally, California poppies enhance mood, enhance sleep quality, and lessen stress and anxiety.

The use of California poppy as a natural stress and anxiety reliever has several advantages. It calms agitation, weariness, sleeplessness, irritability, headaches from tension, stiffness in the muscles, shakiness, and vertigo. The California poppy can also improve mood and ease melancholy or depression.

Carnation Flower

Eastern and central North America are home to the perennial plant known as the cardinal flower (Lobelia cardinalis). The pink, white, or purple blossoms are usually 1 to 1.5 inches broad. The large root system of the cardinal flower can be employed for therapeutic reasons. Using the cardinal flower can help with menstrual cramps, migraines, anxiety, and flu symptoms, among other things.

Sacred Cascara

A rare and powerful substance called cascara sagrada is found in the Pacific yew tree's bark. Native Americans have long utilised the plant as a natural remedy for a variety of health issues, such as joint discomfort, high blood pressure, and seizures.

Numerous advantages for general health have been linked to cascara sagrada. Studies have demonstrated, for instance, that the substance can help decrease blood pressure and prevent the development of cancer cells. Cascara sagrada has also been shown to enhance cognitive performance and lessen signs of stress and anxiety.

Consuming cascara sagrada in extract or tincture form is the most effective method. Before commencing any herbal therapy, be careful to discuss it with your doctor. All supplements should be taken with caution and according to their recommendations.

Animal's Claw

Cat's Claw (Uncaria tomentosa) is a plant that grows in the United States and some regions of Canada. It is also known by the names Indian hemp, badger brush, and yerba santa. Native Americans have traditionally used it as a medicine, and scientists now think it could be healthy. Compounds found in cat's claw may aid in reducing pain and inflammation, enhancing blood circulation, and safeguarding the heart. Additionally, some people utilise it to cure illnesses including arthritis and others.

Catnip

The herb "Catnip" has been used for many years as a cure-all. Sedative, antispasmodic, and analgesic effects are believed to exist in it. According to recent research, catnip has heart-health benefits as well.

Cattail

Many lakes and rivers include the plant known as cattails. This plant has long, thin stems and can reach heights of one to two feet. The oval-shaped leaves have a medium green colour. The white, little blossoms are tiny. Fibre, vitamins A and C, potassium, magnesium, and calcium are all found in abundance in cattail.

Cayenne

The cayenne pepper plant is indigenous to South America. Many different cuisines, including Mexican and French cookery, employ cayenne pepper. It is a wonderful option for individuals who want some heat but don't want to get overheated because of its moderate heat intensity. The flavour of food may be enhanced with cayenne peppers without becoming overpowered.

The following are a few advantages of utilising cayenne peppers:

- They can aid in reducing swelling and discomfort brought on by illnesses like arthritis and others.

- They are effective at reducing cold and flu symptoms like fever and congestion.

- They can increase blood flow and support the immune system.

Cedar

The pine family includes cedar, which may be found growing all around the world. Sculptures, furniture, and construction materials may all be made from cedar wood. Many things may be made with cedar oil, including treatments for hair care and treating skin ailments.

Chamomile

A blooming plant known as chamomile may be found all over the world. Since it has been used for centuries as a medicine, several health advantages have come to light. Effective pain relief, anxiety and tension reduction, and better sleep are all benefits of chamomile. Additionally, it has anti-inflammatory effects that can aid in easing the symptoms of illnesses like arthritis.

Chickweed

Stellaria media, sometimes known as chickweed, is a crucial plant in Native American herbal medicine. Chickweed has been used for millennia and is being used today to cure a variety of illnesses. Numerous healthy substances found in chickweed can contribute to bettering general health.

The capacity of chickweed to lessen inflammation is one of its main advantages. It has been demonstrated that the antioxidants in chickweed can aid in defending the body against the harm done by free radicals, a common cause of inflammation. Chickweed has been used to treat ailments including weariness and sleeplessness since it is a potent stimulant.

Additionally, chickweed contains antibacterial qualities that can help stave against infections. Chickweed not only destroys dangerous bacteria but also has the potential to stop the growth of several fungi. As a result, it works well to treat long-lasting illnesses like Lyme disease and Candida overgrowth.

Chlorella

A single-celled plant called chlorella is well known for enhancing mental performance and lowering inflammation. Additionally, this microalgae can aid in lowering the risk of diabetes, heart disease, and stroke.

The following are a few possible advantages of chlorella:

1) Enhanced mental capacity

2) lessening of inflammation

3) decreased risk of diabetes, heart disease, and stroke

Chokeberry

A shrubby vine with a normal height of 4 feet, chokeberry. Bees pollinate the plant's fragrant pink or white blossoms, which are also present. A dark red berry that may be eaten raw or used in cooking is the chokeberry's fruit.

Taking chokeberry supplements or eating the fruit has a number of advantages. Chokeberry, for instance, has been demonstrated to enhance heart health by lowering inflammation and enhancing blood flow. By enhancing the immune system and preventing the growth of tumours, it can also aid in the prevention of some cancers. Chokeberry may also aid those who have dementia or Alzheimer's disease in improving their memory and cognitive function.

Citrus Bark

A spice with a long history and several applications is cinnamon. The inner, dry bark of certain laurel-family tree species is known as cinnamon bark. The bark has a rich, fragrant scent and is dark brown.

Cloves

The subterranean stem of a Madagascar-native evergreen tree yields cloves, a spice. Foods and drinks frequently contain cloves as a flavouring. However, they may also be used to conventional medicine. Clove has several advantages, including lowering inflammation and discomfort, enhancing mood and memory, and safeguarding the lungs.

Group Moss

The Sioux and other North American tribes have long employed the strong plant club moss. This plant's leaves and stems are used to create a tea or infusion that is considered to provide a number of health advantages. These include addressing respiratory issues, decreasing inflammation, and enhancing the immune system.

The following are some of the special advantages of club moss:

-Reducing inflammation: Club moss may be used as a herbal medicine to lessen inflammation, which can assist with ailments like arthritis.

-Treating respiratory conditions: Bronchitis and asthma may both be successfully treated with club moss. This is because it has ingredients that facilitate better airflow and assist to relax airways.

Club moss may also aid to strengthen your immune system by boosting the generation of white blood cells.

Coltsfoot

Aconitum napellus, a plant native to temperate Eurasia and North America, is a member of the Ranunculaceae family. Coltsfoot was formerly used to cure fever, gastrointestinal issues, and arthritis in addition to its typical usage as a pesticide. The herb is also said to protect the liver, cure depression and anxiety, promote nervous system health, and boost fertility.

Corn

A multipurpose plant, maize may be used for both food and fuel. Dietary fibre, carbs, and other nutrients can be found in maize. The plant provides a good source of protein and it has antioxidant properties. Consuming maize can lower the risk of heart disease, diabetes, and some forms of cancer, among other health advantages.

Cranberry

Small, shrubby, and deciduous, cranberry trees can grow to a height of 10 to 15 feet. Its fruit, which is oval in shape and ranges in colour from pale green to deep crimson, has a smooth, thin bark. The sour fruit is used to make jams, jellies, sauce, and juice. The bloom of the plant is pollinated by bees, and its leaves are arranged in pairs.

Bush, Creosote

Asteraceae is the family of plants that includes creosote bush. The Greek term for resin served as the inspiration for the genus name, Creosote. In Central and Western North America, you may find this plant.

Creosote bushes can reach heights of 1 to 3 metres. It has opposing leaves with whole edges and a serrated edge that range in form from oval to oblong. Up to 50 bisexual or unisexual yellow flowers with five petals reflexed at the base and united at the tip can be found in the inflorescence. Two glossy, dark brown seeds are released as the fruit's capsule opens.

For a number of ailments, the creosote bush is utilised as a natural medicine. The treatment of fever, inflammation, and respiratory issues is regarded to be successful. Additionally, it has been used to treat digestion issues, skin conditions, neurological abnormalities, and joint discomfort. According to certain research, it could lower the risk of cancer.

What advantages does utilising creosote bush offer?

The advantages of utilising creosote bush are as follows:

- It works well to treat fever

- It may lower the chance of developing cancer.

- It has been used to treat digestion issues, skin conditions, neurological abnormalities, and joint discomfort.

Damiana

In Mexico and Central America, damiana (Damiandra Zizanoides), a plant belonging to the mint family, grows naturally. Damiana is a plant whose leaves and blooms are used to create tea, extract oil, and cure a wide range of illnesses. Indigenous people in the region have used daimona for years as a general remedy, but more recent studies have pointed to its potential advantages.

Damiana tea is thought to have stimulant, diuretic, and aphrodisiac properties. It may also lessen tension, anxiety, and sleeplessness. Anxiety disorders, depression, nerve discomfort, menstrual cramps, infertility problems, psoriasis and eczema, memory troubles, and other illnesses have all been reported to be helped by the plant's extracts.

Damiana can also lessen inflammation and increase circulation. Recent studies have revealed that damiana may also benefit older persons' cognitive performance and encourage healthy cell development in addition to these traditional applications.

Dandelion

Dandelion is a superb herb for the body's detoxification process. It is excellent for warding against illness since it is strong in vitamin C. Dandelion also has a lot of antioxidants, which aid in preventing cell damage. enhanced liver function and enhanced digestion are two additional advantages of dandelion use.

Satan's Club

In North America, the Coastal Mountain Range of California and Oregon is where one may find Devil's Club most frequently. The plant, which belongs to the buckthorn family, has a maximum height of 12 feet. The traditional uses of devil's club as a medicine have included the treatment of infections, cancer, and ulcers. Secondary metabolites found in the plant have been demonstrated to have positive health effects, including anticancer capabilities.

Dogbane

A genus of plants in the sunflower family is known as dogbane. The common dogbane (Duguetia Versicolor), dwarf dogbane (Duguetia minimum), and prickly dogbane (Aconitum napellus) are among the native species to North America. Dogbane blooms feature five petals, each with a long filament, and are often purple or blue in colour. The roots have a fibrous, parasitic root structure.

Tea made from dogbane flowers is used to cure a variety of ailments, including fever and inflammation. The herb is also used to cure bug bites and soothe nerve discomfort. Azulene oil, which has anti-inflammatory qualities, is present in the root system. The plant also has flavonoids and tannins that promote healthy skin and hair growth.

Dogwood

Some of the world's most useful and adaptable plants are Native American herbs. These organic treatments can help you live a better life by promoting general health and repairing wounds. Ten of the top Native American plants will be discussed in this part along with their advantages.

Donald Quai

A well-known Chinese herb called dong quai has been used for generations as a natural treatment for a number of ailments. Dong Quai is frequently used to alleviate stress, anxiety, and menopausal symptoms, in particular. Improved nerve function, better sleep, and relief from joint discomfort are some other advantages of dong quai.

Dong Quai oil, dong Quai root extract, and dong Quai bark extract are a few of the plant's important constituents. These three substances have all been demonstrated to possess potent anti-inflammatory activities. They have also been demonstrated to enhance circulation and blood flow, which aids in lowering inflammation throughout the body.

Dong Quai dietary supplements can be consumed in a variety of ways. They are available over the counter and at a few health food stores. They may be found online as well. Imagine you want to consistently consume a Dong Quai supplement. In that situation, it's recommended to first speak with your healthcare physician because frequent use of this herb may result in certain adverse effects.

David Maple

A resilient and quick-growing tree, the douglas maple is found all across the world. It is a well-liked tree for gardening and yields a lot of maple sugar. In addition, the tree is renowned for its hardy branches and resistance to pests and diseases. Douglas maple has been linked to a number of health advantages, including increased circulation, alleviation from joint discomfort, and decreased anxiety.

Skunk cabbage from the East

Native to North America, eastern skunk cabbage (Portulaca oleracea) is frequently used in cooking. The plant is frequently regarded as a potent detoxifier and has a long history of usage as a natural medicine for a variety of diseases. Additionally, Eastern Skunk Cabbage has the ability to heal or prevent digestive issues including indigestion and constipation. The plant is also thought to improve skin health and general brain health and function. Eastern Skunk Cabbage also aids in promoting healthy hair, nails, and digestion, as well as lowering swelling and inflammation.

Echinacea

Native to North America, the "Echinacea" plant has a long history of usage as a remedy. A member of the daisy family, echinacea is well recognised for boosting circulation and warding against infections. Echinacea can help with colds, the flu, sinus infections, and other respiratory conditions while also strengthening the immune system.

Elderberry

A 3 foot tall shrub known as elderberry, it has leathery leaves and clusters of tiny white or pink blooms. The berries have a tart flavour and are edible. Elderberry is a traditional remedy for respiratory illnesses including the flu and colds. In addition to helping treat common ailments, the plant provides additional health advantages. It has been demonstrated that elderberry can lower cholesterol levels, enhance blood sugar regulation, and lower the risk of heart disease.

Eleuthero

A genus of flowering plants in the Araliaceae family is called Eleuthero. The word "generic" comes from the Greek terms "eleutherios," which means "free from fear," and "this," which means "bush." The genus has roughly 30 species, the majority of which are unique to North America and Siberia. Eleutherococcus senticosus and Eleutherococcus palustris are the only two of them that have been found outside of those areas.

Indigenous people have traditionally utilised eleuthero plants as medicine despite their sparse distribution. Their advantages in treating anxiety and stress-related diseases, as well as Russian colds and other respiratory infections, are particularly well-known. Additionally, it has been demonstrated that some species enhance immune response and lessen inflammation.

Terpenes, such as sabinene, cineole, camphene, -pinene, limonene, myrcene, and -terpineol, are the main components of eleuthero plants. These substances display a wide range of therapeutic benefits, such as antioxidant activity, anti-inflammatory effects, and anticancer effects. Some terpenes have lately been found as possible biofuel sources in addition to their historical medical use.

Eucalyptus

Eastern Australia and New Caledonia are the natural habitats of the eucalyptus tree. The tree may reach a height of 30 metres and has smooth, red-brown bark on older trees. The leaves have a pointed apex, a lanceolate shape, and a serrated border. The blooms have five fused petals at the base and are either white or pink. Fruits are capsule-shaped objects that break apart to release their seeds.

Native Americans may benefit greatly from eucalyptus trees in numerous ways. The tree's usage as a natural insecticide is one of its advantages. Due to their antifungal characteristics, the leaves can be utilised to cure common lawn ailments including rust and downy mildew. The eucalyptus tree also has anti-inflammatory effects, which is another advantage. It can therefore be used to treat ailments including arthritis and headaches. Additionally, it has been demonstrated that eucalyptus oil contains antiviral characteristics, making it useful in the treatment of cold and flu illnesses.

Night primrose

The blooming plant known as evening primrose (Oenothera biennis) thrives in temperate climates. It has been established that the plant offers a number of health advantages and has been utilised as traditional medicine. These advantages include lowering inflammation, enhancing heart health, and assisting with joint function improvement.

Bladderpod Fendler

The perennial herb known as Fendler's bladderpod, commonly referred to as the bladderpod lily or the American bladderpod, is indigenous to North America. It may reach a height of 1.5 feet and has oval-shaped leaves that are white on the underside and green on top. The centres of the purple blooms are yellow.

The Fendler's bladderpod is a plant used in herbal medicine for its anti-inflammatory, gastrointestinal-soothing, and infection-fighting qualities. Additionally, it is used to treat skin diseases, reduce anxiety, and control blood sugar levels.

Fennel

You need go no farther than the fennel plant for a natural cure for minor health issues. Since ancient times, Native Americans have utilised fennel to cure conditions including indigestion, diarrhoea, and respiratory ailments. Additionally, the herb is recognised to enhance mental and emotional health. Here are six justifications for include this plant in your normal diet:

1. Fennel combats bloating and gas.

2. It facilitates digestive improvement and constipation relief.

3. Due to its anti-inflammatory qualities, it can aid in the reduction of inflammation and discomfort.

4. Antioxidant qualities help it combat the body's dangerous free radicals.

5. It may lower bodily tension and anxiety levels.

6. Last but not least, fennel is a wonderful source of dietary fibre, which helps support general digestive health and manage blood sugar levels.

Fenugreek

A member of the Fabaceae family, fenugreek (Trigonella foenum-graecum) is a flowering plant. In regions of south-central Asia, including India and Pakistan, fenugreek is a natural plant. Other regions of the world, including as North Africa, the Middle East, and Europe, also plant fenugreek. In many regions of the world, fenugreek has been used medicinally for generations. The seeds and leaves are both utilised medicinally.

Feverfew

Europe and Asia are home to the plant known as feverfew (Tanacetum parthenium). It is utilised as a traditional treatment for a number of medical issues. It is believed that the plant has anti-inflammatory, analgesic, and fever-lowering qualities.

Feverwort

Popular native American plant feverwort has several advantages. Colds, the flu, and other respiratory illnesses are all treated with it. Additionally anti-inflammatory and capable of reducing pain, feverwort. The circulatory system and the heart both benefit from it.

Galangal

Galangal is a spice made from a rhizome that grows in Southeast Asia. In Asian cooking, galangal extract is used to flavour foods. The following are just a few advantages of utilising galangal:

1. Galangal might aid in boosting circulation and enhancing sleep.

2. Due to its anti-inflammatory characteristics, it may be able to lessen pain and inflammation brought on by ailments including arthritis and joint discomfort.

3. Additionally, it can aid with digestion, especially when combined with other herbs like ginger and turmeric.

Cambogia Garcinia

In recent years, garcinia cambogia has gained popularity as a weight-loss product. The usefulness of this extract for weight loss, however, is the subject of scant study. While other studies disagree, some claim that garcinia cambogia can aid in weight loss. The safety and effectiveness of Garcinia Cambogia for weight reduction have not been examined by the National Centre for Complementary and Integrative Health (NCCIH).

Garlic

Due to its numerous health advantages, garlic is one of the most often used plant herbs. Allicin, which is abundant in it, contains antioxidant and antiviral characteristics that shield cells from cellular harm. Additionally, garlic can enhance blood flow and aid decrease inflammation throughout the body. In addition to these conventional use, garlic has therapeutic value.

Gentiana

A genus of blooming plants in the sunflower family is called Gentiana. Native to North America, the genus is frequently observed in arid or sandy environments. The Gentiana genus has roughly 20 species, the majority of which are herbs. The Gentiana genus has a few species that have therapeutic uses.

Gentian plants provide advantages such as stimulating the appetite and lowering stress levels. Some gentian plants are also utilised for their cosmetic qualities, which aid in skin irritation prevention and hair growth promotion.

Garlic Root

A versatile plant with a long history of medical usage is ginger root. Numerous medicinal substances, including analgesic and anti-inflammatory ones, are found in ginger root. It may be used to cure a number of ailments, such as fever, stomach cramps, and headaches. Ginger root is effective in treating infections since it also contains antiviral and antibacterial properties.

ginseng lupulin

A venerable tree called the ginkgo biloba may be found all across the world. Even so, it's particularly well-known for its health advantages for people. Ginkgo Biloba, a plant native to China and Japan, is a favourite herb in traditional Chinese medicine because it boosts stamina, memory, and circulation.

Additionally, diabetes and other illnesses have been treated using ginkgo tree extract in Eastern Europe. Terpenes, flavonoids, and other antioxidants found in it aid in the prevention of illness. Alzheimer's disease and dementia can both be effectively treated with ginkgo biloba extract. Studies have revealed that consistent ginkgo biloba usage can help prevent age-related cognitive decline and keep people intellectually sharp into their senior years in addition to these personal advantages.

Ginseng

For millennia, people have utilised ginseng as a herb to enhance their health. It provides a number of advantages, including increased energy, lowered stress levels, and enhanced mental clarity. Reduced risk of cancer, improved blood circulation, increased libido, and higher immune system performance are just a few of ginseng's health advantages.

Glucomannan

One of the most well-liked and useful plants from Native America is glucomannan. A particular form of fibre called glucomannan aids in controlling cholesterol levels, blood sugar levels, and weight reduction, among other things.

Foods including seaweed, fruits, vegetables, and grains contain glucomannan. However, since most foods don't contain enough glucomannan, it is advisable to take supplements with it. Your general health and well-being can be enhanced by include glucomannan in your diet.

Goldenrod

Native to North America, goldenrod is a perennial with a sluggish growth rate. The plant has been discovered to offer a number of health advantages and has been used medicinally for thousands of years. Inflammation is reduced, anxiety and depression are treated, cognitive function is aided, and circulation is improved, among other advantages.

Goldenseal

A herb called goldenseal (Hydrastis Canadensis) has been used for generations to cure a number of illnesses. Berberine, a compound found in the plant that has anti-inflammatory, antibacterial, and antiviral activities. It has also been successful in treating joint diseases including rheumatoid arthritis. Goldenseal supplements provide a number of health advantages, such as lowering the risk of cancer and enhancing digestion in general.

Gooseberry

Gooseberry is a little shrub that can reach a height of 2 feet. It features low-growing leaves and blue blooms that bees use for pollination. Gooseberries are a kind of berry that may be found globally in temperate regions. Fresh, dried, or processed berries are used to make jams, jellies, syrups, wine, and other products. Due to the presence of antioxidants, fibre, and vitamins C and K, gooseberries provide several health advantages.

Rock Root

Native to North America is the plant known as gravel root. Native Americans have utilised it for medical purposes for ages. It is now being researched for its potential health advantages, particularly for treating depression and anxiety.

Gravel root has been demonstrated to lessen the signs of anxiety and sadness in animal trials. Additionally, it raises GABA levels, a neurotransmitter that aids in mood regulation. Gravel root also possesses anti-inflammatory qualities that may be used to treat arthritis.

Hellebore fern

Native Americans have employed a variety of native American plants for their therapeutic benefits for ages. Numerous of these herbs have been found to be efficient in the treatment of a number of conditions, including arthritis, anxiety, heart disease, and more.

Green hellebore is a perennial plant that is particularly well-known for its therapeutic qualities. Native Americans have utilised this herb to cure a range of ailments, such as anxiety and despair. Green hellebore has been shown to assist in the treatment of cancer and other ailments in addition to its traditional usage.

Reduced anxiety and depressive symptoms, enhanced heart health, decreased inflammation, and cancer prevention are some advantages of utilising green hellebore. If you're searching for a herbal cure that will help you enhance your general health, green hellebore can be an excellent choice for you.

Leaf tea

Green tea has several advantages, both for general health and for specific illnesses. While the catechins in green tea have many health advantages, the antioxidants help shield the body from many ailments.

Green tea can be used as a topical remedy, added to food, or taken as a beverage. Consistent green tea use has been linked to a lower risk of cancer and other chronic illnesses. Green tea is also used as a moderate stimulant for better attention due to its capacity to enhance cognitive function.

The negative effects of drinking a lot of green tea include nausea and upset stomach. Read the labelling when buying green tea and choose varieties produced with organically cultivated leaves.

Guarana

The guarana tree, or Piper guarana, is a shrubby tree that can reach a height of 25 feet. The leaves are oppositely oriented and have serrated edges, and the bark is rough. The fruit is a capsule, and the blooms are tiny and white. Guarana grows in Brazil, Paraguay, and Uruguay and is a native of South America. Indigenous people in these nations have long utilised it as a stimulant and anti-inflammatory drug.

Brazilian natives chew the leaves to get their desired results. Guarana beans contain caffeine, which has long been used to alleviate issues including headaches, exhaustion, anxiety, melancholy, and sleeplessness. Additionally, guarana supports improved concentration and mental clarity during or after physical exertion. Guarana is furthermore used by some people to boost energy levels during exercises and other strenuous activities.

Fitnessnema Sylvestre

Native to North America, the Gymnema Sylvestre plant is mostly found in the eastern and central regions of the country. The plant is used for a number of things, including circulation improvement, anxiety treatment, and memory development.

Native Americans have been using the plant for millennia as a way to improve memory, lessen anxiety, and cure cardiovascular disease. Modern studies have demonstrated that Gymnema can boost blood flow and restore cognitive function in people with dementia or Alzheimer's disease.

Hawthorne

For its therapeutic qualities, the plant hawthorn has been utilised for generations. It is well recognised for enhancing cognitive function, lowering anxiety and depression, and supporting a robust immune system. Hawthorne is also a naturally occurring source of antioxidants, which can aid in lowering the risk of cancer and other illnesses.

Book 4:
Native American Herbalism Encyclopedia Vol 2

Chapter 1:
The Best 200 Medical Herbs To Use For Everything

Indigenous communities from all around the world have been using the plant known as "Heal All" for millennia to treat wounds and illnesses. The plant is beneficial in treating a variety of skin disorders, including eczema, psoriasis, and dermatitis, and is both antibacterial and antifungal. Heal All is also helpful in treating respiratory issues like bronchitis as well as infections like the flu and the common cold.

Hibiscus

Herbs from the American Indian culture are frequently utilised in medicine. Hibiscus, dandelion, and rose hips are some of the most well-known and well-liked Native American herbs. The blooming hibiscus plant is indigenous to North America. The purple blossoms have a yellow centre, and they are used to make juice, tea, or perfume. Also a native of North America, dandelion is prized for its therapeutic qualities. The blossoms may be consumed fresh or dried, and they have been used to cure everything from congestion to hair loss. The antioxidants and vitamins C and A-rich rose hips are a native of both North America and Europe. They are utilised in a variety of baked items, salad dressings, herbal teas, and tonics.

Honeysuckle

The Caprifoliaceae family includes blooming plants like honeysuckle (Lonicera japonica). Although it is indigenous to China, Japan, Korea, and Russia, it is also grown in many other regions of the globe. The plant may grow to a height of up to 10 feet and develop into a small tree or shrub. At the extremities of branches, white or pink flower clusters are formed.

Hops

A blooming plant in the Humulus lupulus family is the hop. It is a climbing plant that may go as tall as two metres. Beer and other alcoholic beverages have a bittersweet flavour that comes from the hop plant. Bees pollinate the blossoms, and hop bines are used to produce items made from hops, such as malt.

Equine Gentian

You have a variety of possibilities when trying to learn which native American herbs are the greatest. Horse gentian is one of these plants. Native Americans have long used this plant, and it has a reputation for helping with a variety of problems. The following are some advantages of using horse gentian:

Energy levels are increased, cognitive function is enhanced, cardiovascular health is supported, healthy skin and hair development is encouraged, and inflammation and discomfort are reduced.

Horsetail

Horsetail is a perennial herbaceous plant with a height of up to two metres. It has strap-like leaves and a tall, slender stem that can turn woody at the base. Over 200 substances, including essential oils that have been used for therapeutic purposes for millennia, are found in the horsetail plant. There is evidence that several of these substances have anti-inflammatory and antiviral activities.

Chinese ginseng

Indian ginseng has been a well-liked natural treatment for millennia in Asia. This plant's root is used to cure a variety of illnesses, such as weariness, depression, and memory loss. Indian ginseng is also believed to increase vitality and circulation.

Among the advantages of utilising Indian ginseng include enhanced focus and concentration, better-quality sleep, and a decrease in worry and stress. Additionally, it is believed to aid in reducing inflammation and fostering general wellbeing.

Native Hemp

Anxiety, depression, and other mental health conditions have all been treated using Indian hemp. Additionally, it has been used to enhance sleep quality and lessen nightmares. Inflammation, seizures, and other medical disorders can all be successfully treated with Indian hemp.

The most popular applications for Indian hemp include:

- Treating depression and anxiety
- Improving the quality of sleep -Decreasing the frequency of nightmares

Native Paintbrush

A blooming plant in the daisy family is called an Indian Paintbrush. It features tiny white or pink blooms, slender leaves, and a height of 3 to 4 feet. The plant can endure in both dry and wet settings because to its robust root structure. Indian Paintbrushes have been used for their therapeutic powers by people for many years.

Pain, inflammation, and fever are just a few of the conditions that Indian Paintbrush cures. Additionally, the flowers aid in the treatment of cognitive issues like memory loss, anxiety, and sadness. Indian paintbrushes are sometimes even used as mosquito repellant.

Native to North America, Indian Paintbrush may be found in the eastern United States, Canada, and Mexico.

Ironwood

North America is the home of the ironwood tree species. Ironwood produces wood that is highly appreciated for being robust and long-lasting. The tree is also well-known for its therapeutic benefits, which include abilities to treat pain and fight infections. Ironwood provides a number of health advantages, including lowering inflammation, preventing cancer, and enhancing cardiovascular health.

Buckwheat from Jame

Eriogonum jamesii, sometimes referred to as Jame's buckwheat, is a wildflower found in western Canada, British Columbia, and the United States. A herbaceous perennial plant with a height of 1 foot, jame's buckwheat. The margins of the ovate-elliptic leaves are smooth. The tops of the stalks are covered in pink or white blooms. The fruit is a capsule with one or two seeds within.

The health of humans and the environment may both benefit greatly from Jame's buckwheat. High quantities of antioxidants in the plant are beneficial to human health because they can shield cells from harm from free radicals and pollutants. The plant also possesses anti-inflammatory qualities that may help treat conditions like arthritis that are accompanied by inflammation. Jame's buckwheat benefits the environment by supplying nutrients essential for plant growth and aiding in the binding of particles to make them more easily removed by rain or snow runoff.

Jiaogulan

Gynostemma pentaphyllum, also known as jiaogulan, is a traditional Chinese herb that boosts vitality and blood flow. It is well known for its potent antioxidant qualities and healing effects on the skin and other organs. Jiaogulan may also aid in lowering stress and anxiety, enhancing sleep quality, enhancing cognitive function, and lowering inflammation, according to new findings by experts.

Jiaogulan is most frequently used as a dietary supplement to enhance overall health and wellbeing. You can consume extract, tincture, tea, or capsules of jiaogulan. Choose the jiaogulan administration technique that is most effective for you from the numerous available options. While some like to take it in the late afternoon or the evening before bed, other people prefer to take it in the morning before breakfast.

Improved circulation, better sleep, less stress and anxiety symptoms, greater cognitive function, and decreased inflammation are some advantages of jiaogulan. Juniper

Juniper is an evergreen plant that thrives in colder areas all over the world. The touchably rough bark has a lot of terpenes. These aromatic compounds give juniper its distinctive flavour and smell. The tree's wood, leaves, berries, and oil are all useful. Products made from juniper offer several health advantages, such as lowering inflammation, improving digestion, and preventing anxiety and depression.

Kava Kava

Up to 3 metres tall, the kava kava plant (Piper methysticum) is a shrub or small tree. Sharp, pointy spines cover its branches. The leaves have strongly lobed borders and are ovate-elliptic in shape, measuring 2 to 10 centimetres long by 1 to 5 millimetres broad. When the capsules from the white, bell-shaped blooms are opened, the kava rootlets fall out. New plants are produced from the rootlets.

This question can't be answered definitively because it relies on the individual who consumes it and their biology. According to some, kava interacts with the brain in a way that promotes relaxation and stress reduction. Some claim that the plant offers advantages for the brain, such as enhancing memory recall and focus.

Some even utilise it to improve their mood when they are depressed or anxious.

Many of the alleged advantages of kava kava intake are attributed to kavalactones. Yangonin and kanavansine are the two compounds that are most well-known. For instance, canavanine seems to have depressive properties, whereas yangonin is known to help decrease blood pressure. We still don't fully understand how kavalactones affect the human body. Nevertheless, research indicate that they're probably harmless if used in moderation.

Koko Nut

African native kola nuts can be found growing naturally throughout central and eastern Africa. In Arabia and Persia, the kola nut gained popularity after being brought to the Old World. In the seventh century AD, Arab merchants brought kola nuts to Europe. Today, kola nuts are produced over most of Africa. The best kola nuts come from Nigeria and are dried after being soaked in cold water for up to three weeks.

Female Slipper

The plant known as lady's slipper (Cypripedium calceolus) is indigenous to North America and some regions of Europe. With strap-like leaves and clusters of tiny, fragrant white blooms in late spring, it may reach a height of three feet. Since the flower petals are just extensions of the pistil, they have no purpose other than to be destroyed once the flower blooms.

Citrus balm

Since ancient times, the herb lemon balm (Melissa officinalis) has been utilised as a natural treatment for a number of diseases. It is indigenous to North America and inhabits both dry and wet environments. An upright, bushy shrub with a height of up to 3 feet, lemon balm. The leaves are ovate-oblong in shape with serrated edges and have short, silky hairs covering them.

Citrus Verbena

Lemon verbena is a native of the eastern United States and is a member of the verbena family. The hardy plant lemon verbena can thrive in a variety of soils and environments. It features fragrant leaves and blooms that may be used to a variety of dishes, including salads and soups. Tea made from the blossoms and leaves of the plant might assist to increase circulation and reduce tension or anxiety.

Lemongrass

Native American herbs are a wonderful supplement to any health routine since they provide a multitude of advantages for the body and mind. One of the most well-liked plants from the Americas is lemongrass. Its numerous advantages include anti-inflammatory effects, heightened mood and vitality, and a reduction in headaches and congestion.

Licorice

The flowering plant licorice (Glycyrrhiza glabra) is indigenous to Eurasia and North Africa. The glycyrrhizin chemical found in licorice root gives the plant its distinctively sweet flavour. Licorice has been proven to provide a number of health advantages and has been used medicinally for millennia. These include of lowering blood sugar levels, enhancing blood pressure control, lowering inflammation, and assisting with weight reduction.

Lobelia

A perennial herb known as lobelia has grass-like leaves and violet blooms. The L. cardinals, L. tenuifolia, and L. perennis species are those that can be found in North America, and each has a unique set of advantages.

American Indians have been using lobelia as a medicine for generations. Studies have demonstrated that it is effective in treating respiratory issues such asthma, bronchitis, the flu, and colds. Additionally, it is thought that the plant promotes relaxation and mood enhancement. Some individuals take it as a stress and anxiety reliever.

Maca

A Peruvian root known as maca has been utilised for generations as a source of vigour and energy. Being an adaptogen, it aids the body in coping with stress. Maca can enhance male sexual performance, libido, and fertility. It also has antioxidant effects.

Maple

Hardy deciduous trees like the maple may reach heights of 30 feet. The leaves are ovate-oblong with serrated edges, and the bark is scaly. The fruit is a little, spherical thing with two seeds, while the blossoms are tiny and white. Despite being a native of North America, the tree has been brought to many other regions of the globe.

Thistle of Martin

Cirsium arvense, often known as Martin's thistle, is a native of central and eastern North America and is a member of the daisy family. The plant may reach a height of three feet, has purple blooms, and bears yellow seeds.

Martin's thistle mostly contains flavonoids, which have anti-inflammatory, antiviral, and antispasmodic properties. The plant has also been demonstrated to protect the heart and lower cholesterol levels. Martin's thistle is utilised as an attractive plant in addition to its medicinal properties.

Mayapple

A shrubby herbaceous perennial plant in the family Berberidaceae, mayapple is often referred to as Indian hawthorn or mountain mayapple. It is indigenous to North America and may be found throughout most of the eastern, central, and southern United States as well as Canada. Small, compound leaves with elliptic or heart-shaped shapes and serrated edges are seen on the plant, which reaches heights of 1–3 m.

Milk Vetch The Rocky Mountains and Great Plains of North America are home to the perennial plant milk vetch (Astragalus bisulfate). Native Americans have long utilised milk vetch as a medicine, and it is currently being researched for its possible health advantages.

The leaves and root of milk vetch have been used to cure bronchitis, hay fever, constipation, diarrhoea, and other respiratory conditions. Chemicals in the roots can also decrease cholesterol and safeguard the heart. Milk vetch stems and blooms can be used medicinally as well. The blossoms have a flavour similar to tea and are occasionally used in place of regular tea when it is unavailable or when consumers do not want to consume caffeinated drinks. You may also use the dried flowers as a recreational marijuana product by smoking them.

The bark of milk vetch has been used to cure a variety of dental issues, including pain, inflammation, fevers, headaches, and toothaches. Additionally, milk vetch fruit is consumed raw or cooked like a vegetable.

Milkweed

One of the members of the daisy family is milkweed. It is a plant that grows throughout Europe and North America, and it is utilised as a natural cure for a number of health issues. A substance present in the plant called milk has been proven to provide a number of health advantages. The benefits are outlined below, to name a few.

Mint

Native American herbs have a long history of healing and are frequently utilised for medical purposes. One such plant with many advantages is mint.

Mint helps reduce bloating and ease gas in the stomach. Additionally, it can be used to treat headaches, fevers, and colds. Mint is also frequently utilised to strengthen the immune system.

Other advantages of mint include lowering inflammation, enhancing digestion, and enhancing circulation. While there are several varieties of mint plants, some of them will offer these advantages.

Alpine Hemlock

The perennial herb known as mountain hemlock, or Conium maculatum, may reach heights of 2.5 metres. The plant has long, thin leaves and hairy stalks. The berries are purple or black, while the blossoms are tiny and white. For Native Americans, mountain hemlock offers several advantages, including the ability to alleviate pain, enhance blood flow, lessen inflammation, and lessen the effects of exhaustion and stress.

The therapeutic potential of mountain hemlock is among its most significant uses. The root can be used to treat inflammation and to relieve discomfort. The leaves can also alleviate tiredness and stress-related symptoms while enhancing blood circulation. Mountain hemlock berries can either be used as a food source or as a medicinal in the form of tea.

Mugwort

The wildflower known as mugwort (Artemisia vulgaris) is found in temperate climates. It belongs to the genus Artemisia. It is used as a herbal remedy to cure toothaches, malaria, and other illnesses. For its euphoric effects, mugwort has also been used traditionally as a smoking herb.

Mullein

Around the world, mullein is a plant that thrives in temperate regions. A tea that is considered to offer various health advantages is made from mullein leaves and petals. Mullein can alleviate anxiety and depression as well as pain and improve circulation. Additionally, eczema, asthma, and other respiratory conditions can be treated with the tea.

Nettle

Let's say you're looking for natural treatments for your health issues. In such scenario, researching American-native plants would be a smart idea. Nettle, wild ginger, and dandelion are some of the most well-liked herbs in America.

Since ancient times, nettles have been utilised as a medicinal plant. Joint pain, muscular pains and spasms, as well as other common symptoms, are frequently treated with it. Nettle is also proven to lessen inflammation and enhance blood circulation.

A common plant in America is wild ginger. It is frequently applied to treat pain alleviation, blood pressure reduction, and digestive enhancement. Wild ginger can also help strengthen the immune system and ease cold and flu symptoms.

Another widely used plant in America is dandelion. In order to cure kidney issues, respiratory issues, anxiety, and menstrual cramps, it is frequently taken as a tea or tincture. Dandelion also aids in lowering cholesterol and warding off malignant cells.

Oak

Oak trees are strong, towering trees with thick, scaly bark. They may reach heights of up to 160 feet and are indigenous to the Northern Hemisphere. The wide, lobed leaves of an oak tree change from green to yellow-green in the autumn. In addition to being a major source of food for animals in the forests where they grow, an oak tree's acorns are also employed in certain traditional treatments.

Avocado Oil

A common cooking oil that is available at many grocery shops is olive oil. It offers a number of health advantages and is manufactured from the fruit of the olive tree.

Consuming olive oil offers a number of advantages, such as anti-inflammatory qualities, satiety, calorie reduction, and high levels of monounsaturated fats and antioxidants, which can help lower the risk of heart disease, cancer, and other disorders. Olive oil also aids in lowering cholesterol, promoting weight reduction, enhancing memory recall, lowering blood pressure, and relieving joint discomfort.

Thyme grape

There are oregano plants growing all over the world. Perennial in nature, it grows in a range of soil types, including sandy soil. Since it has been used for centuries as a medicine, oregano is currently being researched for its potential health advantages. Oregano has a number of health advantages, including lowering inflammation, thwarting infections, and enhancing cardiovascular health.

Santo Palo

The United States is home to a wide variety of therapeutic plants and herbs. Some of the most well-known and well-liked of these plants are referred to as "palo santo" or "holy wood," and include sage, wormwood, rosemary, lavender, and thyme.

Palo santo has therapeutic uses that include mending wounds, lowering inflammation, enhancing emotions, increasing energy, alleviating anxiety and depression, and more. Palo santo is frequently used by individuals to detoxify and cleanse their bodies.

French flower

The plant known as the Pasque flower (Aconitum napellus) has a long history of usage in traditional Chinese medicine and has been proven to offer several health advantages. The pasque flower in particular is known to help reduce stress, improve mood swings, and soothe anxiety. The pasque flower is said to promote healthy blood flow and lessen inflammation.

Lotus Flower

The blooming plant known as passionflower has long been utilised for therapeutic purposes. It has a long history of enhancing emotions and encouraging relaxation. Passionflower is also recognised for its positive effects on health, which include lowering anxiety and depression, enhancing cognitive function, and boosting vitality.

Partridgeberry

In the eastern and central United States, trees and bushes produce the tiny, dark purple-black partridgeberry fruit. Although edible, the berry is not as well-known as other native American fruits like wild blueberries. The fruit, wood, and roots of the plant are all utilised.

Partridgeberry has the advantage of being an excellent source of vitamin C. Antioxidants and other nutrients like potassium and magnesium are also present. These nutrients could assist maintain the body working correctly and shield cells from harm.

Peppermint

The Mediterranean area gave rise to the peppermint plant. Since it has been used medicinally for so long, many conditions may now be treated with it without risk. The main advantages of peppermint include its capacity to act as a natural anti-inflammatory, as well as how it may aid with mood swings and anxiety.

Pine

In the Northern Hemisphere, pine is a tall, thin tree. The needles are scale-like and come in bundles of two. The bark feels gritty to the touch and smells strongly like pine. The tree has a 2–3 m diameter and can reach heights of 20–30 m. The underside of the needles is white, and the top surface is brown. They have a unique scent that is frequently utilised in aromatherapy.

The tree produces copious amounts of sap, which is used to produce syrup, turpentine, and wood tar. Bows, arrows, toys, furniture, and other goods are all made of wood. Bears, squirrels, porcupines, and deer all find cover among pine trees.

Pine can help with weight reduction because to its high calorie content and additional advantages including lowering inflammation, easing arthritis and other joint discomfort, enhancing skin health, enhancing lung health, and raising energy levels.

Plantain

A plant kind that is a member of the banana family is called a plantain. They are widespread across the world and are native to tropical and subtropical areas. Although they are usually consumed as a vegetable, plantains may also be added to savoury meals or served as a side dish. Potassium, vitamin C, and dietary fibre are all abundant in plantains. Magnesium, manganese, and vitamin B6 are also abundant in them.

Prickle Root

For generations, pleurisy root has been used to treat respiratory problems and chest discomfort. It has elements that aid in chest muscle relaxation, easing symptoms including coughing, shortness of breath, and fast breathing. Pleurisy root is also thought to assist in lowering lung inflammation.

Poke

A classic Native American cuisine called poke is cooked using fresh or frozen meats, veggies, and occasionally fish. It is frequently eaten as a side dish and can be served hot or cold. Kale, Swiss chard, mustard greens, collard greens, fruits including mangoes, pineapple, lychee fruit and grapefruit, as well as meats like tuna steak, salmon fillet, chicken breast and shrimp are some of the items most frequently used in poke.

Including some of the vital native American herbs and plants in your diet has several advantages. The therapeutic qualities of these plants have been used for centuries. It has been discovered that they promote general health and wellbeing. Including these plants in your diet has the following advantages, among others:

1) Supporting Healthy Digestion: The fibre content of many of the native plants used in poke helps to support healthy digestion. Fibre is crucial because it keeps your digestive system functioning and aids in the removal of waste from your body.

2) Supporting Heart Health: A number of native herbs and plants that are used to make poke are rich in antioxidants, which help to shield your heart from the harm that free radicals may do. Free radicals are dangerous chemicals that may damage DNA and cell membranes, which can result in illnesses like cancer. You may significantly reduce your risk of heart disease by consuming these antioxidants from plants in your diet.

Cactus Pear

A prickly pear is a tiny shrub or tree that can reach a height of 10 feet. The prickly pear's fruit is a spherical, spiky ball. The fruit can offer a variety of health advantages and is edible. The fruit of the prickly pear is rich in magnesium, potassium, vitamin B6, vitamin C, and vitamin B6. The fruit can also lessen inflammation and aid in better digestion.

Cactus with Spiny Pears

Many of us turn to savoury dishes and warm beverages as the weather cools. The prickly pear cactus is one plant that is frequently disregarded yet has the potential to be incredibly cosy. Native to North America, these cacti provide several advantages for both people and the environment.

The following are some advantages of utilising prickly pear cacti:

When it's chilly outside and there may not be access to wood or other means of heating, the cactus may help a space seem warmer.

Natural anti-inflammatory qualities of the cactus can aid in reducing bodily inflammation and reducing discomfort. As a result, those who suffer from arthritis or joint discomfort might consider it.

Antioxidants found in the prickly pear cactus assist shield cells from harm, which may advance health and fend against ailments in the future.

Husk of psyllium seeds

Psyllium seed husks are full of fibre and provide a host of health advantages. They can assist with digestion, weight reduction, preserving healthy blood sugar levels, controlling heart disease risk factors, and lowering inflammation. Psyllium husks are frequently added to dishes as a filler or as nutritional supplements.

Psyllium is a source of soluble and insoluble fibre that comes from plants. Digestive issues and cholesterol levels are both decreased by soluble fibre. In contrast, insoluble fibre takes up water and lowers blood sugar levels by delaying the absorption of glucose. Psyllium husks also include antioxidants like lutein and zeaxanthin, as well as other minerals like magnesium, potassium, manganese, and copper, in addition to these advantages.

Psyllium husks are most frequently used as an additional source of fibre. This is because they contain a lot of soluble fibre, which helps enhance digestion and lessen symptoms like constipation and diarrhoea. Psyllium can also aid in weight reduction since it lowers calorie intake and enhances satiety, or the sense of being full after eating. Utilising psyllium husks as an additional source of fibre has the added benefit of lowering the risk of obesity and its related health issues, such as type 2 diabetes and heart disease.

Purslane

A typical wild plant that may be eaten as a vegetable is purslane. Numerous health advantages have been discovered after years of research on the plant. It has been demonstrated that purslane can aid with cardiac diseases including high blood pressure and cholesterol. It has also been demonstrated to enhance cognitive function and aid in cancer prevention.

Bunny Tobacco

For millennia, a variety of native American herbs and plants have been utilised as cures and sources of medicine. Some plants, like rabbit tobacco, can help users both physically and mentally.

Native to North America, rabbit tobacco is a plant. It is a tiny tree or shrub that may become as tall as 6 feet. The rabbit tobacco plant has triangular-shaped leaves that are coated in tiny, prickly needles.

The rabbit tobacco plant has white, petalless blooms. They develop on slender stalks close to the plant's base. An oil found in the flowers is utilised to create smoking mixtures.

There are substances in the rabbit tobacco plant's root that have therapeutic qualities. These substances can be used to treat chronic pain, depression, and anxiety. The rabbit tobacco plant's root can also be used to treat varicose veins and asthma problems.

Some individuals think that the plant known as "rabbit tobacco" also has spiritual benefits. It is claimed to facilitate better connection with spirit guides and other extraterrestrial creatures.

Razor Bahia

A West Indian plant called ragleaf Bahia has been used for many years to cure a variety of illnesses. Due to the anti-inflammatory characteristics of this plant, edoema and inflammation may be reduced. Ragleaf Bahia may also aid in enhancing general blood circulation. This herb may also aid to reduce lung inflammation, which is regarded to be advantageous for the respiratory system.

Purple Grass

Red clover is a perennial that can reach a height of one metre. The leaves are soft to the touch and placed alternately. The blooms have five petals, are tiny, and are white. Bees pollinate them when they bloom from early spring to late summer. Dietary fibre, protein, vitamins A, C, and E, potassium, magnesium, and iron are all present in sufficient amounts in red clover.

Redroot

A blooming plant called "Red Root" is indigenous to North America. It belongs to the ginger family and has long been used for medicinal purposes. The plant includes anti-inflammatory chemicals that can be used to relieve cramps and strengthen the heart. The plant also aids in circulation improvement and blood pressure reduction.

Rhodiola

A two-meter-tall, perennial, scented shrub called Rhodiola Rosea. The stem and root are covered in tiny, daisy-like white blossoms. The plant grows well in cold areas and has broad, curling leaves.

Rosavin, salidroside, and Scutellaria baicalensis extract (SBE), which have been demonstrated to enhance mood, cognitive function, energy levels, stress alleviation, and immune system health, are all present in the root and stem. The capacity of the plants to increase blood flow to the central nervous system and oxygen delivery to the brain and other tissues may be the cause of these benefits.

By enhancing communication between the various areas of the brain, rhodiola can further aid in the reduction of anxiety and sadness. It has also been demonstrated to enhance memory performance and alertness.

Romero

North American plants, such as romero, have a long history of usage in traditional medicine. It is well known for its medicinal benefits, which include easing pain and inflammation. Romero is a beneficial treatment for a variety of health issues since it also contains anti-inflammatory and antioxidant qualities. Romero also aids in bettering digestion and circulation.

Rooibos

South Africa is home to the shrubby, perennial plant known as rooibos. The red blooms are tiny and tube-shaped, and the leaves are grouped in whorls of three. Due to the high quantities of antioxidants, flavonoids, and caffeine in Rooibos, it is consumed as tea. Drinking rooibos tea is said to provide a variety of health advantages, such as a decreased risk of heart disease, dementia, Alzheimer's disease, stroke, malignant tumours, and enhanced cognitive performance.

Drinking rooibos may also help with weight reduction by stabilising blood sugar levels, boosting circulation, and decreasing inflammation; enhancing skin health; relieving anxiety and depression; enhancing sleep quality; and assisting with digestion.

Red Rose

Rose hips are an essential component of several traditional Native American cures. They have been used for food for a very long time. These tasty fruits are rich in antioxidants, vitamins A, C, and E, as well as minerals like potassium, magnesium, zinc, and iron. Additionally rich in soluble fibre, which can help control blood sugar levels, are rose hips.

Consuming rose hips has several advantages, including:

- Antioxidants found in abundance in rose hips can help prevent cell deterioration and support heart function.
- Additionally rich in soluble fibre, which can help control blood sugar levels, are rose hips.
- Vitamin A, which is necessary for a healthy immune system and eyesight, is present in rose hips.
- Magnesium, which is crucial for supporting nerve health and general muscular function, is found in abundance in rose hips.

Sagebrush

North American sagebrush (Artemisia tridentata) has been used for millennia as a treatment for a number of illnesses. The plant includes a number of substances that are thought to offer health advantages, such as lowering inflammation, fostering healing, and preventing the development of cancer cells.

Herb of Saint John

The perennial plant known as Saint John's wort (Hypericum perforatum) can reach a height of one metre. It features red berries and purple blooms. An herbal remedy called Saint John's wort is used to cure a number of ailments, such as stress, anxiety, and depression. Additionally recognised for enhancing mood and reducing pain, Saint John's wort.

Saltbush

A succulent plant known as saltbush thrives in arid, sandy soils. It is indigenous to Eastern Canada and the Western United States. Native Americans have traditionally used the herb for therapeutic purposes. Numerous medical conditions, including as arthritis, muscular discomfort, and headaches, can be treated with saltbush. Additionally, the herb possesses anti-inflammatory qualities.

Compounds in saltbush have antiviral and antiparasitic effects. Additionally, the herb can aid in bettering digestion and blood flow. The fact that saltbush is safe to use while pregnant is one of its advantages.

Sarsparilla

The tall herbaceous perennial plant sarsaparilla (Smilax Officinalis) reaches a height of around three feet. The stem has flat, smooth, green leaves on top and white leaves below. The stem is woody at the base. Flavonoids, tannins, saponins, and glycosides are some of the active components of sarsparilla that have therapeutic properties. The plant is used to ease gastric discomfort, enhance digestion, increase appetite, and enhance respiratory health.

Savory

Savoury is a flavour that is frequently connected to various culinary traditions, including Italian, French, and Mexican. Savoury flavours are frequently seen in American cuisine in dishes like beef stroganoff and chicken cacciatore. These meals' flavours are rich and deepened by savoury herbs and plants.

Palmetto Saw

A blooming plant native to Florida and Georgia is called a saw palmetto. It is commonly recognised that the plant can help men's health by lowering their chance of prostate cancer, among other things. Other illnesses including arthritis may be treated using saw palmetto's anti-inflammatory qualities. Saw palmetto is utilised as a natural colour, as well as a component in cosmetic products, in addition to its therapeutic uses.

The plant may reach a height of 3 feet and has green or purple blooms. The fruit is an orange drupe, and inside each one lies a kernel of crude oil with potential medical use. Saw palmetto leaves and bark are also used in cosmetics and cookery.

Snakeroot Senega

Native Americans have long utilised a plant called senega snakeroot. Senega alkaloids, a substance found in the plant, are good for your health. Senega snakeroot has anti-inflammatory properties as well as advantages for the immune system and blood circulation. Seneca snakeroot also possesses anti-inflammatory qualities that might lessen arthritic discomfort.

The Senna Leaf

Use Senna leaves if you want to add some healthy plants to your garden but aren't sure where to begin. These leaves offer a lot of health advantages and are rich in antioxidants. Here are a few advantages of using Senna leaves:

Help Relieve Inflammation: Reducing inflammation is one of the main advantages of utilising Senna leaves. Sennosides, which have anti-inflammatory qualities, are present, which explains why.

Improve Digestion: Senna leaves also have the advantage of enhancing digestion. This is as a result of the tannins and other digestive aids they contain.

Senna leaves can also help the body cleanse by assisting in the removal of toxins and waste products from the body.

Bog Cabbage

Wild plants like skunk cabbage (Symplocarpus foetidus) flourish in disturbed environments such at the sides of roads and abandoned fields. Skunk cabbage may spread far through the soil because to its large root systems, so when utilising it in landscaping, it's crucial to keep the plant's development under control. The root is not dangerous, but the leaves and blossoms are. The leaves are coated in a gooey fluid that, when consumed, causes nausea, diarrhoea, and constipation. Although the stamen contain a sap that can be utilised in herbal medicine, the blossoms are also toxic. Skunk cabbage is a great source of minerals including vitamin C, manganese, potassium, magnesium, and phosphorus as well as antioxidants.

Slithering Elm

The slippery elm, or Ulmus rubra, may be found across most of North America. It is frequently employed as a natural treatment for respiratory issues, coughs, and arthritis. The oil produced by slippery elm, which has been utilised for millennia in traditional Native

American treatments, is also well recognised. The oil has been demonstrated to have anti-inflammatory qualities and may be used topically or consumed.

Upland Sumac Smooth

Hardy shrub Rhus glabra, sometimes known as smooth highland sumac, may reach heights of 6 feet. The leaves have a serrated edge, are opposite, simple, and elliptical in shape. At the terminals of the branches, there are spikes with tiny, white flowers. The fruit is a capsule-shaped dry fruit with one to four black seeds within. The majority of Illinois is covered by the smooth upland sumac, which is a native of the Great Lakes region.

For millennia, people have utilised the leaves for medical purposes. Psoriasis, eczema, and dermatitis are among the skin ailments that smooth upland sumac is known to effectively cure. The dried capsules can also be brewed into a tea to treat fever or arthritic symptoms or used as an insect repellant.

Stevia

Stevia is currently among the most well-liked plants on the planet. It is a tiny tree or perennial shrub with flavorful blooms and short leaves. Although stevia is endemic to tropical areas all over the world, it was initially found in South America. Commercial stevia cultivation is now practised in a number of nations, including Taiwan, China, Paraguay, Brazil, and Uruguay.

In Asia and South America, stevia has been used as a sweetener for millennia. It has also gained popularity in recent years in North America. Like other artificial sweeteners, stevia has no nutritional flaws but is 200 times sweeter than sugar. Stevia furthermore has no calories, gluten, or sugar alcohol.

The following are a few advantages of stevia use:

Because it has no calories, it may be substituted for sugar or other high-calorie meals without causing weight gain or unhealthful calorie demands;

Because it doesn't contain any sugar alcohols that may build plaque, it doesn't induce tooth decay;

Since it has a low glycemic index, it won't cause blood sugar levels to rise as much as ordinary sugar does.

Since it is non-toxic, anyone can drink it without fear of negative effects.

Bitter Nettle

In North America, stinging nettle (Urtica dioica) is a typical weed. Since ancient times, it has been used in traditional medicine to treat a wide range of conditions, including pain, inflammation, and infection. Additionally recognised for its ability to sting, stinging nettles are useful as a deterrent to pests and predators.

An annual plant, stinging nettle may reach a height of two feet. The edges of the long, curving leaves are razor-sharp. The silky petals of the tiny, green blossoms are a bright colour. Be cautious when handling the nettle plant since its stinging hairs are extremely sensitive to the touch.

Diosgenin, a substance found in the root of the stinging nettle, is assumed to be in charge of the plant's stinging properties. Additionally, diosgenin may be transformed into the active substance diosmin, which has anti-inflammatory qualities.

The following are some advantages of stinging nettle use:

1) It can aid in reducing inflammation and discomfort.

2) It may act as a natural repellent for pests and predators.

3) It contains anti-inflammatory characteristics that may be used to lessen the signs and symptoms of a number of illnesses or injuries.

Stoneseed

A perennial herbaceous plant known as stoneseed belongs to the Asteraceae genus of daisies. Stoneseed is a plant native to North America that thrives in the arid regions of the Rocky Mountains and Great Plains. Stoneseed is a natural remedy that has historically been used to cure a variety of ailments, including asthma, bronchitis, heart disease, arthritis, and varicose veins. Herbal treatments employ the blooms and leaves. Online and health food stores both sell stoneseed.

Sumac

North America and Eurasia are home to the shrubby tree or tiny bush known as sumac (Rhus typhina). The fruit, a vivid crimson drupe, may be used to make beverages and sauces. The leaves have a strong flavour and smell. Astringent and anti-inflammatory, sumac possesses these qualities. It cures illnesses such as colds, the flu, toothaches, and diarrhoea. Additionally, the bark is used to cure boils, rashes, eczema, and psoriasis on the skin. Sumac can also ease headaches, sadness, and anxiety.

Sweetflag

Native American plants and herbs can be used to promote health and well-being. For instance, the common plant Sweetflag (Asarum canadense) is utilised for therapeutic reasons. Many advantages of the sweet flag include pain relief, infection prevention, and the reduction of inflammation. The local plants elderberry (Sambucus canadensis), poke root (Phytolacca americana), and wild ginger (Asarum viride) have also been utilised as medicines.

Let's say you wish to supplement your diet with natural plant and herb extracts to boost your health. The finest alternatives in the situation can be found in Native American culture. These herbs provide powerful cures for common maladies in addition to several additional advantages including increased circulation, boosted immunity, and deeper sleep. The following list includes the top five Native American plants and herbs:

1) Sweetflag (Asarum canadense)

2) Poke Root (Phytolacca americana)

3) Elderberry (Sambucus canadensis)

4) Wild Ginger (Asarum viride)

5) Lavender (Lavandula angustifolia)

Sweetgrass

Although sweetgrass may be found all around the world, it is particularly common on American Indian reservations. Due to its sweet flavour and relaxing qualities, it is utilised in rituals and as a tea. Sweetgrass comes in a variety of forms, and some of them are more therapeutic than others. Five of the more advantageous kinds are listed below:

A kind of sweetgrass called blue grama is mostly used medicinally. It can alleviate pain, indigestion, and anxiety and has anti-inflammatory qualities.

Toothwort

In North America, toothwort is a low-growing plant that is frequently found in wet places. The plant has lobe-like leaves and a stem that may reach a height of two feet. The seeds are tiny and black, while the blossoms are tiny, white, and fragrant. The plant is a natural therapy for a number of issues, including the treatment of cold and flu symptoms as well as pain relief and fever decrease. There are several toothwort kinds, each with unique advantages.

An efficient method of pain alleviation is toothwort. Inflammation in the body is brought on by oligosaccharides, which are substances found in the plant. By attaching to receptors on nerve cells, oligosaccharides prevent the brain from receiving pain signals. Toothwort is said to help lower fever in addition to being a potent pain reliever. Compounds in the plant have antibacterial and anti-inflammatory properties.

Also regarded as an antibacterial plant is toothwort. One of the toothwort's constituents prevents germs from growing by destroying their cell membranes. This makes it challenging for germs to grow and spread illness. Toothwort extract also works well for treating cold and flu symptoms. Toothwort is an effective remedy for various ailments due to its antiviral characteristics.

Horned honeysuckle

Hardy perennial trumpet honeysuckle (Lonicera sempervirens) can reach a height of 30 feet. The trumpet-shaped blooms have white petals that alternate with black sepals, and the leaves are lance-shaped. Native to North America, trumpet honeysuckle may be found in large portions of the eastern United States, Canada, and Mexico. Native Americans treat a variety of illnesses with the plant's juice from the blooms, which they use to treat indigestion, cold and flu symptoms, and other maladies. The flower's high concentration of essential oil also makes it an efficient insect and mosquito repellant. Trumpet honeysuckle's lovely blooms and tendrils make it a common landscaping plant.

Usnea

Usnea is a genus of lichen that is present in both North America and Europe. Usnea is a fungus that lives in symbiotic relationships with algae, and lichens are renowned for having antiviral qualities. Native Americans have employed lichens for medical purposes for thousands of years, and many tribes still do so today.

There are more than 100 species of Usnea, the majority of which have medicinal uses. Antiviral, antibacterial, antifungal, anti-inflammatory, and antioxidant capabilities are a few examples of these advantages. Usnea can be consumed as a supplement or added to meals.

Usnea has been demonstrated to lessen human anxiety symptoms and enhance cognitive performance. It is also thought to shield the liver from harm brought on by drug and alcohol usage.

Usnea bark (Auricularia auricula-judge), usnea leaf (Lichenomphalia coronaria), usnea fruit (Lobaria muralis), and usnea sponges (Dictyocaulus filiformis) are a few common usnea supplements.

The Ursi

The eastern and central regions of the United States are home to the uva ursi plant. The plant is employed as a natural treatment to cure a variety of diseases. There are substances in uva ursi that are anti-inflammatory, anti-cancer, and antiseptic.

The Venus Slipper

Over 2,000 distinct plant species that Native Americans value greatly may be found in the United States. They have a historical and cultural tie to these plants, which contributes to this in part. Many of these plants and herbs have been utilised in rituals and ceremonies, while a few have been used for therapeutic purposes for many years.

Venus' slipper is one of these plants. The anti-inflammatory and antifungal qualities of this plant are only two of its many advantageous traits. Additionally, it can aid in bodily detoxification and better blood circulation. Venus's slipper also strengthens the immune system and lowers stress and anxiety levels.

Aquatic Birch

The deciduous water birch (Betula papyrifera) can reach heights of 30 feet. It features little, white blooms in the late spring and smooth, green leaves. The wood is a light brown colour, robust, and firm, with wrinkly and rough bark. Native to eastern North America, the water birch is widespread in Ontario and Quebec.

The water birch is significant because it offers people food, shelter, and resources for tools, construction supplies, and other items like medications and tools. The following are a few advantages of water birch:

The water birch provides nourishment. The tree produces nuts that are rich in vitamin E and protein. They can be used to manufacture flour or oil, consumed raw or roasted, or both.

- Animals are protected by the water birch. Its slick, emerald leaves shield the sun during the day and deflect rain during the night from crops. The tree also shields against cold and windy conditions.

The water birch serves as a supply of raw materials for construction goods. Its hardwood may be used to make logging equipment, bridges, furniture, tools, weapons, and other things.

- Medicines can be found in the water birch. The tannins in the bark have been utilised for ages to cure a variety of illnesses.

Watercress

Leafy green watercress is a native of North America. It is sometimes known as curly dock or water spinach. It may flourish in drenched rivers, lakes, and streams. Vitamins A, C, and K, vitamin B6, and minerals like potassium and magnesium are all abundant in watercress leaves.

Fresh or dried watercress leaves can be used as a garnish or in salads. It can enhance heart health and has anti-inflammatory qualities. Additionally, the herb provides cognitive advantages that help with brain health and Alzheimer's disease prevention.

Occidental Hemlock

The Pacific Northwest's hilly areas are home to the towering western hemlock tree. The branches and trunk are covered in enormous slabs of scaly, severely raked bark. The blooms are white or light pink, and the ovate leaves have pointy points. One to four tiny seeds are contained in the cylinder-shaped fruit. Western hemlock has a wide range of applications in both medicine and spirituality.

Western hemlock roots have been used for generations to cure a wide range of illnesses, such as fever, arthritis, and renal issues. Additionally, the bark may be cooked to create a tea that is said to be anti-inflammatory and aid in improved breathing. Additionally, furniture, tools, and other goods are made of wood.

Also having spiritual importance is western hemlock. It was regarded as a holy plant by Native Americans since it was believed to have potent curative effects. They would apply burns as an ointment or bind wounds with the sap from the trees. Today, some individuals turn to western hemlock juice or tincture as a natural treatment for conditions including ADD/ADHD, depression, seizures, exhaustion, nasal troubles, and anxiety.

Occidental Skunk Cabbage

Western skunk cabbage, wild ginger, dandelion, garlic, and yarrow are some of the herbs and plants that are most frequently employed in Native American medicine. Symplocarpus foetidus, a native of North America and a member of the Brassica family, is also known as Western Skunk Cabbage. The plant has been used for millennia to cure a variety of diseases, including skin disorders, gastrointestinal difficulties, respiratory problems, arthritic pain, heart problems, and mental and respiratory problems.

Western skunk cabbage has several advantages, including:

- The herb has anti-inflammatory properties and eases arthritic pain and swelling.

- It can aid in breathing improvement by enhancing airflow and reducing irritation.
- It can aid in bettering digestion by lowering intestinal inflammation and enhancing nutrition absorption.
- It can enhance mental health by easing symptoms of anxiety and despair

Stoneseed in the West

Western stoneseed (Astragalus membranaceus) is a perennial herb with white, pink, or yellow blooms that can reach a height of 1.5 metres. The leaves form a significant component of the Native American diet, and the root is a medicinal herb. High concentrations of minerals including potassium, magnesium, calcium, iron, and zinc have been detected in flowers. Additionally, several research have indicated that flowers might lessen inflammation and enhance blood circulation. The leaves are frequently used in soups and stews and can be consumed fresh or dried.

Pine White

Overview and advantages of several important native American plants and herbs

Herbal medicine has been utilised by Native Americans for a very long time, and it is currently being researched. Some of these plants are now recognised as being crucial to both human and animal health. Some of the most significant herbs and plants used by Native Americans are listed below:

Pinus strobus, a white pine

This tree is a wonderful option for treating arthritis because of its well-known anti-inflammatory effects. Additionally, it has been used to treat nausea, sadness, anxiety, and respiratory issues.

(Betula papyrifera) birch

Birch bark was used by Native Americans to manufacture birch wine and beer. Beta-carotene, which lowers the risk of skin cancer and eye problems, is also abundant in the tree.

Additionally, the bark and leaves can be used as a natural remedy for burns, mono, pneumonia, sinusitis, toothaches, acne, eczema, and other skin problems.

Clear Sage

One of the most popular and commonly utilised plants in Native American medicine is white sage, or Salvia apiana. Numerous ailments, such as headaches, anxiety, menstrual cramps, toothaches, and colds, are treated by the leaves and branches. The herb is also renowned for its ability to reduce inflammation. It has been used to relieve joint pain, including arthritic discomfort.

Untamed buckwheat

Wild buckwheat is a widespread wildflower that grows all throughout North America. This flower is endemic to Eurasia, and it is believed that the ancient Greeks cultivated it. High quantities of protein, fibre, and antioxidants may be found in wild buckwheat. The edible blooms can be eaten as a single grain or in salads.

Fresh Ginger

The plant known as wild ginger (Zingiber officinale) can be found throughout North America, portions of Europe, and Australia. Wild ginger's root and stem are used to produce medicine.

Wild ginger has anti-inflammatory, pain-relieving, and circulation-improving properties. Additionally, some people take it to raise blood pressure and enhance cognitive function.

Online or at health food stores, wild ginger is available for purchase. It ought to be kept in a cool, dark location.

Wild Ham

One of the most popular herbs and plants in America is wild gammon, often known as berry-of-the-wool. This plant frequently thrives in unnatural environments like fields and by the sides of roadways. Although some people perceive the wild gammon plant's fruit to be sour, it is a delicious purple berry.

The wild gammon plant has several advantageous traits in all of its components. The leaves and young shoots are added to foods and beverages, whilst the roots are used to manufacture medicine. Additionally, the bark has been utilised to cure a variety of illnesses, including infections and skin disorders. The fruit may be consumed raw or cooked, delivering nutrients including vitamins A and C, in addition to these advantages.

Leaky Lettuce

An annual plant known as wild lettuce, often known as lamb quarters, thrives throughout the United States. It has a lengthy history of usage as a medicine, and researchers are now looking at whether it could have health advantages.

The Asteraceae family, which includes several plants with therapeutic qualities, includes wild lettuce as one of its members. Wild lettuce can be prepared as a tea, tincture, or extract using its leaves and blossoms. Additionally, the leaves are used to create a salad dressing called "wild balsamic vinaigrette."

Consuming wild lettuce can reduce inflammation, strengthen the immune system, control blood sugar levels, combat cancer cells, and slow down the effects of ageing on cognitive function.

Willow

The willow tree is a typical sight in many regions of North America, from the tropical rainforests to the high heights of the Rocky Mountains. Many things are made from willow tree wood, including furniture and building materials.

Using goods made of willow has a lot of advantages. The use of willow bark as a natural remedy for fever, inflammation, and other illnesses has proven to be successful. The willow tree's leaves and branches can be utilised as a source of nourishment, medicine, and shelter.

The willow tree is adaptable enough to be employed in a variety of contexts and grows swiftly. It can be utilised in parks and nature preserves as a source of wildlife habitat or planted close to residences or businesses to offer shade and save air conditioning expenditures.

Hazel Witch

Witch hazel (Hamamelis virginiana) is a tiny tree or shrub that can reach heights of 8 to 12 feet. Its leaves are scale-like underside and sparsely haired on the top surface. White blooms and a brown pod serve as the fruit of this plant. Witch hazel is used to treat a variety of skin issues, including sunburn, dryness, irritation, and itching.

Witch hazel also has anti-inflammatory, antiviral, antibacterial, and detoxifying properties. Additionally, it might aid in boosting circulation and lowering edoema. It has also been used to treat tension headaches, stress reduction, and pain alleviation.

Wormwood

Mugwort, often known as wormwood (Artemisia absinthium), is a plant that grows wild all over the world. For ages, native populations in North America and Europe have utilised wormwood as a medicine. Colds, the flu, TB, and other respiratory illnesses have all been treated with wormwood. Additionally, it can be utilised to lessen inflammation and aid with pain relief.

Wormwood is frequently regarded as a powerful herbal treatment. They should only be used with care and under a healthcare professional's supervision, as with other herbs. The adverse effects of wormwood include disorientation, sleepiness, and dizziness. Before using wormwood supplements, see your doctor if you're pregnant or nursing.

Cao Yan

Yan Cao is a North American plant with the scientific name Cynanchum wilfordii. It belongs to the mint family and thrives in wet regions next to rivers and streams. There are rumours that the leaves and blooms may be eaten and are also used medicinally.

Yarrow

A common herbaceous blooming plant found in temperate regions of the world is yarrow (Achillea millefolium). The opposing, oblong to lance-shaped leaves have serrated edges. The blooms have five petals and are tiny, blue or purple. Yarrow is a significant medicinal plant that has been used for many years to cure a wide range of illnesses.

Yarrow tinctures and teas can be made from the plant's leaves and blooms. The dried leaves can be used to flavour herbal treatments or dried and made into tea. Additionally, infused oils or capsules containing the flowers can be utilised topically. There are several uses for the yarrow plant's root, including as a diuretic, bitter extract, tonic, and emetic.

Orange Dock

The blooming plant known as the yellow dock (Veronica anagallis) is indigenous to the eastern United States. Making a tea from the yellow dock's roots is thought to have therapeutic properties. Yellow dock has a number of advantages, such as lowering inflammation, enhancing digestion, and treating numerous illnesses and disorders.

Golden Gentian

Native to North America, many healthy plants can be utilised as medicines. The yellow gentian (Gentiana lutea), which has been used medicinally by Native Americans for generations, is one of these plants.

The perennial yellow gentian may reach heights of two feet. The alternating, 1 to 3 inch long leaves have serrated edges. The bell-shaped blooms have brilliant yellow petals with reddish-brown markings on the interior.

The diuretic and antioxidant properties of the yellow gentian's root system are advantageous for renal health as well as general vigour. The plant has also been used to cure a variety of other diseases, including arthritis, anxiety, and fever.

Yucca Mate

The leaves of the yerba mate plant are used to make the traditional tea known as yerba mate. In South America, yerba mate is well-liked and is viewed as a sociable drink. It offers a lot of advantageous qualities, such as caffeine and antioxidant activity.

Yerba mate is thought by many herbalists to boost circulation and cognition. Yerba mate also contains catechins and polyphenols, both of which have anti-inflammatory qualities. These substances assist a healthy body and mind by lowering stress levels. Additionally, some research indicate that yerba mate helps lessen the signs of anxiety and despair.

A. Yerba Sant

The leaves and blossoms of many different plants, including sage, yarrow, mint, peppermint, and calendula, are used to make the popular and healthful tea known as yerba sant.

Improved circulation, increased concentration and mental clarity, lowered stress levels, improved digestion, and other advantages are some of the often cited advantages of yerba sant tea use. Additionally, some individuals utilise it as a natural treatment for sadness and anxiety.

Sagebrush (Artemisia tridentata), goldenseal (Hydrastis Canadensis), lambsquarters (Chenopodium album), mullein (Verbascum thapsus), peppermint (Mentha piperita), and calendula (Calendula officinalis) are some of the particular herbs used to manufacture yerba sant.

Yucca

Native Americans employed a variety of plants for medical purposes. One such plant is the yucca. Numerous civilizations have used yucca for medical purposes for a very long time. Compounds found in yucca have been shown to improve neuronal function, cure respiratory problems, and reduce inflammation and discomfort.

Numerous ailments, including respiratory problems, inflammation, and discomfort, have been treated with yucca. It works well to reduce both acute and chronic inflammation. Studies on animals revealed that it was successful in lowering the pain brought on by different illnesses and traumas. It was also discovered to aid enhance general nerve and functional function.

Asthma and other respiratory conditions can be treated naturally using yucca. Studies on asthmatic animals revealed that it was successful in easing symptoms and enhancing lung function. Additionally, it aids in clearing congestion and enhancing general breathing.

Aziz Zizzi

Including native American herbs and plants in your health and wellness regimen has several advantages. Among the most prominent are:

1. For millennia, Native Americans have utilised these herbs to enhance their health and wellbeing.

2. They offer a variety of qualities, including as anti-inflammatory, antibacterial, detoxifying, and analgesic actions, that can enhance general well-being.

3. Due to the natural antibiotics and antioxidants they contain, these plants help strengthen the immune system.

4. Some plants' naturally occurring constituents, such flavonoids and terpenes, can also enhance mood and cognitive performance.

Book 5:
Native American Essential Oils Vol 1

Chapter 1:
An Overview of Essential Oils

These days, essential oils are quite popular, and for good reason. These minute components are used often in herbal treatments and personal care products since they provide several health advantages for the body and mind. What exactly are essential oils and what do they accomplish? An overview of essential oils and their numerous advantages will be given in this section. Additionally, we will offer advice on how to utilise them wisely and successfully. Read on for all the information you need about essential oils, whether you're trying to relax more or enhance your health.

How Do Essential Oils Work?

An example of a plant-derived oil is essential oils. By using steam distillation, they are extracted from aromatic plants. Lavender, chamomile, thyme, and lemon balm are the plants that are most frequently utilised to make essential oils.

Over 100 distinct essential oils have been employed in food flavouring, vitamins, soaps, lotions, fragrances, and other products. Lavender oil, peppermint oil, tea tree oil, and ginger oil are a few popular essential oils.

What Advantages Do Essential Oils Offer?

Utilising essential oils both inwardly and physically has a variety of advantages. Among the advantages are:

Headaches and migraines can benefit from the use of essential oils.

They can be beneficial for respiratory conditions including bronchitis and asthma.

They are also helpful for skin problems including psoriasis and eczema.

They can aid in elevating emotions and general feelings of wellbeing.

They can aid in reducing tension and stress.

Considerations Prior To Using Essential Oil

There are a few things to consider if you want to add some essential oils to your arsenal for aromatherapy. Make sure you get high-quality oils first; avoid diluted or chemically enhanced versions. Second, exercise caution since essential oils may be quite strong and should only be used sparingly. Finally, try new oils on a tiny area first before applying them to bigger ones.

What Is the Best Way To Pick The Right Essential Oil For You?

It's critical to select the best essential oil for your needs while making your selection. There are several varieties of essential oils, and each one performs well under particular circumstances.

Start by reviewing the oil's uses to determine which one is best for you. It's critical to comprehend the functions of essential oils before making a purchase because they are frequently employed as supplements or medicines. Additionally, before making a purchase, examine the qualities of each oil.

Some essential oils might be dangerous when consumed or applied to the skin. Always be sure you use oil according to the safety instructions provided.

When choosing an essential oil, it's crucial to also take your climate into account. While certain oils perform better in hot climes, some perform better in cooler ones. Before buying any essential oils, check the weather forecast to be sure they will function in your specific location.

What Are Some Risks Associated with Improper Use of Essential Oils?

The risks of utilising essential oils improperly are numerous. Toxic exposure, skin inflammation, and hormone disruption are a few frequent issues. When essential oils are combined with other substances or used topically, toxic exposure may result. applying oils that are unsafe for topical use or applying excessive oil can both result in skin irritation and inflammation. If essential oils are consumed in large amounts or applied to regions where hair grows rapidly, hormone disruption may ensue.

Native Americans and Essential Oils

People have utilised essential oils, which are derived from plants, for thousands of years. There are plants all around the world that are used to make essential oils. Native American civilizations are among the best areas to discover essential oils.

For thousands of years, Native Americans have utilised essential oils for a variety of purposes. Treatment for infections, illness prevention, mood enhancement, and relaxation are a few applications. Many of these uses are still being researched today, and most likely will never be fully understood.

There are several different essential oil combinations that can be employed. Before using any essential oil, it is crucial to seek expert advice to make sure it is safe and suitable for your individual requirements.

Chapter 2:
How Using Oils Can Help You Feel Better

Natural medicines like essential oils have been used for millennia to treat headaches. Lavender, peppermint, and lemon essential oils are among the most often used remedies for headaches.

Lavender oil, which is a relaxant, works wonders for alleviating headaches when applied directly to the scalp. Additionally, the analgesic qualities of peppermint oil might help lessen pain and inflammation. Lemon oil's anti-inflammatory characteristics make it useful for treating headaches as well.

Aids in Reducing Nausea

The secret to finding oils that work best for you when it comes to reducing nausea is to experiment. Some of the most popular essential oils used to treat nausea are lavender, ginger, and peppermint.

Each oil has unique advantages that are particularly helpful for easing nausea. It is well known that lavender oil is calming and good in lowering anxiety and stress levels. By increasing hunger, ginger oil can help alleviate nausea and enhance digestive function. Because it serves to activate the central nervous system, peppermint oil is also beneficial in the battle against nausea.

It's crucial to choose an oil that reduces nausea for you. However, combining different oils can also improve their overall efficacy.

Helps Lower Inflammation

The use of essential oils has a variety of advantages, one of which is the reduction of inflammation.

According to one study, using lavender oil to treat eye irritation may be beneficial. The oil's anti-inflammatory qualities are probably to blame for this.

Inflammation-reducing essential oils include thyme, ginger, and tea tree. Due to the antibacterial and antifungal qualities of these oils, the development of bacteria and fungus that might lead to inflammation may be slowed down.

Helps You Sleep Better

Sleep quality can be enhanced using essential oils. Here are a few of the numerous advantages:

You may relax and sleep more easily with the aid of essential oils. Some essential oils, such as lavender, can aid those who have trouble falling asleep by lowering anxiety and stress levels. Others, like peppermint, aid in relaxing and speed up the process of falling asleep.

Throughout the day, essential oils may also lift your spirits and give you more energy. Lavender and lemon balm are two essential oils that work well to lower stress and encourage a happier view on life. These essential oils, when used with other all-natural treatments like exercise, may support greater mental health throughout the day.

Over time, using essential oils can also help you sleep better. Reduces Anxiety and Pain By progressively including essential oils into your bedtime routine, you may discover that they encourage improved sleep hygiene, which may result in longer periods of undisturbed sleep.

Aromatherapy is one of the most popular ways to use essential oils, especially to treat pain and anxiety. Certain essential oils (like lavender) have been shown in research on the use of essential oils for anxiety treatment to help lessen symptoms including anxiousness, tension, racing heart rates, and insomnia. Additionally, some essential oils (such tea tree) are well renowned for their ability to effectively reduce pain and combat infection.

Helps Decrease migraines

According to the Cleveland Clinic, up to 75% of people worldwide have headaches, making it one of the most common pain-related health issues. Around 12% of Americans suffer from migraines, a more severe type of headache, according to Johns Hopkins Medicine. As the Cleveland Clinic notes, headaches are a significant reason why people miss work and school. They may exacerbate anxiety and depressive emotions.

There has been relatively little research on the benefits of peppermint essential oils, which some individuals use to treat headaches. One review claims that just dabbing peppermint oil on the head and temples helps ease headache symptoms. The primary active component of peppermint, menthol, may be to blame for this. Menthol gives a cooling feeling that is hypothesised to have an analgesic (pain reducing) impact, according to an uncontrolled study of 25 people that examined the degree of migraine headache after applying a 6 percent menthol gel to the pain location. Two hours after application, people who used the gel for migraines saw a substantial decrease in the severity of their headaches.

Helps to restore hormone balance

Your levels of oestrogen, progesterone, cortisol, thyroid, and testosterone can be balanced with the use of hormone essential oils.

Clary sage, geranium, and thyme are a few oils that help control oestrogen and progesterone levels, which helps with conditions including infertility, PCOS, PMS, and menopausal symptoms.

The amounts of oestrogen in women's saliva may be affected by geranium and rose, according to a 2017 research that was published in Neuroendocrinology Letters. People who are suffering menopausal symptoms brought on by reduced oestrogen production could find this helpful.

Certain oils have been demonstrated to reduce cortisol levels, which can help you feel better, lessen the symptoms of depression, and increase testosterone levels, which boost a man's libido.

Enhances Skin Condition

A natural and efficient way to maintain your personal care routines without using products with chemicals and hydrogenated oils is to use essential oils on your skin, in hair and beauty products. Essential oils can reduce wrinkles, clear up acne, protect skin from UV damage, and thicken hair, among other things.

Evidence-Based Complementary and Alternative Medicine reports on research that "at least 90 essential oils are suggested for dermatological usage, with at least 1,500 combinations." These oils' benefits for the skin come from their ability to combat the bacteria that cause dermatological illnesses.

Oils may also enhance the general look of your skin and speed up the healing of wounds. They can also assist with inflammatory skin conditions including dermatitis, eczema, and lupus.

Numerous studies have also demonstrated the positive effects of essential oils on hair growth. In a 2015 study, the impact of rosemary oil on those suffering from androgenetic alopecia, or male or female pattern baldness, was examined.

For a six-month treatment period, patients were randomly assigned to receive either rosemary oil or minoxidil (a medication often used to treat hair loss). Researchers found that both groups' hair counts had significantly increased after six months. They also discovered that the minoxidil group had more itchy scalps.

Reduces Body Toxicness

Essential oils can assist in reducing pollutants by promoting detoxification of your home and body. All of us breathe in and ingest different chemicals and environmental toxins, which may be bad for our hearts, brains, and general health.

Some oils have moderate diuretic properties that increase urine production and cleanse the body. Studies show that certain oils enhance digestion and remove toxins that build up in the body.

Oils that detoxify the body can assist in eliminating these toxins while purifying the air in your home. In fact, by eliminating dangerous germs and toxins, essential oils—unlike the majority of chemical-laden household cleaning products—might organically clean your home.

Essential oils such as grapefruit, orange, lemon, lemongrass, eucalyptus, and cinnamon can help reduce pollutants in your home or office.

Chapter 3:
How to Use Essential Oils

How Does Aromatherapy Work?

Essential oils are used in aromatherapy to enhance mood, relaxation, and overall health. Essential oils are organic plant-based extracts. They have been employed for many years to treat a wide range of illnesses. There are several varieties of essential oils, each with special advantages.

Lavender, chamomile, peppermint, frankincense, and myrrh are some of the most popular essential oils used in aromatherapy. These oils can be used directly on the skin or breathed. Essential oils can be combined with a carrier oil (like jojoba oil) to create a cream or lotion for topical application.

People of all ages have been proven to benefit in different ways from aromatherapy. It can ease anxiety and depression, lessen stress, enhance sleep quality, and do much more.

It's crucial to understand your body chemistry and medical issues before utilising essential oils in aromatherapy. Before using essential oils therapeutically, it's crucial to check with a healthcare provider since some people are sensitive to particular compounds they contain.

By the Inhalation of Steam

The best method to use essential oils is by steam inhalation. The oils can be directly inhaled using a steam inhaler or diffused. While inhaling the oils directly allows you to absorb more of the fragrance in your nose, diffusing the oils aids in spreading them across the space.

Using A Diffuser for Essential Oils

Let's say you're searching for a quick and simple approach to include essential oils into your daily routine. A diffuser is the ideal solution in that situation. Diffusers function by distributing the oil into the air, making it simple to use and breathe.

Determine the sort of diffuser you want before you do anything else. There are devices called ultrasonic diffusers that spread the molecules of the oil into the air by breaking them up with high-frequency sound waves. This diffuser works best for people who want a little misting of the essential oil instead of a full-on diffusion and it also operates more quickly than other diffusers.

If you're searching for something more powerful, think about an electric diffuser. These appliances heat the oil by heating electrical currents, which causes the oil's molecules to disintegrate and disperse into the air. They frequently have longer running durations and tend to be more potent than heat- or ultrasonic-based diffusers.

Gather your materials, including distilled water, essential oils (which may be purchased already diluted or diluted yourself), and your diffuser after deciding what kind of diffuser you require. Pour the mixture into your diffuser after thoroughly combining 2 tablespoons of distilled water per cup of essential oils (or the appropriate dose). Prior to adding your oils, turn on the machine and let it warm up.

We may utilise essential oils in a variety of ways throughout our everyday lives, so try out several applications to see which ones suit you the best. Using essential oils can be more fun and easy if you incorporate a diffuser into your regimen.

Bathing With Essential Oils

Essential oils can be precisely what you need if you want to give your bathtime ritual a little extra zing. Many of these oils are renowned for their healing qualities and can promote physical and mental relaxation.

Four techniques are shown below for using essential oils in your bath:

1. To give the soap an additional layer of relaxation, add one or two drops of oil. Because it has been demonstrated that lavender helps to foster a sense of calm and tranquilly, it is a fantastic choice for this.

2. To increase the water's energising effects, apply oil before bathing. Because it is believed to be antibacterial and antiseptic, tea tree oil is a popular choice for keeping your skin healthy while you soak.

3. To create a calming effect, add a few drops of oil immediately to a hot bath. The benefits of chamomile, lavender, and ginger in this situation include better sleep and the reduction of tension, headaches, and discomfort.

4. For better relaxation and better-quality sleep, use essential oils as aromatherapy in your bedroom at night before you go to sleep. Here, a few drops of rosemary, chamomile, or lavender work wonderfully!

Employing Topically

Essential oils are easily absorbed by the skin since they are fat soluble. Applying essential oils to your skin for absorption is a common approach, but you should never put them directly on your skin. A carrier oil, such as sweet almond oil or apricot kernel oil, is always used to mix and dilute it.

Always dilute your essential oil with a common neutral carrier oil (often referred to as base oil) before application if skin irritation is a concern. Unlike essential oils, carrier oils do not evaporate and are generally cold-pressed oils. They can nevertheless deteriorate in ways that essential oils cannot. Your choice of carrier oil will depend on your preferences for fragrance, texture, and sensitivity in order to prevent allergic reactions. Coconut oil, sweet almond oil, jojoba oil, avocado oil, sunflower oil, and grape seed oil are examples of common carrier oils.

Common areas for application of essential oils include the feet, ears, wrists, and temples.

Breathing In the Scent

Your essential oils can be gently inhaled. Open the essential oil container, dab a few drops on your nose or a tissue, and take a long, satisfying breath. Use only one drop when using an essential oil for the first time to prevent sensitivity or a response.

Try to keep your breath quiet as you inhale. Check to see if it enters and exits the body readily or if it becomes caught there. A sniff is not the same as a deep inhale. Your head will be alerted by taking slow, deep breaths that your body needs to relax, and your entire body will comply. Your body and mind are one and the same, therefore it's frequently helpful to trick your body into relaxing first to prepare your mind for sleep.

You are conscious of the importance of breathing to your survival. When it is easy, natural, and necessary, deep breathing can improve one's health and well-being. It is one of the easiest and most effective ways to relax and restore your composure when you are feeling stressed. Deep belly breathing is the key. Such breathing can also help to balance our nervous system and lessen stress in our life when paired with aromatherapy using essential oils.

Chapter 4:
How to Store Essential Oils

It's crucial to preserve essential oils properly while storing up on them. Oils that are not properly kept can be hazardous as well as giving off unpleasant odours. The best methods for storing essential oils are described in this section, along with tips on how to prevent frequent blunders. This section provides all the information you need to keep your essential oils secure and efficient, including how to store them correctly in a cool, dark area and keep them away from heat and light.

What Leads To The Degradation Of Essential Oils?

Numerous plant-based compounds that make up essential oils are liable to decompose over time. The progressive decomposition of essential oils can be caused by a variety of environmental variables, including air pollution, light exposure, and climate regulation.

The following are a few typical reasons why essential oils degrade:

- Exposure to air conditioning or heating systems: These systems frequently change the humidity and temperature in a space, which can harm essential oils. This may cause the oils to degrade over time into smaller molecules that the air can more readily absorb.

- Heat exposure: The degradation of essential oils is also influenced by sunlight and heat. The oil will begin to break down some chemical components when heated over 150 degrees Fahrenheit. This might hasten the oxidation process, which is how essential oils lose their healing powers.

– UV radiation: Skin cells and tissues are susceptible to harm from ultraviolet (UV) radiation. The molecules of essential oils are also harmed by this kind of radiation, which may cause gradual deterioration over time.

Things to Consider When Storing

Make sure to keep them away from heat and light at all times.

Always be sure to keep essential oils out of the light and heat while storing them. The sensitive characteristics of the oil may be harmed by exposure to either. Pack your essential oils in a dark, cool spot if you're taking them with you on the road.

Wooden storage boxes are used

Because they are natural and don't release any dangerous chemicals, storage boxes made of timber materials are ideal for keeping essential oils. Essential oils like lavender oil, peppermint oil, and eucalyptus oil may all be kept in wooden storage boxes.

When keeping essential oils in wooden boxes, always adhere to the manufacturer's guidelines. Some essential oils, like lavender, may be kept in low temperatures for storage. Others, like peppermint, can, however, be kept at a greater temperature. Additionally, keep in mind that some essential oils, like lavender, could produce an aroma if they are kept in a wooden box.

Utilising Storage Boxes for Fabric

You could think about using cloth boxes suitable for the type of oil while keeping essential oils. If the oil is light, like rose or lavender, a box made of thin cardboard can do. For stronger scents like peppermint or ginger, a stronger box constructed of wood or metal is required.

The size and form of the oil should be taken into account while choosing a cloth storage box. While certain oils can fit in a tiny container, some need a bigger one. Determining the degree of protection the oil will require is also crucial. More security is offered by a box with a tightly fitting lid than by one with a loose cover.

Keeping Things in Kitchen Cabinets

One of the most vital and most neglected areas in your house is the kitchen. A crowded kitchen can result in a dirtier home overall in addition to making cooking challenging. Because of this, it's crucial to take the time to keep your essential oils correctly so that they're simple to identify and use when you need them.

Always keep essential oil bottles upright while storing them to prevent oil spills. Label each bottle with the appropriate scent(s) as well. You may either use a little sticker that you can place on top of the bottle or write the smell name on a piece of paper and tuck it inside the bottle to do this.

To prevent colour fading or rancidity, consider airtight, glass-lined storage containers for your oils. Additionally, it's critical to keep your oils in a cool, dark location away from sunshine and heat. Ask your Essential Oil Guide if you have any questions about how to store essential oils safely!

Keeping in Air-Tight Containers

To maintain their efficacy, essential oils should be kept in a cold, dark, and sealed environment. Direct sunshine, extremely hot or low temperatures, and excessive humidity are not the best conditions for storage.

To prevent leakage and contamination, it's crucial to keep the bottles of essential oils completely shut. Some individuals like keeping their essential oils in glass containers for storage. Others use plastic containers instead because they are more airtight. Periodic stock rotation is also beneficial to avoid utilising tainted or outdated oil.

Keeping Things in Fridges

Make sure the bottles of essential oils are properly closed and positioned on a level surface when keeping them in a refrigerator.

Oils shouldn't be kept in the freezer. They won't last as long and will clump up. Pack your essential oil supply in a cold, sealed container if you're travelling with it.

Keeping Things Cool and Dark

To keep their efficacy, essential oils should always be kept in a cold, dark location. This indicates that the bottle should be kept in the refrigerator if it won't be used for more than two weeks and in a cold, dark cupboard otherwise. If the oil won't be used right away, put it in a little glass container with a tight-fitting cover. If the oil has no scent after you pour a small amount onto your hand, return it to the container. Label your bottles with the name of the oil and the date that they were filled.

Before purchasing, check the expiration date.

The expiration date must be considered while keeping your essential oils. If maintained over their indicated expiration dates, essential oils are prone to oxidation and degradation. Oils with adequate storage will often have a longer shelf life than oils without proper storage.

Some recommendations for good oil storage include storing oils away from heat, light, and moisture in dark glass or stainless-steel containers. Before buying oil, it's crucial to verify the expiration date to determine how long it will last.

Book 6:
Native American Essential Oils Vol 2

Chapter 1:
List of All Crucial Essential Oils

The use of essential oils in the home and for our health has numerous positive effects. Lavender oil is one of the most often used essential oils. We will look at some of the main applications and advantages of lavender oil in this section. This essential oil offers several advantages that may be enjoyed both internally and externally, from reducing anxiety to encouraging relaxation. We'll also look at some typical applications for lavender oil, such topical uses and diffusers. Lavender is the best essential oil to use if you want to get a variety of advantages.

Oil of cedarwood

The aroma of cedarwood oil is sweet, woodsy, and spicy. Since ancient times, it has been used as a home cure for a number of illnesses, including cedarwood oil for acne. Additionally, cedarwood oil is said to support emotional harmony and relaxation.

Lemongrass Oil

Popular essential oil for aromatherapy and for its calming effects is lavender oil. It has a lovely, herbal aroma and is made from lavender plant blossoms. A number of ailments, such as anxiety, stress, depression, and sleeplessness, can be treated with lavender oil.

Oil of Sweet Grass

The blooming tips of many varieties of grass are the source of the essential oil known as sweetgrass oil. Its warm, anchoring aroma encourages relaxation and reduces tension. Additionally, anxiety, sadness, and other mental health conditions are treated using sweetgrass oil.

Spruce Oil

Native American sage oil is a strong essential oil that has been utilised for many years to advance health and happiness. The leaves, stems, and blossoms of the sage plant are used to make this oil. It is frequently used as a natural treatment for a number of ailments, including as respiratory problems, depression, anxiety, and chronic pain.

Additionally, sage oil successfully heals skin conditions including eczema and acne. Asthma, menstrual cramps, and headaches are a few more ailments that some people take it to address.

Oil of Peppermint

Indigenous people all throughout the world have utilised peppermint oil, a popular essential oil, for generations. It has a cooling impact on the body and contains a lot of menthol. Utilising peppermint oil can help with nausea, migraines, and anxiety. Additionally, it may be added to mouthwash or massage oil.

Oil of Eucalyptus

Blue gum oil, often known as eucalyptus oil, is a pure, natural essential oil made from the eucalyptus tree's leaves and branches. Colds, bronchitis, and asthma are just a few of the diseases and respiratory conditions that the oil addresses. Additionally, it can be used to reduce swelling and irritated skin.

Rosmarinic Oil

Native Americans have utilised rosemary oil, a well-known essential oil, for generations. The antioxidants beta-carotene, lutein, and zeaxanthin are abundant in rosemary. Additionally useful for inflammation and respiratory issues.

Cypress

Strengthening gums, preventing infections, getting rid of body odour, calming inflammation, and enhancing the respiratory system are all possible with cypress essential oil.

Eucalyptus Eucalyptus essential oil aids in the treatment of respiratory issues, muscular aches, fever, diabetes, and mental fatigue. It is also very beneficial for skin and dental health.

Frankincense

For wounds, infections, scars, digestion, coughs, and colds, frankincense essential oil works best. Additionally, it can help elevate one's spirits, reduce anxiety, and encourage cell renewal.

Geranium

In addition to stopping bleeding, geranium essential oil also stimulates cell renewal, heals scars, tones the body, kills parasites, and removes body odour.

Ginger

Ginger essential oil is well known for its ability to relieve pain, protect the skin, prevent bacterial development, enhance memory, clear phlegm, enhance stomach health, and remove toxins.

Grapefruit

This essential oil can increase urination, stop infections, lessen depressive symptoms, improve mood, and flush out pollutants.

Helichrysum

This essential oil helps to regenerate cells, combat allergies, stop microbial development, lessen spasms and inflammations, heal scars and wounds, and encourage proper bile discharge.

The essential oil of hyssop hotspot causes muscles, gums, and skin to tighten. It promotes good digestion, lessens spasms, reduces excess gas, and increases urine and perspiration.

Jasmine

Jasmine essential oil is effective in treating a variety of conditions, including depression, the blues, sexual dysfunction, increased libido, menstrual flow regulation, increased milk supply, labour pain relief, and cough and phlegm relief.

Juniper Juniper essential oil cleanses blood, treats rheumatism, lessens gas, promotes brightness to the skin, enhances urine and sweating, and hastens wound healing.

Lavender

The neurological system, respiratory system, urination, immunological system, sleeplessness, and skin are all efficiently treated by lavender essential oil.

Book 7:
Native American Spirituality

Chapter 1:
Native Americans' Beliefs and Practises

Knowledge Of Native American Beliefs and Customs

One of the most intriguing features of the culture is the beliefs and practises of Native Americans. It's hardly surprising that they still have a significant presence in contemporary culture given the rich history and significance they carry. Some of the most prevalent Native American beliefs and customs will be covered in this section. You will learn all you need to know about these intriguing ancient societies, from animal symbolism to healing practises.

Native American Spirituality Definition

Native American spirituality has its roots in the religious practises of North America's original inhabitants. These customs reflect a strong kinship with nature and respect for the dead and supernatural beings. The spiritual practises of Native Americans include ikéyátsoyii, Diné bizaad, and animism. According to animism, even inanimate objects have a spirit. The idea that commonplace items and natural occurrences have a spirit or force is known as diné bizaad. Ikéyátsoyii translates as "the way of the heart." This phrase alludes to the notion that everyone possesses a mechanism that enables them to communicate with their spiritual Source. Native Americans communicate with their spiritual selves and pay tribute to their ancestors via ceremonies and rituals. To gain insight and understanding about life, the cosmos, and human nature, they also rely on sweat lodges, dream questing, and other rituals.

Beliefs And Spiritual Practises

They don't distinguish between the physical and spiritual worlds.

The relationship between the spiritual and material worlds is at the centre of Native American spirituality. The spiritual and material worlds are not separated in their minds. Everything has a spirit, and everything is interconnected.

The tribes hold that everything has a spirit that is both alive and active. This applies to inanimate items as well as living things. According to the Sioux, everything in the universe possesses a spirit, and it is crucial to show respect for these spirits.

Additionally, tribes have the notion that there are several kind of spirits. While some people are kind, others are evil. These wicked spirits may do a lot of damage to individuals and their houses, so it's crucial to keep out of their way.

Native Americans Practise a Wide Range of Religions

Native Americans practise a variety of religions, some of which are rooted in their ancestors' ancient spiritual practises. The creator deity, the thunder god, the moon goddess, and other great spiritual entities are among the pantheon that many Native Americans believe in. Animism, a belief that all living things have souls, is practised by several cultures. Other tribes employ ceremonies, traditional medicines, and shamanic practises to seek spiritual direction.

Recognising their attitudes towards death

The views of Native Americans about death differ from those of the majority of people. Death is not a finality to North American indigenous people. Instead, it is viewed as entering a new reality or condition of being.

Native Americans in North America frequently hold the belief that after death, a person passes through four stages: travel to the deceased's realm or spirit village, encounters with significant spirits, trials by ghost warriors, and eventually entrance into the everlasting world.

Natives go through a variety of tests and difficulties at each stop along the way to demonstrate that they are deserving of accessing the afterlife.

Some theories contend that we receive visits from several departed family members and friends while we are still on earth. These stops enable us to pick up some of the lessons we need to know in order to continue on to our ultimate goal.

Another idea is that a person's soul can stay with them after they pass away and communicate with their loved ones. This implies that even if a loved one passes away unexpectedly, you could still be able to interact with them through other ways, including dreams or visions.

Native Americans frequently hold this belief as well. After passing away, a person's spirit could take up residence in another body and carry on living. Pre-birth incarnation, which holds that everyone has had at least one previous birth, is really a common belief in many civilizations. Some of the pain and suffering we go through as we age and get older on earth may help us get ready for the next world.

1. Fresh-picked vegetables is a well-known practise for many people all around the world, but what about Native Americans? The harvest or planting season is commemorated by the following five festivals.

2. The Navajo Harvest Festival, which takes place in September, honours the abundance of the previous year's harvest. Traditional dances, ceremonies, and singalongs are all part of this celebration.

3. October sees the annual Cherokee Oktoberfest, which honours German history on Cherokee territory. This event's main draws are local beer, cuisine, and music.

4. The Hmong New Year Festival is celebrated in November to mark the conclusion of the harvest season and to ask for abundant harvests the following year. There are several celebrations, such as a parade, cultural performances, and a fireworks display at dusk.

5. December is the Hawaiian Festival of Aunty Lilo, which honours lady plants and fertility spirits connected to hula dance and agriculture. Throughout December, a

number of festivities are hosted throughout the chain of islands, including pig races, luau dances, concerts by marching bands, fireworks displays, etc.

6. In San Francisco, where Filipino immigrants reside and work, October is the time for the Pilipino Harvest Festival. This event offers karaoke, Pinoy Pong (a board game similar to checkers), food booths offering Sinigang (a sort of soup made from fermented hog blood), colourful floats portraying scenes from traditional Filipino culture, and nocturnal fireworks displays.

Native American Pipes Ceremony

Although the origins of the ceremonial use of pipes are unknown, it is thought to be very old. Pipes are associated with a variety of myths and legends, but one popular one holds that they were formerly employed as a means of spirit contact. Some people think the pipes were used to call ghosts through music.

For Native Americans, the contemporary pipe ceremony is a spiritual occasion. It is a chance to commune with the natural world and the cosmos. While each ritual has its own special components, drums and smoke sticks are frequently used. Participants can communicate with their ancestors and other spiritual entities through the pipe's smoke.

Smudging

Smudging is a customary ritual that many Native American tribes still use today. It speaks with the spirits of the natural world while clearing and sanctifying spaces or things.

Smudging rituals come in a wide variety of forms, but they all have several things in common. Participants first assemble in a circle around a dirty object or space. They then pick a burning substance, such sage, cedar wood, or sweetgrass, and set it ablaze. The heat from the fire aids in the airborne release of the plants' aromas. The spirits of nature are supposed to be attracted to these aromas and may help to cleanse and guard the place or item being smudged.

Participants frequently chant or sing prayers while waving their hands in front of the flame once the incense is lit. The smoke is more evenly dispersed throughout the space and across the item or area being cleaned thanks to the dancing and movement. In order to induce relaxation and reduce tension, individuals occasionally rub oils (like lavender) over their bodies while engaging in this practise.

Traditional rites like sweat lodges and dream journeys frequently include smudging. Together, these ceremonies foster human-nature relationships, which are fundamental to Native American culture.

The Search For Vision

In several Native American tribes, vision quests are a widespread practise. Young men typically take them on to develop their spiritual strength and wisdom. A vision quest often consists of a set of tasks that the participant must complete in order to achieve understanding of his or her identity and life's purpose. These difficulties can come in numerous forms, such as fasting and protracted prayer sessions, as well as solitary travel across severe terrain. The purpose of a vision quest is to acquire spiritual knowledge, physical might, and endurance that may be applied later in life.

Beliefs Relating to Death

In terms of death, Native American religion generally followed the same path as the majority of other civilizations throughout the world. They believe in a spirit that lives on after the death of the physical body.

It will go for another planet or the hereafter, where it will lead a life like to the one it had while it was a human being on Earth. The idea of travelling to another dimension makes logical given that various tribes initially spent so much time travelling. They could consider travelling to be a normal aspect of life. But occasionally, a spirit gets stuck on Earth or never makes it to the spirit realm.

In order to facilitate the spirit's passage to the next life, funeral rites and ceremonies were developed. But this is not so unlike from other world religions. For instance, ancient Egyptian pharaohs were mummified and interred with material possessions in order to "live" blissfully after death. "Last Rites" and prayers said during a funeral serve the same purposes in Catholicism.

Exercise Lodges

Sweat lodges have existed for generations, dating to a time when Native Americans engaged in a type of physical, spiritual, and visionary cleansing. Sweat lodges, sometimes referred to as purification lodges, are locations where you may reenergize and create a solid connection with the spiritual world. This goal is attained in various ways by various tribes, but it always starts with a little wooden frame, some sheets or skins to cover it with, and a heat source. They are organised and choreographed by spiritual leaders in the community, who provide specific directions based on the circumstances or goals of each scenario.

Every sweat lodge ceremony includes burning several types of tobacco, cedar, and sweetgrass as well as making offerings and praying. A fire is built outside the lodge to heat the rocks, which are then hauled inside for the duration. Water is applied to the pebbles to unleash the fragrant, sometimes hallucinogenic vapour. They might be finished individually or collectively.

The Pipes Ceremony

Different types of smoke and steam play a significant role in Native American rites. Since it was in the air, it served as a bridge between the earth below and the heavens above. Anyone who has seen a vintage "Cowboys and Indians" film or animated series has probably seen American Indians burning a peace pipe as part of a rite. These examples of the spiritual importance of pipe rites are unrealistic and oversimplified.

The use of tobacco is also common in religious rites and celebrations. Several tribes participate in these rites by passing or smoking different pipes in the four cardinal directions. The rituals are as diverse as the tribes who perform them and the settings in which they are performed. Pipe smoking is a part of personal prayers, naming ceremonies, and peace negotiations. When there are more people attending an event, a professional pipe carrier supplies the pipe and manages the praying procedure.

Chapter 2:
Indigenous Peoples Religion and Medicine

Ancient Native American healing techniques are still used today. Many cultures have methods for treating its members by fusing roots, herbs, and other plant components. This does not imply that just plants were used in Native American medical techniques, though.

Travelling from tribe to tribe, no healing method is the same. However, you will find many similarities in their rituals, knowledge, and ceremonies. Health was a representation of Native Americans' spirit, but there were no therapeutic guidelines. They believed that unless they restored the spirit, mind, and body, no one would live. To avoid disease and harm, they had to stay in their native habitat. Naturally, they understood that in order to improve their health, they had to address their physical problems.

Their primary component, which went beyond physical aches and pains, was the herbal remedies that went along with these therapeutic techniques. Naturally, they also advised the patient to concentrate on their spirituality and internal peace while they were attending to their physical state, which gave many Native Americans the motivation to endure a variety of ailments.

Both the plants utilised and the functions they served are still well known today. That doesn't imply that everything is as clear-cut as it was when it was first passed down from one person to the next over the years.

The term "Native American Medicine," as it is used now, relates to the many indigenous tribes that inhabited North America before the advent of Europeans. Each tribe had its own beliefs and practises, but there was a common understanding that harmony between the patient, the patient's family, the community, and the natural environment was essential for health and wellbeing.

Native American medicine might date back more than 40,000 years. However, until the arrival of the Europeans 500 years ago, the majority of it remained undocumented and kept a secret among numerous tribes. The majority of Native American elders are hesitant to divulge medical information out of concern for the safety or integrity of sacred knowledge. Some tribes, like the Cherokee, preserved some knowledge of medicine. However, the bulk was verbally transmitted from one generation to the next.

Before Europeans could see some of this medical expertise, many healers who had it perished. Ancient and contemporary Native American tribes care about maintaining their culture, and many healers are interested in finding more about customs and how they handle particular ailments. Even if some elders think that revealing health secrets and cures to non-natives will help maintain it, the majority do not have confidence in doing so. Therefore, there is still plenty to learn.

The US Pharmacopoeia has at some time made reference to Americans, suggesting that pharmaceutical corporations had exploited them in the past and still do so to produce today's medications.

Why Spirituality Is Important

As it has been throughout human history in the majority of the world, spirituality was essential to Native American healing. In rites and ceremonies, singing, dancing, and prayers were employed. This element of spirituality sets conventional medicine apart from Native American healing practises. The goal of traditional medicine is to improve a person's physical condition. Native healers, on the other hand, believed that spirituality and the psychological health of the person, family, and community were crucial for healing.

Medicinal Wheel

The goal of the medicine wheel, like that of the Sacred Pipe, was to bring the different elements of one reality together to acknowledge their unity.

The several personalities that make up each of us live together in the same body. You contain several different personas within you, including the child, the caring mother, the wise, the irritable adolescent, the hunter, and many others.

Without each, you wouldn't be who you are now. There will be parts of you that are angry with you for not thinking about and paying attention to them appropriately in the past, as well as parts of you that speak out much too often.

It is essential that you build trusting relationships with each of your constituents over time and give them the freedom to express themselves in a way that makes them happy and feel appreciated.

Instead of working against your interests because they are resentful or unhappy, you want them to be your life partner. Your life's activities depend on this totality.

It's surprising how much Carl Gustav Jung's Analytic Psychology resembles this ages-old, intuitive Native American concept. Rather from being a location where separate memories and complexes were "stored," according to Jung, the subconscious was an intricate collection of many archetypal figures.

Each personality interacts with other personalities as well as the conscious ego and has its own set of desires and skills. The interactions and conflicts between personalities as well as between each personality and consciousness shape everyone's psychic dynamics.

This idea makes self-destructive behaviour and any psychological inversion action understandable.

Native Americans were fully aware of this idea before to Jung, and the majority of their religious rituals were focused on bringing opposites together to become oneself.

The results and improvement in your day-to-day life will be astonishing, even if it could take some time each day for a few months:

Find a peaceful area where you can spend 10 minutes each day by yourself. Sit comfortable and take two or three long breaths to relax.

Imagine that you are ambling across a meadow. On this bright and beautiful day, the sky is clear and blue. The only sounds you hear as you cross the lawn are the wind and the rustle of the grass. There's only you.

You eventually come to a dilapidated house in the middle of some fields. You are welcomed with a sizable room with a sizable circular table in the middle as soon as you open the front door.

The table has chairs available. While some are stolen by people or animals, others are not. This is your private group.

Try to find a comfy chair. Take a seat, and say hello to everyone else here.

Who are they exactly? What history do they have? What are they after? What can you do to help them?

Try to get an understanding with each of your identities. If you stop hurting yourself and being selfish, you'll be surprised at how quickly things in your life start to get better.

This idea—that we are a totality made up of several parts—is reflected in the medicine wheel. To survive in this life with balance and harmony, we must figure out how to live in close relationships with each of them.

From your individual oneness to the oneness of your family, society, and so forth, all of creation may be viewed as being one.

The basic concept of "the many that are one" was comprehended by Native Americans. To bring life back to its full potential, they created the medicine wheel ceremony.

For this ritual, the practitioner must build a stone circle. All the elements of life merge to form this sacred world of oneness and harmony as a result of this straightforward action, which starts an upward spiral of positive energy.

The practitioner gives back part of the order and harmony he got by creating a peaceful and harmonious environment for himself.

Each stone represents a member of the community or a facet of your personality who is free to enter and express himself or herself.

The biggest stone in the Circle, which is situated at its centre, represents the Spirit, the essence of all things.

Four gates, one for each of the four directions (North, South, East, and West) are part of the Circle of Stones, and each gate represents a distinct archetype.

South: Denotes a fresh start, youth, springtime, optimism, and vitality. It stands for rebirth.

West: Youth, conflict, and the quest for meaning and identity. It illustrates our trips into our deepest personality traits, or as Carl Jung called it, our voyage "into the shadow," to learn who we really are. In this circular part, we are robbed of the things we value. The West serves as a metaphor for the painful collapse.

North: This is the era of middle-aged balance, compassion, and selflessness.

In the East, it is the season of old age, repose, wisdom, and enlightenment. You reach this level when you completely reject the earthly world and start to develop a spiritual sensitivity.

The sacred pipe and the medicine wheel conceal more than meets the eye. Every component has a deeper significance and function that may be used to enhance people's wellbeing.

Native American medicine now

There has been a spike in interest in Native American medicine as a result of the general concern of the adverse effects, toxicity, resistance, and addiction caused by pharmaceutical drugs, surgery, and other modern therapies. Herbal remedies are in demand as a means of treating illnesses and diseases. Over time, high-quality herbal remedies have been created, the majority of which were inspired by Native American healing practises. Compared to pharmaceutical goods, herbal treatments are less harmful and more effective.

Choose herbal remedies that have been formulated using conventional pharmaceutical ingredients.

Although Native American medicine was outlawed, many modern pharmaceuticals have their roots in it. Many of the herbal cures used by Native Americans are included in the United States Pharmacopoeia, according to Laurance Johnston, who studied diverse medical systems from throughout the world.

Native Americans, for instance, used willow tree bark as a painkiller. In this bark, acetylsalicylic acid was discovered. Acetylsalicylic acid is known under the brand name aspirin.

But there are also notable philosophical differences between contemporary medicine and indigenous medicine.

Book 8:
Native American Natural Medicine

Chapter 1:
The Cherokee Legend

The Cherokee mythology is one of the most alluring and fascinating stories in Americana. It relates the tale of a people that endured numerous hardships over the course of centuries, including battle, sickness, persecution, and displacement. Here, we'll go into great detail about this mythology and provide you all the information you need to comprehend it. This book will take you on a tour through some of the most well-known Cherokee legends, from their beginnings to their characters.

The Cherokee Legend: An Overview of History

The Cherokee Legend is a well-established tale with a lengthy past. It has been handed down through the generations and is still a hot topic of conversation today. According to a narrative, Coyote and Trapper, two brothers, were banished from their tribe for disobeying the rules. They travelled the world in quest of a new home, but they never found tranquilly. They finally constructed their own dwellings in the skies after years of travelling.

Coyote and Trapper faced several difficulties as they constructed their house. They had to first get beyond the perils of the untamed world below. Second, they had to deal with the challenges that their tribesmen brought. To finally construct their cottage high in the mountains, they had to struggle against nature. Coyote and Trapper eventually started their own clan, though.

The Cherokee Legend is rich with allegory that alludes to the human condition. Coyote and Trapper, for instance, stand for bravery and tenacity since they can conquer all obstacles despite being outsiders. The tree that leads them to their house stands for development and change; it is always ready to assist people who are eager to make use of its advantages.

The Cherokee Legend is a motivational tale that honours tenacity and independence. It reminds us that, whatever the challenges life presents, we can always find a way to overcome them.

The Moccasin Maker: The Making of an Epic Legend by the Cherokee

The Cherokee moccasin maker mythology is a grand tale rich with tradition and history. The mythological figure known as the moccasin maker is credited with making the original pair of moccasins.

Mother Earth is the central figure in the mythology. She was enraged because people were ruining all she had built and cluttering her property. She then cursed them with unfavourable climate, poor health, and difficult lives.

A guy by the name of Thunderer went hunting one day in the woods. He stumbled upon a deer that had been ensnared in a human-made trap. The hunter who had placed the trap may be killed, and the deer could be released. Thunderer earned the title of "the great hunter-warrior who saved humanity from Mother Earth's wrath" in recognition of his feat.

Thunderer had a romantic encounter with Sky Woman when he was out hunting. He was informed by Sky Woman of Mother Earth's fury and how humanity were to blame. If he wed her, she would help him preserve mankind. Thunderer concurred, and shortly after that, they were wed.

Together, they set off to Mother Earth's home planet in order to make an apology for humanity. Mother Earth listened to their tale and gave in, allowing them to reside on her land as long as they did not harm it or disobey any of her laws.

So that people's feet wouldn't suffer when walking on the surface of the earth, Sky Woman started producing moccasins for them to wear. She also showed them how to construct houses and raise vegetables.

Despite having learnt their lesson, humans still did not treat Mother Earth with respect. A new myth was concocted by Thunderer and Sky Woman about a great moccasin maker who would show them how to coexist peacefully with nature.

This fabled person was referred to as the formulate maker. According to legend, he or she used the skins of animals that had passed away naturally to make the first pair of moccasins. People were also taught how to weave baskets and create other things out of natural resources by the formula makers.

The Cherokee moccasin maker mythology is a grand tale rich with tradition and history. The mythological figure known as the moccasin maker is credited with making the original pair of moccasins.

The Journey That Changed the Cherokee Nation Forever: The Vision Quest

One of the most beautiful, culturally diverse, and historically significant tribes in North America is the Cherokee Nation. From the Appalachian Mountains to the Gulf of Mexico, their territory, sometimes referred to as "Cherokee Country," is located. The lengthy and treasured history of the tribe includes a special vision quest ritual called the "Path of the Arrow."

For Cherokee males, the Path of the Arrow is an initiation ceremony that signifies the passage from boyhood to adulthood. It entails a trek through the wilderness and tests participants' ability to withstand physical adversity in order to achieve spiritual enlightenment. They are taken on a journey that takes them out of society and deep into the forest, where they must confront fear, isolation, and self-discovery.

Cherokee culture has been significantly shaped by the Path of the Arrow. Generations of Cherokees have drawn inspiration from it, imitating it, and embracing their cultural heritage. It is still a significant part of the tribe's identity today. It is regarded as being a crucial component of their history and traditions.

A significant turning point in the Cherokees' fight for independence was the Battle of Horseshoe Bend.

Many people believe that the Battle of Horseshoe Bend was a turning point in the Cherokee people's fight for freedom. On September 14, 1814, the conflict took place close to the modern-day Arkansas community of Horseshoe Bend. The Creek and Cherokee tribes were inspired and thought they could beat American forces once more after defeating the American Army at the Battle of Tippecanoe in 1811. However, General Andrew Jackson staged a tactical surprise attack at Horseshoe Bend against a lesser Cherokee army that was preparing for an assault. Following the victory, a series of military triumphs served to bring the American colonies together and ultimately led to the War of 1812.

The Cherokee Nation's Legacy After the Revolution

One of the earliest countries in North America is the Cherokee Nation. After many years of battle, the country was able to retain its independence and sovereignty.

A rich cultural history has been passed down through the generations to the Cherokee Nation, which now appreciates it. Traditional American values include close family ties, a great respect for nature, and a dedication to democracy.

Long after the last of the Cherokee Nation's inhabitants have died away, their heritage will still be honoured. The Cherokee Nation continues to play a significant role in American history and culture as a result of their efforts.

Chapter 2:
Sacred Medicines for Native Americans

A centuries-old method of medicine with roots in indigenous Native American culture is known as "Sacred Medicine." Modern medical concepts are being incorporated into and being expanded upon by sacred medicine.

Sacred Medicine is not a method but a state of consciousness. To comprehend it better, you must be aware of this.

Sacred Medicine: What Is It Exactly?

Many people associate medicine with frigid, sterile settings, drugs, operations, and professionals in white coats working to better a patient's physical condition. On the other hand, ancient societies, notably among Native Americans, used medicine as a complex, interrelated system of spiritual and physical well-being.

The physical, mental, social, and spiritual components of our bodies are divided into distinct categories. When these elements are out of balance, we experience sickness and illness.

The indigenous people viewed medicine as a means of restoring harmony and balance to nature's fundamental forces. It entailed being aware of our ability, which permits us to exist in the world as entire, complete beings.

The lives of the native people were not governed by interpretations or restrictions made by the Holy Scriptures because they did not practise any Abrahamic faiths. Instead, they looked to nature for guidance, studying the environment they inhabited and its cyclical patterns to help us defend our stance.

According to them, life occurs in cycles or circles, much like the sun and moon's phases, the seasons, and the cycle of life, rather than in a straight line as we define it in terms of time and days. Our lives are a part of a cycle, much as the lives of animals, plants, and herbs.

This understanding of existence led to the creation of sacred medicine. It has a holy circle that has healing properties that may benefit our bodies, minds, and souls.

The Four Sacred Medicines of Indigenous Culture

The four Sacred Medicines that make up the medicine wheel, according to the Native Americans, are composed of four organic plants.

The medical wheel operates in four directions, giving it four distinctive properties. It is impossible to express the essence of the universal one or divine essence, which is represented by the centre of the wheel. Native American culture refers to it as the "holy secret" in general.

Different tribes have their own unique definitions of the four directions on the wheel. They contend that many facets of existence are represented by each direction. As a result, it has distinct connotations for many tribes.

The wheel is split into numerous colours, each having a unique meaning, including red, yellow, black, and white.

The medical wheel is illustrated in the following ways:

It depicts several stages of life, including conception, youth, adulthood, and death. The four seasons of spring, summer, winter, and autumn are also represented by it. It may also be a reflection of a person's physical, mental, spiritual, and emotional traits. Additionally, it shows components from nature like earth, water, fire, and air. Some people think that the different orientations represent different human racial groups, including black, white, Asian, and American Indian. The wolf, buffalo, bear, eagle, and other animals can also be represented by it (Sol, 2021).

The medicine wheel's most fundamental representations are the Four Sacred Medicines.

The first plant ever given to native peoples by the Creator was tobacco. They believe that this plant spirit is the one that ignited all others. Sage, cedar, and sweet grass are among more plants that are revered as holy medicines. These plants are all considered to be one of the four Sacred Medicines.

Native Americans employ these Sacred Medicines in both their daily lives and rituals. White sage, cedar, and sweet grass are among the herbs that are all utilised in smudging. The native people believe that each plant symbolises a distinct entrance. The eastern door is reached by tobacco, and the western door is reached with sage. Sweet grass has taken up residence at the southern door, while cedar has taken up residence at the northern door. These holy plants are burned in order to release their fragrant smoke, which is said to appease the spirits they honour and adore (Ojibwe Journal, n.d.).

Sacred Medicine Movement in the Modern Era

Although it incorporates certain contemporary ideas, the present Sacred Medicine movement is based on ancient ideas. Adherents of this movement describe it as partnering with the body, mind, and spirit. It lays a focus on the heart, values intuition, and works to empower those who practise it. It also supports a more feminine strategy for healing. This kinder strategy covers our lives as a whole, including our physical and emotional wellbeing. These include aspects that many medical professionals ignore, such as our capacity to sustain interpersonal connections, financial stability, spirituality, and professional well-being.

These variables have a long-term effect on the health of our bodies, and contemporary Sacred Medicine aims to address all of these problems at once.

According to the modern Sacred Medicine movement, a balanced body may be able to cure itself. This is not meant to belittle the advantages of modern medicine. It means fusing the finest of conventional beliefs with the best that contemporary medicine has to offer. We all possess the amazing capacity to heal ourselves thanks to the marvellous nature of our bodies; all we need to do is learn how to activate it.

The goal of this movement is to reduce our dependency on synthetic medicines. Modern Sacred Medicine practitioners want to enable their patients to access their own healing intuition and start the healing process.

Practitioners of contemporary Sacred Medicine place equal weight on their role in the healing process as do physicians. Nobody understands our bodies as well as we do. We can help our doctors create effective treatments by providing them with information on how we prefer to be treated.

A increasing trend among individuals and healthcare professionals is called "Sacred Medicine." What's the aim of the movement? To "reclaim medicine's lost heart," as the phrase goes. They believe that medicine has become a profession that is cold and heartless, and they wish to bring compassion and spirituality back into the field (Rankin, n.d.b).

Practitioners of Sacred Medicine passionately believe in the curative power of love. Though they admit that science may treat symptoms, they believe that only love can bring about real healing. Adhering to Sacred Medicine does not involve discounting the therapeutic benefits of modern medicine, surgery, or other forms of care. Instead, it implies that just managing a symptom or getting rid of an organ does not equal healing. According to modern Sacred Medicine, you need to deal with the root of the issue in order to heal correctly. You must locate the issue, figure out why you are uncomfortable, and try to address it from the inside since only you are aware of the condition of your heart (Rankin, n.d.a).

Holy Medicine in Daily Life

Some Sacred Medicine concepts of today can be applied to our everyday life. Their names are as follows:

1. If we are prepared to embrace our suffering as an essential component of our development, we may use diseases, injuries, and trauma as chances for spiritual awakening.

2. Our bodies are capable of self-healing. Still, persistent stress impairs our capacity for healing and interferes with the body's normal processes.

3. This includes your social life, career, sexuality, religion, finances, diet, and daily activities.

4. The bare minimum requirements of exercising, eating correctly, getting enough sleep, and taking your medicine won't get you to the pinnacle of wellness and health.

5. Despite your claims to want to get healed, your inner saboteur prevents you from becoming better.

6. You are the authority on your body, not anybody else.

7. Believe in the curative power of love.

8. Believe in the strength of circles.

9. You may take life energy from other people when you run out of your own.

10. You may heal yourself by using your energy and life force to help others.

11. To be in the best possible health, you must develop your own life energy.

12. Stable connections may be strong healing factors.

13. You need a refuge or a safe haven to recover.

14. Laughing and having fun are the best forms of rehabilitation.

Chapter 3:
The Main Medicinal Plants Used by Native Americans

Every person who is serious about their pastime of maintaining a herb garden must grow therapeutic herbs and plants at home. The apothecary philosophy of medicinal plants may be a natural step for you into medicine if you enjoy gardening! Make a beautiful herb garden that provides you with healthy vitamins. High-quality herbs may be used to create delicious anti-inflammatory and immunity-enhancing ointments and beverages. You and your family will be on the path to better health if you have some knowledge. Herbs for therapeutic purposes are simple to cultivate in pots, gardens, and even small places.

Basil

Basil is easy to grow and versatile enough to thrive both indoors and out. It can transform ordinary foods into culinary masterpieces! Fresh basil tastes and feels different than dried basil. Basil is a medicinal herb that can help with indigestion, cuts, scrapes, and other mild illnesses (in addition to flatulence).

- kinds of basil you can grow at home
- Cinnamon basil has extremely lovely and fragrant blooms and has a sweet spice scent.

- Citral, an aromatic molecule in citrus fruits that gives them their distinctively lemony flavour and perfume, is a component of lemon basil.
- In addition to its aroma and blooms, purple basil is frequently grown for its decorative attributes.
- The lovely African Blue basil, which has blue veins in its leaves, and Thai basil are examples of perennial basils that thrive year after year. However, most other varieties are annuals that must be replanted every year.
- Although considerably more difficult to cultivate, globe and Greek basil mature into charming tiny shrubs that stay in their designated areas.

Start growing basil by planting seeds four to six weeks prior to the year's last day of frost. Basil needs warm air and sunlight to grow, thus it is usually more practical to start the seeds indoors rather than outside to prevent damage from cold. Maintain a moist but not wet soil. In a day with 6 to 8 hours of sunshine, basil plants thrive.

Cayenne

Cayenne, a fantastic plant to have in your pharmacy arsenal, but not a herb according to botanical definition. The king of therapeutic plants, according to many people, is the cayenne pepper. For thousands of years, people have used these peppers to treat a variety of illnesses. Cayenne peppers are wonderful for cooking and include a number of beneficial ingredients, which add to their medicinal properties.

Many meals contain cayenne peppers. They are closely related to bell peppers and jalapenos and belong to the same family of flowering plants as nightshades. They were first brought to Europe in the 15th century by Christopher Columbus, who had discovered them in Central and South America and returned with them.

Cayenne peppers have been used medicinally by early South American civilizations for hundreds of thousands of years in addition to being a common spice used in many different regional kinds of cookery. The excellent nutritional profile of these peppers includes a variety of antioxidants that are beneficial to your general health and wellbeing.

Capsaicin, the cayenne pepper's primary ingredient, is what gives the peppers their healing properties. Additionally, it adds to their peppery flavour. The spiciness of a dash of cayenne pepper depends on how much capsaicin is present. The level of heat is dependent on the quantity of capsaicin present. Cayenne pepper has been proven to have a number of health benefits, including those that increase metabolism, lower ghrelin production, lower blood pressure, aid digestion by delivering digestive enzymes to the stomach, and reduce pain by reducing the amount of substance in the body.

Chamomile

A blooming plant called chamomile has little, daisy-like blossoms. These flowers may be dried and used into soothing and medicinal herbal beverages, hot compresses, infused oils for cosmetics, and other products. This adorable and practical little herb is very simple to grow in your yard. You may start seeds indoors or outside. After then, until the flowers are ready to be picked, you must take meticulous care of your chamomile plants. These plants benefit from frequent irrigation and a sunny location.

The apple aroma of chamomile is well-known. It greatly aids in skin healing, lessens dryness, itching, and inflammation in skin that has been inflamed. Additionally, the herb is quite effective in reducing indigestion, stress, anxiety, and tension.

Lavender

One herb that has medical benefits merely from breathing it in is lavender. Lavender works even when someone merely choose to smell it, unlike other plants that are only effective when consumed. One of the main reasons people use the herb in baths, hospitals, and in beds to relax is because it provides a calming and sedative effect when breathed in. Lavender is the key component in aromatherapy if you're interested in it. The majority of clients receive lavender-infused accommodations, towels, and pretty much everything clothing. Lavender is used externally to treat burns and abrasions.

Sage

The term "sage" comes from the Latin word "salvia," which meaning "to heal." Sage is being utilised as a spice as well as a herb. Early on, the plant was mostly valued for its therapeutic uses; it was very infrequently acknowledged as a delicacy. According to studies, sage can assist with mood swings, blood cholesterol problems, memory problems, and sore throats.

Salvia officinalis, a hardy perennial with a flavorful aroma that grows in zones 5 to 9, has a savoury and somewhat bitter taste. Sage can endure temperatures as low as 0 degrees Fahrenheit (32 degrees Celsius) and thrives in a variety of climes. It has a nice look in the yard and blooms all summer long with exquisite purple, pink, blue, or white flowers. Sage plants should only be watered when the soil feels completely dry.

With its lovely blooms and pleasant perfume, lavender (Lavandula) is a welcome addition to any garden. It is very simple to cultivate. The Mediterranean herb lavender grows best in hot, sunny climates. Choose a spot in your garden that will receive direct sunlight for the plant.

Citrus balm

Lemon balm may be grown at home for a number of uses, including the treatment of skin conditions and small wounds as well as the reduction of insect bite pain and swelling. Lemon balm is particularly repellent to mosquitoes. It can help control blood sugar and relieve painful muscles and cold sores.

Rosemary

For growing in a rock garden or on top of a dry stone wall, rosemary is a great option. In Zones 7 and above, the plant can be grown as a perennial shrub. It should be cultivated in pots and taken indoors during the winter if you live in a colder region. Repot the plant when the roots fill the pot as the plant grows and the soil feels dry. Rosemary benefits from 6–8 hours a day in direct sunlight.

Thyme

Thyme is an evergreen herb that belongs to the Lamiaceae family of mints and is incredibly adaptable. It thrives in direct sunlight. When planting thyme, make sure the soil has a pH of around 7.0 and is well-drained. You may also fertilise the seeds with limestone, oyster shells, or crushed eggshells.

Parsley

In the past and present, parsley has been praised for its antioxidant flavonoids, which combat free radicals. Some of them have been demonstrated to stop (or delay) the growth of certain malignancies. Vitamins L, 812, K, and A are just a few of the abundant vitamins found in parsley. Parsley strengthens bones, soothes the neurological system, and supports a healthy immune system.

Since parsley takes a while to sprout from seeds, plant them in the spring, eight weeks inside before the last freeze. Also, to hasten germination, immerse seeds in warm water for 24 hours prior to planting. The plant will have plenty of time to adjust by starting from seed in the spring before autumn arrives and the first frost strikes. Plant in either full or partial light; both environments will be beneficial. For optimum growth results, a loamy soil fertilised with natural substances is necessary.

I strongly advise taking into account St. John's wort if you struggle with mental health issues like depression. The plant's leaves and yellow blossoms are only two of its many functional components. Care must be taken, though, as this plant is also linked to some components of danger and injury. When used with other treatments, especially modern ones, this plant, along with other therapeutic herbs, appears to have an effect. Therefore, you should refrain from combining it with any other medications and instead take it on its own if you're seeking to treat any mental health issues.

The plant is most common from the middle of summer till the end of the year. The key advantage of this plant is its ease of environmental adaptation, which allows it to flourish in virtually any location under ideal conditions. Most people are amazed by the herb's persistence because it may be found in the driest locations, such as areas where cactus are often located.

Marigold

The herb marigold may be helpful for a number of skin issues, including sunburn, acne, pimples, ulcers, and gastrointestinal issues. Calendula, often known as marigold, is one of the best all-purpose skin care products. It works particularly well on minor injuries, burns, insect bites, dry skin, and acne. Calendula tea can be used topically twice or three times daily as an astringent face rinse to treat acne. There are several over-the-counter (OTC) medications available, including salves, creams, and lotions.

Even though marigolds are quite easy to grow, they come in a variety of colours. White, yellow, orange, red, and blended colours are among them. Marigolds come in a variety of sizes as well, from little varieties that are under a foot tall to enormous varieties that may grow up to four feet tall. Even though marigolds are hardy plants, cold weather can cause them to perish.

Marigolds are relatively easy to grow from seed and do well in full sunlight and typical garden soil. They may also be grown in pots or other containers, which is why they are sometimes known as "pot marigolds." To ensure a longer blooming season, the calendula plant's sticky blooms must be plucked every two to three days. Calendula often self-seeds unless it is completely mulched. Although it is typically planted yearly, warmer conditions may allow it to become a short-lived perennial.

Book 9:
Native American Stones & Crystals

Chapter 1:
Basic Information About Healing Stones and Crystals

Probably one of the most talked-about subjects in the world right now is healing crystals. There is no doubting that these stones have strong affects on our physical and mental wellbeing, whether you believe in them or not. This article will provide you a general overview of healing crystals, including what they are, how to utilise them, and their advantages. We also have some suggestions for the top healing stones for a variety of problems. Discover everything there is to know about healing gemstones by diving in.

It's remarkable (and depressing) to think of how frequently cultures with strong relationships to stones have been assaulted by colonisers and explorers for their "barbaric" and "uneducated" practises given our contemporary adoration for crystals and their medicinal possibilities.

The "Code of Indian Offences" endangered the traditional role of medicine men and women in indigenous culture in the late nineteenth century, despite more severe fronts having been made for prior generations. These healers might end up in jail or worse if they are forbidden from using healing tools like crystals.

Native American diamonds have a long history of ceremonial use that includes viewpoints from more than 2,000 different indigenous groups in North America alone.

While we are unable to discuss every aspect of crystal meanings and uses in Native American healing rituals, our goal is to highlight this significant variation and offer a look into the enormous variety of holy stone connections.

The Value of Healing Stones in Native American Culture

Native American gemstones serve as tools and totems that help unify indigenous civilizations and cure people. Health in indigenous cultures represents the continual work to maintain and enhance spiritual life as well as the physical body's balance with the natural world.

Personal Healing Stones Therapy

Many indigenous people hold the view that health is a balance with the natural world, and that disease and injury arise when a person loses contact with and harmony with it. A person's views and actions lead to discord. A person who practises bad habits, thinks poorly, or feels unpleasantly invites the negative effects of an imbalance with nature's flawless, beneficial gifts.

In these natural healing systems, one might seek treatment from a medicine man or woman. In indigenous tribes, medicine people conducted therapy utilising complementary therapies including crystal healing and the use of sacred symbols. As was previously said, crystal connections are extremely delicate and particular to each person. Indigenous healing systems that use individual treatment techniques make this connection clear.

A highly private and intimate experience, healing using holy objects like crystals and other spiritual rituals is shared between the healer and the patient. Regarding how to approach and combine various ways into treatment, the patient's wishes should take precedence.

The medicine person respects and tunes into the person's vibrations before beginning any healing using crystals or other talismans.

Stones of Healing for Social Cohesion

The close-knit community of a tribe is strongly affected by an individual's sickness. As a result, both men and women who practise medicine are interested in community healing.

They help the neighbourhood comprehend how one person's discord knocks the whole neighbourhood out of balance with nature. An individual's bad energy may extend to the entire neighbourhood. Rather than only as a result of a single sick person, the community may suffer as a whole as a result of collective decisions and behaviours.

Native American jewels, potent symbols, and plants like sage or palo santo are used in rituals and ceremonies officiated by traditional indigenous healers that purge the community of the residual energy of disease and weakness in order to reenergize it and bring it back into harmony with nature.

Native American tribes have employed highly evolved techniques for aeons, as evidenced by the incredible ability they acquired to work with healing stones and crystals.

Long lines of practise produced the ability to weave intricate patterns, carve features in stone, and polish smooth crystals. Native American healing stones had many uses in their civilization as a result of these qualities.

A connection with spirit guides

Native American jewels provide a physical link between people and spirit guides. Some stones are said to call spirits and entice them to interact with people.

By keeping crystals, Native Americans create a natural, balanced protection with the Earth. Crystals and other holy objects, like peyote, can be used to enter different heavenly worlds.

Keeping a Record of History

Crystal jewellery and pendants worn as amulets depict stories from indigenous history and long-standing oral traditions. Some elements of Native American culture are preserved via the meticulous engraving of symbols onto crystals and gemstones.

Finance and Trade

While crystals and stones have always held a spiritual value for indigenous people, their skill of using these materials in jewellery and other applications has evolved over time to integrate new patterns and manufacturing technologies that have been made possible by commerce.

These impacts resulted from the mobility of people and economic networks. Not every migration into these cultures had positive effects, such as the spread of disease and famine. However, native people did succeed in finding sizable markets for their painstakingly produced crystal artwork.

How Do Crystals Work?

A naturally occurring material, crystals are composed of atoms that are organised in a particular pattern. These materials can be either solid, liquid, or gaseous. Crystals come in a wide variety of sizes and forms and frequently have special qualities that make them effective for healing. Crystals may shield against radiation and other poisons, enhance good energy, and aid with physical and mental wellness. They may also facilitate communication with the spiritual realm.

Knowing which crystal varieties are most appropriate for your particular requirements is crucial if you want to utilise crystals for healing. Quartz, jasper, turquoise, apatite, amethyst, peridot, chalcedony, calcite, rose quartz, and onyx are a few examples of common crystals. Knowing the characteristics of the crystal you are utilising is also useful. For instance, rose quartz is useful for enhancing emotional well-being while quartz shields against radiation harm.

What Are Some Regular Healing Crystal Benefits?

Using healing gemstones for your health and well-being has a lot of advantages. There is evidence to support the efficacy of these stones, which have a long history of usage in healing. The following are a few of the most widespread advantages of utilising healing crystals:

Crystal Healing Can Help Lower Stress

High blood pressure, heart disease, and diabetes are just a few of the health issues that stress can contribute to. By restoring balance to the body's energy, heating stones can help lower stress levels. They can also encourage restful sleep and a more laid-back attitude.

Healing Crystals Can Help with Depression and Anxiety

Both sadness and anxiety are serious mental health conditions that can be challenging to manage. By supplying soothing energy and encouraging optimistic thinking, healing gemstones may be beneficial. They can also reduce pain and strengthen your immune system.

Healing Crystals Can Aid with Pain Relief

Many individuals turn to healing crystals to get relief from bodily discomfort like headaches, backaches, or rheumatism. The body's energy may be balanced, inflammation may be reduced, and the nerves that regulate pain may be stimulated by heating crystals.

Enhancing Mental Health with Healing Crystals

Numerous individuals utilise healing stones to enhance their mental well-being. They could offer vigour and inspiration, which helps lessen anxiety and sadness. Additionally, crystals may strengthen your immune system and reduce discomfort.

How Can You Pick the Perfect Crystal for You?

When looking for a healing stone, there are many different crystal kinds to consider, but not all crystals function in the same manner. It's crucial to choose the ideal gemstone for your requirements.

Asking yourself the following questions can help you determine which crystal is suitable for your situation:

What do I require to recover?

What do I want to achieve?

Do I use this crystal as my main tool or as a supplement?

What will I use it for?

Let's say you're attempting to recover from a condition like bereavement, anxiety, or depression. In that situation, quartz is a wise choice since it may assist to eliminate energetic barriers and amplifies energy. Amethyst or tourmaline might be preferable if you utilise this crystal as part of a ritual or meditation practise since they encourage calmness and peace.

Any form of calcite or apatite would be suitable if your only goals are to boost your energy or soothe your nerves. Keep in mind that certain crystals draw more negative energy than others, so you should experiment with several stones to see which one is best for you.

How Do Crystals for Healing Function?

Crystals have the ability to heal because of their special structure and the way the energies of the cosmos resonate with them. Molecules are organised in precise patterns and structures to form crystals. They can now store and release energy thanks to this.

Crystals have been utilised for thousands of years as decorative, meditative, and therapeutic items. They are considered to possess a number of qualities that might enhance our wellbeing. We may connect with our spiritual side and become more aware of our inner energies with the aid of healing crystals.

Before employing a healing stone, it is crucial to learn about its qualities. Depending on a person's specific health demands or difficulties, certain stones may function better. Additionally, keep in mind that owing to their sensitivity, not all stones are suited for everyone. It is usually advised to evaluate a crystal for compatibility with your energy body on a small scale before utilising it for healing.

Utilising Your Crystal

When using crystals for healing, there is no one right way to do it. However, a few fundamental principles might aid in your initial steps.

It's crucial to understand your energy level and the ailment you're seeking to address before employing crystals for healing. Consider the characteristics of the crystal you are utilising as well. Use a crystal with Heart energy capabilities, for instance, if you're trying to fix a heart problem. Use an earth-based crystal like turquoise or amethyst if you're trying to let go of tension or anger.

Before utilising a crystal for healing, it is crucial to cleanse and charge it after deciding what sort you require. To achieve this, add some rose petals or lavender buds to a basin of warm water and submerge the crystal in it. After letting the crystal absorb the water, give it a thorough rinsing. Before using it, make careful to properly dry it off.

Visualisation is a crucial component of utilising gemstones for healing. When considering what you wish to heal, see your health improving as well as the healer stone(s)' energy. When utilising crystals for healing, this might assist you in tuning in more fully to the result you want.

How To Safely Store Your Crystals

Many individuals have a lot of questions about crystals. How do they function? What advantages do they have? How do I utilise them to cure myself?

The ideal way to keep crystals for each individual depends on their requirements and tastes. There are several ways to do this. Here are some recommendations for safeguarding your crystals:

- Keep crystals out of the sun's direct rays and extreme heat.

- Check the crystal container's airtightness to ensure that moisture and other elements won't get inside.

- Avoid leaving crystal storage containers exposed to the air; doing so may cause the crystals to get contaminated with dust and other substances.

- If you're taking your crystals on the road, be careful to pack them safely and shield them from light and moisture.

Chapter 2:
Common Stones and Crystals

For generations, Native Americans have used crystals and rocks to cure both themselves and their environment. These organic materials may do everything from heal wounds to balance the body's energies. As more individuals look to nature for solutions to their health issues, the popularity of crystals and rocks is rising nowadays. This section will examine a few of the crystals and rocks that Native American shamans utilised for their healing rituals. You can experience a variety of advantages tailored to your body chemistry by adding crystal healing into your own health regimen. Continue reading to discover one of nature's most adaptable healing methods!

Blue Jasper

A common healing gem used by many Native American cultures is red jasper. It is thought to aid in mental clarity, focus, and stress reduction. The jasper is also said to be lucky charm material and protective.

Quartz

Native Americans have long employed quartz crystals and rocks to improve their physical and spiritual wellbeing. The stones are claimed to enhance good vibrations, eliminate energy obstacles, balance bodily energies, and promote optimistic thinking. Quartz is said to provide a number of health benefits, including improving energy flow and lowering stress, anxiety, depression, and other mental health disorders.

Turquoise

The gemstone of choice for many Native American healers is turquoise. The Mayans employed a blue form of turquoise called "malachite" to colour their ceramics and tombs; the Aztec term for turquoise, chalchihuitl, means "turquoise stone." Turquoise is a significant stone for Native Americans today.

The unusual colour and toughness of turquoise have led some people to think that it possesses mystical qualities. It is also said to be helpful in resolving psychological and emotional problems. Some tribes use it as a charm to stave against illness or bad karma. Others, though, utilise it to improve focus and mental clarity.

Turquoise was regarded by the Cherokee as having protective and visionary properties. It is frequently used as a safeguarding stone against stress and negative energy.

Granite

A type of rock called granite may be found all over the world. For generations, Native Americans have employed granite to cure their bodies and their communities. There are a lot of factors that make granite such a potent healing stone.

Minerals including feldspar, quartz, and mica can be found in granite. These minerals boost the immune system and aid in the body's detoxification process. Strong energy vibrations in granite can aid in removing emotional barriers and fostering healing.

Different kinds of granite are used by Native American tribes for various purposes. For instance, the Navajo employ red granite to reduce tension and enhance focus. The Mohawk people utilise white granite as a medium to communicate with and cure their spirit guides.

Sandstone

Fine-grained minerals make up the sedimentary rock type known as sandstone. This kind of rock may be used to make sculptures, structures, and jewellery decorations. It is frequently discovered close to the Earth's surface. Sandstone has long been used by Native Americans to carve tools and other items with medicinal uses.

Sandstone helps to eliminate energy blockages and aligns the chakras, according to Native Americans, who also think it has specific therapeutic powers. To promote wellness and reestablish equilibrium, many individuals massage their temples and other body regions with sandstone. Additionally, some cultures employ sandstone to expel evil spirits from their buildings.

Some individuals think that the vibrations of sandstone might aid in enhancing psychic skills. Others, though, think it can aid in reducing stress or anxiety. In either scenario, sandstone use is thought to be advantageous for the body and mind as part of a holistic approach to wellbeing.

Azurite

Azurite is a vibrant mineral that may be discovered all over the world. It helps to boost the immune system, which is why it is frequently used to treat wounds. Azurite is used by Native Americans to cure wounds and ailments. They think it has the capacity to expel harmful energy from the body.

Grey Onyx

A quartz variety called black onyx is mostly found in Mexico and Peru. Native Americans frequently utilise it to treat wounds, free up energy blockages, and promote peace since it is said to have spiritual characteristics.

The ability of Black Onyx to absorb negative energy and change it into positive energy is one of the key factors contributing to its popularity among Native American healers. This makes it the ideal stone for expelling any bad energy that could be aggravating your discomfort or causing you tension.

Black onyx has several advantages, one of which is that it may balance your chakras. Chakra balancing can enhance general wellbeing and help you find your spiritual path.

Panther's Eye

Numerous American Indian groups frequently wear jewellery made of tiger's eye. It has been worn as an amulet for ages and is thought to have protective qualities. The tiger's eye can be any shade from deep blue to black, although deep blue is the most common.

The tiger insignia that appears on the coats of arms of numerous European dynasties inspired the name of the stone. 'On stones,' a Greek text from the second century BC, has the name's earliest known use. It was referred to as topaz in Asia. It was employed by Alexander the Great and his army in 327 BC when they conquered India.

About how the gem came to be connected to specific abilities or ideologies, there are several stories. According to one legend, an Indian prince who was out hunting found the mineral and kept it a secret because he believed it would give him enormous power. When a princess discovered it, she fell in love with him, but he refused to give it to her since he understood that only royalty could use it to its full potential. She eventually conned him into giving her the stone and got married to someone else.

Some cultures regard tiger's eye as holy, and only those deemed worthy may wear or carry it. Additionally, it has served as a lucky sign for nuptials and fresh beginnings.

Amber

For ages, Native Americans have utilised healing stones and rocks to support their mental, emotional, and spiritual health. According to popular belief, these natural resources contain potent energies that can aid in restoring harmony and balance in the user's life.

Due to its astringent qualities, fossilised resin known as amber is frequently utilised as a healing stone. Clarifying mental and emotional concerns, assisting with the removal of energy system obstacles, and easing unpleasant emotions are all capabilities of amber. It can also serve as a charm for protection against evil spirits and destructive spells.

Turquoise, quartzite, tiger's eye, amethyst, peridot, topaz, bone china, tourmaline, opal, jadeite, and pearls are other common stones utilised by Native Americans for healing. Each has special abilities and advantages that the user may employ to advance their health and wellbeing.

Carnelian

A kind of chalcedony known as carnelian is regarded as one of the most spiritual healing stones. Carnelian was utilised by Native Americans in North America to treat both physical and mental ailments. Additionally, it was believed to strengthen psychic skills and offer safety. Carnelian is renowned for dissolving energy obstructions and promoting constructive development.

Howlite

A kind of chalcedony and fluorite called howlite. It comes in a variety of hues, but is most frequently white or light in colour with black speckles. Native Americans have long utilised it as a healing gem and rock.

According to Native Americans, howlite fosters bonds and aids in spiritual connection. Howlite is used by them to release energy blockages, improve focus and clarity of thinking, and encourage tranquilly.

Another property of howlite is its capacity to treat medical conditions. It can strengthen the immune system, alleviate inflammation, and lessen discomfort.

Jasper the Leopard

Native Americans have a long history of using rocks and crystals as medicines. In order to heal themselves and their loved ones, many individuals use these natural resources. People seeking for a useful stone frequently choose leopard skin jasper.

According to legend, leopard skin jasper is particularly helpful for relaxing and soothing the mind and emotions. Additionally, it is thought to encourage inner serenity and aid in opening up clogged energy pathways. When dealing with bodily problems including pain alleviation, inflammation reduction, and stress reduction, this stone can be quite beneficial.

If you're seeking for a crystal that might boost your general health and well-being, leopard skin jasper can be a perfect choice.

Pyrite

Native American tribes have long exploited the stone pyrite. It may be used to enhance vision, fertility, and protection from harmful energies. It is considered to have therapeutic powers. Turquoise, amethyst, topaz, and onyx are a few more stones that are frequently used with pyrite.

Frosted Obsidian

For making healing crystals and rocks, Native American cultures frequently use obsidian. There are many various colours of obsidian. Nevertheless, the snowflake kind is particularly sought-after since it is said to possess qualities that support mind, body, and spirit healing.

According to legend, obsidian has the innate capacity to concentrate spiritual energy, cleanse, and energise the Chakras. Indigenous people have long utilised it as a tool for meditation, healing, and connecting with the spirit world.

Obsidian is frequently used by hunters to create tools, decorations, and ritual objects like blades and pipes. Obsidian is frequently employed in artistic jewellery making because of its clear clarity and sharp edges.

Book 10:
Native American Herbal Gardening

Chapter 1:
Primary Gardening Tools and Herbalist Equipment

You may take the subsequent tiny step of cultivating your herbs as you construct your collection. Or it may be a tiny herb garden in a window of your house. Depending on how comfortable you are with the notion, you can choose.

It's possible that you already plant herbs for cooking. I'm aware that Grace always had parsley on hand for cooking and for use in her delectable soups. I always brought her a bunch of parsley or basil when I visited. You are a beginning herbalist if you are already cultivating them.

Several considerations will determine what you choose to produce. Find out what will grow in your climate if you're thinking about having an outdoor garden. If you are unable to find the information you want through an internet search, contact your local county extension agency.

Once you've decided which herbs to cultivate, you should get guidance on the best soil, amount of sunshine, and other growing conditions to enhance your chances of success.

Although gardening can be quite labor-intensive, it can also be incredibly satisfying to watch your plants flourish and bear fruits and vegetables. Make sure you have the appropriate instruments in order to make the procedure as easy and fun as possible.

My husband took his time showing me all the different instruments of the trade. Each gardening instrument is more crucial than the previous one and plays a vital part in the area of gardening.

You will learn about the many and most crucial equipment in this chapter as you begin your gardening journey.

Spade

You need a spade to garden. One of the most crucial tools a gardener has is a spade. It is the ideal instrument for aerating the soil and preparing the ground for the growth of new plants and flowers. A decent spade can also tackle smaller rocks and roots. Here are five spades that every gardener needs:

Hoe

Another traditional gardening equipment that has been around for millennia is the hoe. Spades and hoes both have a similar form, while hoes often have a more pointed end. They can cultivate gardens, eradicate weeds, and loosen soil, making them perfect for soft soils. Only soft soils should be utilised with it since hard surfaces might be damaged by them.

Trowel

One of the most crucial tools a gardener may have is a trowel. It makes it easier to shape plants, loosen up compacted materials, and change the soil. A decent trowel has a long, ergonomic handle and a blade that is sharp at the end.

Ground Knife

To put it simply, a soil knife is necessary for removing compacted or dried-out dirt from your garden bed. This not only helps your plants perform better but also keeps your soil healthy and guards against root rot.

Lawn Rake Rakes are excellent for clearing snow, leaves, and other debris off your yard. Additionally ideal for pruning hedges and maintaining flowerbeds.

Fork Spade

This straightforward device is necessary for transferring dirt and breaking up clumps. It may also be used to dig up huge boulders or tree roots.

A Hoe Fork

These make it simpler for you to get the most out of your plants by enabling you to Till and grow your garden precisely. You may select a hoe fork that works for you because they exist in a range of sizes and forms.

Hand Scythe A hand scythe is a multipurpose implement that may be used in the garden for a variety of jobs. It works well for getting rid of weeds and tall grass as well as for attacking tiny plants. Fruits, vegetables, and other plants may all be harvested and trimmed using a hand scythe.

When selecting a hand scythe, there are a few aspects to take into account. Both the handle and the blade should be comfortable. Additionally, the blade needs to be movable to accommodate various cutting jobs.

Scuffle Hoe A scuffle hoe is a gardening implement used to eliminate weeds and loosen soil. It is also referred to as a cultivator, hoe-shovel, or a weed shredder. The long metal handle of this instrument features tines on one end and a V-shaped blade on the other. It removes weeds and undesirable plants by scraping the soil's top layer.

Stake Rod It's crucial to use a stake rod to anchor plants when gardening. A stake rod makes it simpler to raise plants and prevents them from shifting or tumbling over. Stake rods come in a wide variety of styles, so it's crucial to pick one that works with your gardening equipment and the sort of garden you're working in.

Cutting Saw

Branch, shrub, and other plant trimming and removal are made easier using a pruning saw. It may be used to tidy up your garden's trees and plants. It may be used to trim other plants and flowers as well.

Broom A broom removes dirt and insects from the soil's surface, keeping them from building nests and hurting plants. Effective broom use aerates the soil and ensures that it is sufficiently wet.

Watering Can A watering can is a crucial piece of gardening equipment. It not only makes it simpler to avoid wetting your feet, but it also makes it easier to water your plants more effectively. The best watering can for your needs should be chosen among the several that are offered on the market.

The capacity of the water reservoir is one of the most crucial aspects to take into account when buying a watering can. There are reservoirs that can contain up to three gallons of water and others that can only hold one. Get a reservoir that can contain enough water if you intend to use your watering can frequently.

The type of hose connector supplied is a crucial consideration when buying a watering can. There are certain cans that incorporate connections for common garden hoses. Others, on the other hand, have connections that snap into particular gardening hoses. It's crucial to pick a watering can with a connection compatible with the kind of hose you already own.

Last but not least, be sure to read the reviews of the watering cans that are on the market. Reviews can assist you in choosing the watering can that best meets your requirements.

You might also require: pruning sheers, garden scissors, a hand hoe, a mower, a cultivator, and a wheelbarrow.

Tools That Herbalists Need

You are probably already familiar with "herbalism" as a herbalist. What does it actually imply, though? What are the fundamental equipment for the job? And how do they assist you in giving your patients the finest treatment possible? In this section, we'll look at the fundamentals of herbalism and talk about the key equipment that every herbalist needs. Read on to discover more about the things that will help you provide your patients the finest treatment possible, from healing plants to necessary equipment.

Baskets And Scissors

If you work as a herbalist, you are aware of how important baskets and scissors are to your job. Herbs and other plants are cut with scissors, and when they are cut, they can be stored in baskets.

Always keep your scissors sharp, and make sure you're using the appropriate size for the job. For instance, a bigger pair of scissors will be required for cutting large pieces of herbs than for cutting little portions. Additionally, baskets may be altered in a number of ways to increase their usefulness for your task. For instance, some herbalists like baskets with huge mouths that make it simple for them to pick up many of plants. Others, however, like lighter, more portable baskets that are smaller.

Mesh Sieve In herbalism and aromatherapy, plant material—typically flowers or leaves—is strained using a mesh sieve. It can be produced from a variety of materials, including cotton, silk, or gauze, and often has a fine mesh surface.

For herb harvesting, mesh sieves are frequently combined with other instruments like a basket or collection jar. They make it possible to take out the tiny particles from the plant material, which might enhance the final product's potency and quality.

Carrot Ricer

It's true, if a weird requirement for a student studying herbs. However, a potato ricer is essential. I choose to utilise this rather the more costly tincture press. The tincture is under pressure from the press and my ricer to extract all the liquid from the plants.

Pestle and Mortar

Every healer should have a few basic instruments available when it comes to herbalism. The mortar and pestle is one of these. This straightforward device can make soups, stews, and mixes that are finely pulverised.

A bowl and pestle are attached to one end of a mortar and pestle, which is commonly constructed of stone or hardwood. The user adds the components to a bowl and stirs them until they are combined into a paste or powder. This is a simple method for producing herbs in large quantities or finely grinding spices for cooking.

To add to smoothies or drinks, the pestle may also grind seeds or fruits. Additionally, using a mortar and pestle can help you prevent any unpleasant side effects because many plants contain volatile oils that might irritate the nose and throat.

Therefore, have a mortar and pestle close at hand if you're searching for a simple approach to start practising herbalism.

A Spice Mill

For a herbalist, a spice grinder may be a very helpful instrument. For cooking or herbal medicines, you may grind up dry herbs, spices, and other items. Spice grinders come in a wide variety of styles, so it's crucial to pick one that meets your requirements.

A tight cover that keeps herbs from leaking while in use, an easily detachable grinding mechanism, and a large hopper that can hold a variety of ground herbs are some common features of a spice grinder. Some types allow you to customise the powder's fineness by having various speeds.

Read online reviews and evaluate several models before making a purchase of a spice grinder. Additionally, think about how frequently you'll use the grinder and the kinds of spices or herbs you'll use it for.

Canned Goods

Any herbalist needs canning jars as a basic tool. They can be employed for preserving fruits and vegetables, producing tinctures and potions, and keeping dry herbs.

Although there are many different canning jar varieties, the wide-mouth jar is the most common. This jar features a sizable top opening that makes it simple to add ingredients and take them out once they have been canned.

When choosing canning jars, additional crucial characteristics include a robust wall construction and a solid seal. The wall should be substantial enough to prevent breaking during high-pressure canning, but not so substantial as to make cleaning it challenging. A strong seal keeps oxygen out of the jar and stops the contents from spoiling.

Cooking Scale

For any herbalist, a kitchen scale may be a crucial tool. Herbs and other things can be weighed with it. It may also blend herbal tinctures or treatments with exact measurements. Finding a scale that meets your needs might be challenging because there are so many different models on the market.

While some scales only have one weighing mode, others have several, including ounces and grammes. Additionally, be sure the scale has a sufficient capacity; some versions can hold up to 10 pounds. Last but not least, check the scale's reading; ideally, it should show grammes and ounces.

Pressed Tea

This is one of my favourite herbal tools, much like my potato ricer. It greatly simplifies the process of brewing a lot of tea. Additionally, it works well for infusions. Use a coffee press if it is the only thing you have at home. It accomplishes the same goal. A word of caution is necessary, though. It is advisable to have one solely for your herbal hobby. Your teas won't have any residual coffee flavour this way.

Tea Infuser

For only one cup of tea, a tea strainer is the ideal tool.

Powerful Teapot

Making tea fast and conveniently is made possible by electric teapots. You can select one that suits your needs because they are available in different sizes. To set the time for your tea, some electric teapots feature timers, while others have alarms that sound when the tea is prepared. You won't ever have to be concerned about creating a mess in your kitchen again because to the simplicity of cleaning electric teapots.

Knife

Knives are available for purchase in a variety of styles and sizes. Knives are a crucial instrument for gathering plants for many herbalists. Herbalists should keep a few specific types of blades on hand:

- -An herbalist's knife is made specifically for cutting up herbs. It features a long, frequently curved or serrated blade that makes it simpler to cut through thick branches.

- -A scalpel: A scalpel is a tiny tool intended for use on finer plant material. It resembles a hermit knife in appearance.

- -A garden shear: Garden shears are typically used to cut stems or leaves from plants. They come in various shapes and sizes, so select the correct model for your needs.

Chopping Block

Every herbalist needs a good cutting board, and there are several variations on the market. While some boards are made of food-grade plastic, others are constructed of wood.

Whatever kind of cutting board you select, bear the following points in mind:

1. Size - The cutting board has to be big enough to fit your knives and ingredients comfortably, without being too big to make your workplace congested.

2. Select a cutting board made of a sturdy and cleanable material. While plastic boards are frequently simpler to keep clean, wood boards may discolour readily.

3. Look for a cutting board with a style that suits your tastes, whether they are modern or traditional. Cutting boards of all shapes and sizes are also readily available today.

A Two-Boiler

Double boiling is probably something you've heard of if you're a herbalist. To eliminate germs and other organisms, double boiling is a common component of traditional medicinal techniques. Additionally, it's an excellent technique to boost the potency of tinctures and potions. This is how it goes:

Set a big pot of water on the stove to boil.

In a small, heat-resistant container (such as a glass jar or an earthenware mug), place the herbs or other things you wish to cure. Place this container in the boiling water.

Simmer the mixture for around 20 minutes on low heat.

Remove the little container with care from the boiling water and place it on a cold surface or in an ice bath.

Pour the whole contents of the tiny container into a different saucepan or dish.

Make sure the tiny container of herbs or other ingredients is well submerged in the saucepan of boiling water before adding it back.

This liquid should be gently poured into an ice bath or onto the chilly ground after 5 minutes of boiling.

Cups And Spoons for Measuring

Measuring spoons and cups are necessary instruments for herbalists to use in their practise. These come in various sizes to meet any purpose and may be used to measure liquids or dry herbs.

Consider the elements that will matter the most to you when choosing a measuring spoon. Some of these considerations are the spoon's construction material (such as stainless steel), its form, and how simple it is to grip and use.

For herbalists, cups might be crucial. There are several varieties of cups, including silicone cups that are non-toxic and flexible enough to accommodate a variety of forms and ceramic cups that can resist high temperatures. It's crucial to choose a cup suitable for the herbs you'll be dealing with; for instance, if you're measuring dry herbs, use a porcelain cup rather than a plastic one.

It's crucial to account for both the liquid's volume and temperature when measuring liquids. Use a smaller cup to measure honey that is at room temperature rather than hot off the stove, for instance. Similarly, if you're making tea with hot water, use a larger mug rather than a little one because hot water takes up more space in the latter than the former.

Finally, to prevent infection, wash your measuring spoons and cups before using them.

Oversized Mixing Bowls

Searching for the ideal sizable mixing bowl? Look nowhere else! These bowls may be used for a number of things and are ideal for herbalists. In addition to serving meals, they may combine ingredients and store dried herbs.

The KitchenAid stainless steel bowl is one preferred alternative. It is a fantastic option for any kitchen due to the bowl's strength and beauty. Additionally, it has an ergonomic design that makes using it simple.

The glass bowl from Amazon is a fantastic additional choice. For preserving delicate herbs or spices, this bowl's resistance to heat and cold makes it the perfect choice. Additionally, it includes a convenient silicone grip on the bottom that makes moving it about your kitchen simple.

Consider the ceramic mixing bowl from Nordic Ware if you want a bigger bowl that can accommodate more ingredients. This bowl is an excellent alternative for anybody searching for a high-end solution because it is both attractive and practical. Additionally, it has a nonstick surface that makes it simple to combine ingredients without sacrificing moisture or flavour.

Chapter 2

The Two Types of Beginner-Friendly Gardens

As you can see by now, there are many different kinds of gardens. But if you're just getting started, I advise choosing either container gardening or raised bed gardening. The rest of the book will go further into these two categories of gardens and detail how to customise them to your preferences. I've outlined my reasoning for picking these two gardens for this book in the paragraphs below.

The Benefits of Container Gardening for Novices

There aren't many things more fulfilling than witnessing the small seeds you only a short while ago planted steadily grow into healthy, vitamin-rich food for you and the people you care about. Today, sadly, not everyone has a sizable garden with soil ideal for producing veggies. Not all of us even have a garden! A lovely and successful container garden may be accommodated on even the tiniest patio, back porch, balcony, or doorway.

From the earliest Egyptian, Roman, and Asian civilizations, people have been growing plants in pots. Henry VIII was so enamoured with the Hampton Court Gardens that he had its owner imprisoned and claimed them for himself, even though the Hanging Gardens of Babylon were regarded as one of the Seven Wonders of the World.

Container gardening is really straightforward and simple.

Beginners should consider container gardening since it is straightforward and uncomplicated. A container, some plants, and some dirt are all you need. Even better, you may use empty food or drink containers that you can buy at the grocery store or pre-made containers that are available at most garden supply stores. Once you have your container, place your plants in it after filling it with dirt. After that, you'll take care of them by giving them water and other garden-related maintenance. The best method to start gardening is with containers, which are also a terrific way to keep your garden well-organized and simple to maintain.

Offers A Wide Range of Choices

Because container gardening is easy to set up and maintain, it is ideal for novices. As you gain experience, you may expand your garden from a little container. You may discover a container garden that matches your style among a broad selection available to you.

Vertical gardens, 12-pack gardens, herb gardens, and succulent gardens are a few examples of well-liked container gardens. Due of their small footprint, vertical gardens are ideal for those with limited space. Additionally, they need less maintenance because all the plants need is water. The 12-pack garden is ideal for those with lots of room. Nevertheless, they don't want to spend all day planting and caring for each plant. For folks who wish to add fresh herbs to their cuisine or some scent to their house, herb gardens are fantastic. For those who wish to add some greenery to their houses but don't have much space, succulent gardens are ideal. They require very little room and are simple to water.

Water Use Is Lower with Container Gardening Than with Traditional Gardening

The best method to learn how to cultivate without wasting water is through container gardening. With a container, you can plant in lesser quantities and stop extra water from evaporating and being wasted. Furthermore, you only a fraction of the space needed for conventional gardening techniques. Last but not least, containers make it simple to transfer your plants as you decide where they should be placed.

Gardening in containers uses less water

The best method to learn how to cultivate without wasting water is through container gardening. With a container, you can plant in lesser quantities and stop extra water from evaporating and being wasted. Furthermore, you only a fraction of the space needed for conventional gardening techniques. Last but not least, containers make it simple to transfer your plants as you decide where they should be placed.

You can grow plants anywhere you choose.

At the beginning of the planting season, seasoned outside gardeners usually describe experiencing an insatiable want to get started. The time may change based on where you are. In temperate places, it often occurs when winter draws near and the first signs of life emerge beneath the frozen earth. However, in the tropics, as the first rainfall hits the sun-baked Earth at the beginning of the rainy season, the aroma of new Earth fills the air. Contrarily, individuals who like container gardening don't have to wait for these outside indications.

If you use containers, you can start a garden whenever you want, especially if you can cover the container to make a little greenhouse. Young plants may be started without waiting for exceptionally warm weather since a container can be used to generate the best growing conditions.

No Problems with Space

You might think your yard is too small for a vegetable garden. The lack of outside space may be an issue for those who live in townhouses and flats, but if you use container gardening, this shouldn't be a problem.

The availability (or lack thereof) of yard space has no bearing on container gardening. A garden is not necessary. On a balcony, a window sill, or a sunny area close to a window, many plants can flourish. Keep in mind that many plant species might grow in the same container. The common practise of companion planting in containers results in a high yield and enables the majority of people to garden.

Perfect For Gardeners Without Experience

In-ground outdoor gardening comes with some unpleasant truths. The first one discusses weeds. Their seeds are dispersed far and grow more quickly than the ones we plant. Because of this, seasoned gardeners invest a lot of importance, time, and effort into setting up the veggie bed. People who plant their gardens carelessly face the danger of having their beds quickly taken over by weeds. Particularly for novice gardeners, this is really discouraging.

Pests, illnesses, and natural occurrences are other variables that might impact outdoor gardens. Many novice gardeners give up after failing and never give it another go. Container gardening has certain dangers, although they are rather small. Weeds are uncommon, and illnesses and insect problems may be found and treated quickly. Containers may be relocated to safer areas when a protracted period of poor weather is a possibility thanks to their portability.

No-Till Agriculture

Tilling the soil is back-breaking, even for the most enthusiastic outdoor gardeners. Furthermore, many of the natural creatures necessary for a healthy garden have been shown to be disturbed by tilling. For this reason, a no-till garden is becoming increasingly popular.

Without having to alter the soil or worry about tilling damage, container gardening enables you to establish a proper growth environment full of nutritious ingredients.

Reduces The Cost of Fertiliser

Container-grown plants require fewer fertiliser treatments each year when it comes to feeding. Chemical or organic fertilisers used on potted plants stay longer because, like water, they remain concentrated in the little amount of soil inside the pots. Additionally, potted plants do not have to share fertiliser with weeds that are competitors. For the same reasons why fertiliser should only be used sparingly in garden beds, large quantities of fertiliser might burn the roots. Make your own compost or use an organic fertiliser of the highest calibre. Get more for your money and spend less on fertiliser.

Simple Pest Management

Pest problems in garden beds usually require pesticide treatment since you don't have access to certain plants. Plants cultivated in containers make pest management easier and may not require chemical pesticides.

The bigger aphids and scale insects can be manually picked off with a toothbrush or cotton bud bathed in rubbing alcohol. Another excellent technique to get rid of numerous bug pests in the delicate sections of the plant is to move the pots to the bathroom for a periodic shower. Even dipping individual pots in warm water will kill undesirable soil organisms. Ants won't be able to go inside the pot and start aphid farms on your precious plants if you keep it submerged in water. A coating of diatomaceous Earth surrounding the pot would serve as a barrier against slugs and other soft-bodied pests.

Harvesting Is Quite Easy

Harvesting is significantly simpler when growing fruits and vegetables in containers. Grow blueberries, strawberries, and root tubers like potatoes, carrots, and sweet potatoes in pots. When the product is ready to be harvested, just flip the pots over on a plastic sheet rather than digging them up and perhaps destroying the priceless crop. To make sure every tuber is in excellent shape, agitate the soil.

You Can Change the Growing Environment

Without substantial soil additions, giving your container plants the optimal habitat is straightforward. You may provide a slightly acidic medium for your blueberries and rhododendrons without affecting the pH of the soil in other containers or garden beds.

Plant placement can be changed to accommodate seasonal variations in light intensity. As long as they are kept in distinct pots, plants with comparable watering needs can cohabit.

You Can Transform Quickly

You may alter the appearance and concept of your garden by just switching out the containers. For instance, using large stone pots in various architectural designs may give the garden a timeless appearance. Metal containers, whether real or imitation, with rust or a copper patina, on the other hand, can take you back in time. Your yard may be made more colourful with acrylic pots in jewel tones. However, using the same material in a monochromatic design may be sophisticated.

Imagine you want to establish a garden but are unsure of where to begin. If so, container gardening could be the ideal choice for you. Although it is simple to get started, you may modify your garden to suit your own requirements and tastes. Additionally, container gardening might be a fantastic alternative if you have a small yard or worry about the weather where you live.

The Benefits of Raised Bed Gardening for Novices

Because raised bed gardening is simple to put up, requires little care, and produces a good crop, it is ideal for novices. A raised bed is a large soil-filled container that is then supported by legs or poles. This prevents weeds from developing in between the plants and makes it simple to reach into the bed to dig up the plants. You may purchase raised beds already constructed or construct your own out of materials like stone, PVC tubing, or timber.

No-Till Agriculture

A raised bed gets your soil ready for "no work" gardening, which is the easiest sort of gardening. Instead than annually tilling up the soil to add fertiliser and additives, gardeners often maintain their raised beds by placing materials on top. In a plot with seaweed mulch on top for nutrients and weed control, bush beans flourish.

Without the need for strenuous labour, compost, mulches, manures, and other soil conditioners may be put straight to the top few inches of soil. Additionally, the earth can perform its tilling as worms and roots make their way through. Regular human tilling destroys the soil's structure, whereas leaving your soil alone gradually builds up its organic content.

Not a Back Breaker

Weeding a garden, especially a big one, may really cause a surprising amount of back and knee strain, which can have major long-term effects. Debilitating back and joint discomfort can be relieved by using a raised bed, especially one that is at least 12 inches tall. Even young individuals who are considering farming as a career should take into account the possible back harm that organic farming might cause through hand weeding. Consider raised beds to be an investment in your health.

More Attractive

Despite what can seem like sheer vanity, having superior bedding might be useful. In the city, a raised bed could be required to maintain good relations with your neighbours, particularly if you intend to produce vegetables in your front yard. Because there is a distinct border separating the bed from the route, raised beds also make walkways easier to maintain.

Raised beds deter pests and animals.

Although slugs may climb, a raised garden box's tall edges slow them down and provide them a place to halt. Slugs won't crawl over copper flashing, which you may use to border your box, according to several gardeners. If you want to prevent crawling animals like groundhogs from taking your root crops, you may also line the bottom of the box with hardware cloth. Due to their height, dogs are also less likely to urinate directly on your plants. If deer are an issue, you can purchase a box with a built-in deer fence or put deer fencing directly to your bed. Additionally, it is much simpler to incorporate plastic hoops into raised garden beds for cold frames, row coverings, and bird barriers.

Raising Facilitates Drainage

In places that are prone to floods or have marshy yards, a raised garden bed can be the only option for a complete growing season. The most typical raised bed depth is 11 inches, or one inch lower than the walls of a garden box with a 12 inch height. This is sufficient drainage for the majority of crops and gives plants over a foot of additional breathing room above damp conditions. In general, raised beds drain better, even during heavy downpours.

Many Ergonomic Choices

By allowing you to construct higher-level beds, these containers help to lessen the typical back, neck, and shoulder pain brought on by conventional, non-container gardening techniques.

The most discouraging aspect for both novice and seasoned gardeners is physical strain. Raised beds, on the other hand, can help you get over that hurdle and maintain your love for gardening rather than making you feel worn out and suffer every time you think about it.

Easy Control of Weed

You lessen the chance of weed seeds spreading throughout your growing environment and, consequently, weed development, by keeping the earthy components of your garden isolated from the untamed surroundings outside its cosy enclosure.

Especially if your soil mix is weed-free, you are increasing your defence against weed invasion by bringing in your own mix in the first place.

Last but not least, it will be significantly more challenging for plants and weeds growing outside the container to get in if your kit or building includes bottom protection that defends against the Earth underneath it!

Higher Root Growth

Faster root development is possible with low-set containers with ground contact and/or those contain a finer-textured growing medium than with plants planted solely in backyard sod or hard-pan.

Such soils affect plant appearance, health, and harvest periods and make it more difficult for roots to form. Not if you use your own blend, particularly one that is better suited to supporting delicate plant development.

Higher yields and healthier plants are the results of greater root development, according the University of Missouri Extension.

Leaner soil compaction

It is best for both plant and soil health since the soil in containers is never compacted by foot traffic. Kits with protection from a lot of rain can aid in reducing compaction.

Compacted soil is the scourge of all crops, as several of my farming mentors have informed me, and a raised container nearly ensures that it never will be.

It's a smart addition to your garden, according to the University of Georgia Cooperative Extension, especially if there is a lot of foot traffic (and the presence of unruly, inattentive kids nearby).

Higher Yields

For gardeners who wish to grow their own food, the appeal of improving vegetable and product yields through intensive plantings is undeniable.

Raised beds are perfect for crops that are considerably more densely grouped, such as those used in square-foot gardening, bio-intensive planting, and other techniques.

You utilise ALL of your area in a much smaller container garden rather than having a typical garden with several walkways or places for traditional row planting. As a result, you can grow a lot more in a small amount of area.

Chapter 3:
Explains How to Prepare and Plant Your Herbs.

The Right Location

When it comes to finding a good location, first and foremost. This is due to the fact that most herbs need lots of sunlight to grow well and develop to their full potential. Therefore, you should first survey your property and take note of the sunny areas and how long the sun shines on your garden before beginning any preparations. You may cultivate your herbs in a more effective location if you are aware of this. Plants can be grown in a location that receives morning light and afternoon shade if the summers there are warm. Other herbs like the shade, though. Apart from parsley, very few of them are useful in cooking.

You should cultivate your herb garden outside your backdoor or in front of your yard because it is also meant to be viewed. Herbs are incredibly eye-catching and will make a gorgeous display, not to mention that they will smell delicious every time you pass by them. Additionally, having a nearby garden will make it simple for you to get to your culinary herbs whenever you need them.

Getting the Soil Ready

Although herbs are simple to produce, this does not mean that you can grow them anyplace. When growing herbs, you must make sure that plants have access to light, easily worked soil that is well-drained. This is so that herbs may grow better in soil that drains efficiently.

How can you tell whether your soil is properly drained? Simply use a hose pipe or other equipment to run water through your garden for a number of minutes. If the water pools, your soil requires amending because it is poorly drained. Compost, peat, and soil may be added to it to make it better. Be cautious when adding compost; if you accidentally add too much, your soil may become overly rich and your herbs may become weak and susceptible to disease.

Loamy soil, which is composed of sand, silt, organic matter, and clay, is the ideal kind for growing herbs. This kind of soil has the right balance of potash, phosphorus, nitrogen, and trace minerals to encourage healthy development. But what if your garden doesn't have this kind of soil? After enhancing its quality to match that of loamy soil, you can continue to use the sort of soil you now have. Clay soil's structure and fertility may be enhanced by adding organic elements, such as compost, coarse sand, green hummus, peat moss, and well-aged chicken or cow dung. Your soil's friability is a result of the mix of these organic components.

You may analyse the soil PH, which is a crucial element, with the use of soil testing. If nutrients are not effectively dispersed in the soil, having acidic or alkaline soil may prevent them from reaching your plant. The PH of most plants should be neutral, between 6.5 and 7.5. So how do you calculate the PH of your soil? Take a few soil samples—at least 2 cups— from various garden areas, and then deliver them to the testing facility, which may be your local county extension, a landscaping business, or an independent lab. When the findings come in, balance your soil's PH by adding agricultural lime if it is below 6.5 and sulphur if it is greater than 7.3.

Growing Herbs

Each herb plant requires a hole that is approximately 8 inches in diameter. You'll need the following instructions for cultivating various herbs:

- 1 foot: Cilantro, Parsley, Dill, Chives,

- 2 feet: basils, savoury, tarragon, and thyme

- Marjoram, oregano, mints, sage, and rosemary – 3–4 feet.

Start planting after you have the necessary number of feet of the kind of herbs you wish to grow by doing the procedures listed below:

1. To loosen the soil, which has been compacted for a while, begin digging in your garden. By enabling water to seep into the soil and making room for plant roots to expand, this enhances the drainage system.

2. The next step is to top your garden soil with compost, about an inch of it, and mix it all together. This will benefit your soil by boosting its nutrient content and enhancing drainage.

3. Prepare some ditches for sowing using a trowel. Remember that if you don't have a trowel, you can still use your hands.

4. Next, quickly disperse your seeds along the trenches, aiming to attain the specified spacing. To make the seeds simpler to handle, you may also stir in some sand.

5. After lightly covering the seeds with dirt, irrigate the seeds well. If you are overseeding when dispersing, don't worry. If your plants get too numerous, you can thin them out later.

Mulching

Simply said, mulching is the process of covering your farmed soil's top layer with various materials. Mulching not only keeps your garden tidy, but it also enhances the soil surrounding your plants and cuts down on the time needed for weeding and watering. The next step is to cover your garden with a 3–4 inch layer of mulch to lessen the need for cultivation and weeding.

Watering

Generally speaking, herbs need a lot of water. As a result, you will periodically need to water your herb garden if it doesn't rain. When watering herbs, you must wet your garden once or twice a week. A soaker hose is the ideal tool to utilise when it comes to watering herbs. This is because utilising a soaker hose makes it simpler for you to soak the plants with the inch of water that herbs require once a week to thrive effectively. while it's hot and dry outside and while your plants are actively developing, different amounts of water are required. Due to the two circumstances' high evaporation rates, you will need to increase your water supply.

A word of caution: you should avoid lightly misting your garden with water since it will push the herbs' roots to the surface.

Drip irrigation is another technique you may use to irrigate herbs. For producing herbs, this technique greatly lowers the quantity of water wasted through evaporation. When it comes to irrigation, the type of soil utilised in your garden is equally important. You may need to water your herbs more frequently if you choose sandy soil as opposed to heavy dirt.

Staking

Some of the plants you cultivate might not be strong enough to support themselves. These plants require staking, or support, in order to grow comfortably. Stakes of various sizes will be required in your garden. You may bind a tall plant with bamboo sticks by using a lot of them and raffia or green tape. The herb will penetrate the grid and finally fully envelop the sustaining sticks. You must choose a stake that doesn't obstruct the herbs' development in order to get the greatest results. A metal ring with a grind within is a nice illustration of less obvious staking.

Word of advice: Before your herbs get too tall, consider installing a staking system. When you stake the plants early, they will grow more organically.

Weeding

Weeds will always grow as long as you water your plants and provide them with necessary nutrition, as those are their preferred growth circumstances. They will thus arrive and engage in conflict for the nutrients and moisture that the earth is providing for your herbs. Unfortunately, this will simply restrict your herbs' ability to develop healthily. For your herbs to thrive without using up resources, make sure you periodically examine your garden and remove all the weeds. Perennial, annual, or biennial weeds are all possible. The best method for weeding a little garden (which I assume you are just beginning) is to pull them out by hand after the soil has been watered.

Gathering and Keeping

When the plants are ready to be harvested, pluck the leaves or blossoms with your fingers or, for a cleaner harvest, cut them using kitchen shears. Avoid picking the stems naked and only take the mature stalks and blooms at the top of the plant. You should let the plants develop again. To preserve freshness, it is recommended to gather the herbs right before using them. Wash them well to get rid of the soil, soil, and pests. Herbs can be frozen or dried if you need to save them for later use. You must gently wash them, then blot off the extra water with a paper towel.

Herb stems should be cut at soil level, tied in a group at the stem's base, and hung upside down to dry for a week or two. When the leaves or blooms have dried, take them from the stem and store them in a dry, airtight container. They ought to last a year this way. Excellent teas and food flavouring may be made using dried herbs.

Herbs should be cleaned and chopped before being placed in teaspoonfuls into ice cube trays to freeze. Place water in the tray and then freeze. Herbs keep their flavour from the moment they are gathered when frozen. When necessary, remove one ice cube and place it in a pot or cup similarly to how you would with fresh herbs.

Chapter 4:
Tips for Growing Herbs In Your Garden

Whether you are producing flowers or fresh fruit, gardening can be a pleasant hobby. But there are a few things you need to know if you want to clean up your garden without spending a bunch. This section will offer advice on growing herbs in your yard, including how to choose the best plants and how to water and fertilise them. We'll also offer advice on how to set up the ideal growing conditions for herbs so they may thrive and add flavour to your food.

A General Summary

If you want to savour fresh herbs or add a little spice to your food, growing your own is undoubtedly the best option. Herbs are not only simple to grow, but they also provide a lot of health advantages. Here are six recommendations for cultivating herbs in your garden:

1. Pick the proper spot: Herbs love moist, well-drained soil with lots of sunlight.

2. Plant them early: Before the first frost in early spring, herb seeds should be put outside as soon as the ground can be handled.

3. Mulch them: After planting, cover the herb plants with a layer of mulch to help keep weeds and moisture at away.

4. Regular harvesting involves cutting off the dead leaves and blossoms and harvesting the herbs while they are actively producing blooms, which is generally six weeks after planting.

5. Cut cuttings from established plants and propagate them in moist perlite or sponges before planting them back into the soil.

Plant Your Herbs on Soil That Drains Well

Herbs may be grown in your garden in a number of ways, but the most common is in well-draining soil. Herbs planted in raised beds or in containers demand less water and assist to maintain wet soil.

Check the pH of your soil and add lime if necessary to modify it for herb cultivation. When preparing the soil, include organic material like old manure or compost. Slowly add water until the soil's surface is moist but not soggy. For container plants, check the water level each day and top it off as necessary.

Here are a few pointers for growing herbs:

1. Pick a sunny location where your herbs will receive lots of light and sufficient drainage.

2. To fit your environment and garden area, blend tough and delicate plant kinds. In warm weather, many plants may be cultivated in pots outside; in cooler weather, they can be moved inside; and in colder locations, they can be planted straight into the ground.

3. Equally space plants to allow for tall development; a crowded arrangement might result in nutritional deficiency and fungal infestation. Before replanting young plants into separate pots or cells, carefully break apart huge clumps with your hands.

Fertilise Your Herbs Minimally

You can grow your own herbs quickly and easily by giving them a little fertiliser once a month. They will grow more quickly as a result, and they will stay strong and healthy as a result. The following advice will help you fertilise your herbs:

1. Around your herb plants, sprinkle a thin layer of compost or manure on the soil. They will receive the nutrients they require from this, enabling them to develop quickly.

2. When employing organic techniques like composting, put in some organic materials high in nitrogen, such straw or green leaves. The addition of these supplements will assist ensure that your herbs receive all the nutrients they require because nitrogen is crucial for plant growth.

3. If artificial fertilisers are being used, make sure to dilute them before adding them to the soil where your herb plants are growing. You must exercise caution while fertilising since doing so too often can harm both the environment and the plants.

Plant And Combine Similar Herbs

You're probably familiar with cultivating a few basic herbs, like parsley, rosemary, or thyme, like the majority of gardeners. But what about the countless more herbs that gardeners can use? We'll show you how to produce 16 popular herbs in your garden together in this part.

Because both basil and carrots have robust flavours and can be used fresh or dried, they make an excellent combination for gardening. Because they have flavours that are comparable and may be used fresh or dried, thyme and parsley make wonderful partners. Given that they all have potent aromas, lavender, oregano, and mint make for fantastic herb pairings. Plants that require an easy-to-grow container include chamomile, hyssop, and lemon balm. The last benefit of using rosemary with tomatoes is that it deters pests from the plants.

Understand the Varieties of Your Herbs and Their Particular Needs

There are many different types of herbs, making them a terrific way to add flavour and nutrition to your yard. The following advice will help you cultivate herbs in your garden:

Pick the proper kind of herbs. Selecting the appropriate herb for your garden is crucial since they all have distinct requirements. Basil, cilantro, chives, dill, fennel, lavender, mint, oregano, parsley, rosemary, sage, and thyme are some of the most popular herb kinds.

Compared to warm-weather plants, cool-weather herbs require more light. The majority of herbs will thrive in some shade as well as full or partial sunlight. During dry spells, be careful to give them regular waterings and, if necessary, fertiliser.

Herbs like garlic mustard need lots of organic materials and wet soil to thrive. These plants should be planted after adding compost or manure. In warm regions, garlic mustard may also be cultivated outside in pots or containers.

Keep Herbs That Grow Quickly Apart

If cultivated in a comparable soil type, quickly growing herbs like curly parsley, rosemary, and thyme may readily coexist in the same pot or container. It is preferable to keep fast-growing herbs apart from slower-growing plants to avoid them from overpowering one another. This may be accomplished by planting them in various pots or containers or by cultivating them in various garden locations.

Depending on the need, plant your herbs during cool seasons and at the appropriate time.

When growing herbs in your yard, there are a few considerations to keep in mind: the temperature, the season, and the kind of herb.

Climate: Herbs thrive in hotter climes as well, but they favour chilly seasons (between 59 and 86 degrees Fahrenheit).

Herbs grow most effectively between early Spring and late Autumn.

Herbs may be cultivated in any type of soil, although they like dry, sandy soil the most. Additionally, they enjoy both full and light shade.

Book 11:
Herbal Recipes For Your Child's Health

Chapter 1:
Common Medicinal Herbs and Their Properties

Throughout history, medicinal plants have been employed for both culinary and therapeutic reasons. They are still used today to treat a wide range of illnesses, both mild and serious. You may find a guide to some of the most popular medicinal plants, their qualities, and how to utilise them in this area. This guide will assist you in getting the most out of these natural cures for everything from headaches to colds and everything in between.

Anti-anxiety Herbs

For millennia, a variety of plants have been used to treat anxiety. Lavender, chamomile, skullcap, and ginger are among the most well-liked herbs. Some of the most popular herbs for anxiety are listed below:

Lavender: For millennia, people have used lavender to help reduce anxiety because of its calming effects. It can be consumed as a tea or used as an oil to cosmetics.

Chamomile: For generations, herbal medicines have used chamomile because of its well-known relaxing properties. It can be taken orally as a pill or capsule.

Skullcap: Skullcap has a reputation for enhancing mental performance and lowering anxiety. It can be taken orally as a pill or capsule.

Ginger: Ginger efficiently manages anxiety's bodily and psychological effects. It may be consumed raw or made into foods like soup or gingerbread cookies.

For Arthritis, Herbs

For years, many different plants have been utilised to cure ailments like arthritis. Here are some of the most well-liked:

Ginger: Ginger is a natural anti-inflammatory that helps reduce inflammation, discomfort, and stiffness. It may also aid in enhancing joint performance. Eat raw ginger root or drink ginger, clove, and honey tea to benefit from ginger's therapeutic properties.

Another all-natural anti-inflammatory that can help lessen joint discomfort and swelling is cayenne pepper. Add cayenne pepper to meals or beverages as desired to utilise it medicinally. When eaten in the prescribed dosages, capsaicin, the primary chemical in cayenne peppers, is typically harmless but may cause mild skin irritation in some individuals.

Turmeric is a potent plant that has been used for generations to alleviate pain and inflammation all throughout the body. According to studies, it might potentially be used to treat arthritis. Take capsules or tablets with pulverised turmeric combined with water or an oil (such as olive oil) to utilise it medicinally. Additionally, you may add ground turmeric for flavour and health benefits to dishes like curries or soups.

Cancer-Fighting Herbs

Historically, several plants have been used to treat cancer. Research has demonstrated that several of these plants have anti-cancer effects. The following is a list of some of the most popular herbs for treating cancer:

Using basil, you can successfully cure skin, prostate, and lung cancers. Tumour development may also be halted with its assistance.

Echinacea: Due to its anti-tumor characteristics and ability to hasten healing, echinacea is a well-liked herb for the treatment of cancer.

Ginger: Ginger's anti-inflammatory qualities can help lessen the signs and symptoms of cancer. It is also thought to strengthen the immune system and aid in the destruction of cancerous cells.

Goldenseal: A herbal treatment long used to boost immunity and stave against illness is goldenseal. Additionally, it has been successful in battling malignant cells.

Herbs For The Flu And Colds

For the treatment of the flu and cold, several plants are employed. These herbs can be ingested, used topically on the body, or combined with water to make tea. Here is a list of some popular medicinal plants that can be used to treat the flu and the common cold:

Garlic: Studies have revealed that garlic has antiviral qualities, making it a potent remedy for colds and the flu. Garlic can be consumed orally, topically applied to the skin, or brewed into a tea.

Ginger: Studies have revealed that ginger has antiviral qualities as well, making it a successful therapy for colds and the flu. Ginger can be consumed orally, topically applied to the skin, or steeped in water to make tea.

Additionally known to possess antiviral qualities, cayenne pepper works well as a cold and flu remedy. You may consume cayenne pepper orally, apply it directly to the skin, or make tea by combining it with water.

For Digestion: Herbs

Many herbs might be useful if you want to enhance your digestive system. These five herbal supplements can help with digestion and regularity: licorice (Glycyrrhiza glabra), fennel (Foeniculum vulgare), dandelion (Taraxacum officinale), and chamomile (Matricaria chamomilla).

A multipurpose plant, chamomile is used for a number of things, including supporting the digestive system. This blooming plant includes camomile oil, which has been shown to promote nutrient absorption, ease constipation, and reduce inflammation in the intestines.

You only need one cup of chamomile tea every day to get rid of digestive problems including diarrhoea and cramps.

Another common plant for supporting the digestive system is ginger. This vegetable that resembles a root has been demonstrated to enhance gut health by encouraging the development of helpful bacteria, lowering discomfort, and reducing inflammation. Ginger aids in digestion and reduces nausea and vomiting brought on by gastrointestinal conditions. Include ginger in food or supplement form numerous times each day to get the most out of its advantages for gut health.

Another plant that is good for digestion is fennel. This fragrant vegetable includes the anethole essential oil, which successfully reduces IBS (irritable bowel syndrome) symptoms.

Hormone Imbalance Herbs

The hormone system of the body can be balanced again with the use of several medicines. The following are some of the most well-liked herbs for hormonal imbalance:

A well-known herb for bringing the body's hormonal system back into balance is St. John's wort. It has reduced symptoms related to menopause, PMS, anxiety, and depression.

Another herb that is frequently used to reestablish hormonal balance in the body is licorice. Symptoms including hot flashes, mood swings, osteoporosis, and infertility have all been helped by licorice.

It has been demonstrated that the herbal treatment ashwagandha helps both men and women maintain appropriate hormone levels. Traditional uses of ashwagandha include enhancing sexual performance, relieving stress and anxiety, and enhancing general wellbeing.

You probably don't know much about medicinal plants if you're like most people. We'll try you clarify these plants and their potential health benefits in this guide. We'll discuss each herb's background and describe the ailments it can be used to cure. Finally, we'll offer advice on how to recognise and buy therapeutic plants from reputable vendors. You will have a fundamental knowledge of the advantages of utilising medicinal herbs and where to locate them by the conclusion of this book.

Chapter 2: The Best Herbs for Kids' Health

There is no doubt that children have undergone many changes in recent years. They have a lot to learn, between school and extracurricular activities. It is crucial that kids receive the greatest treatment available because of this. And adopting natural medicines is the best method to achieve that. This section will discuss some of the healthiest herbs for children and how they may benefit them. We'll talk about issues like respiratory comfort and fever lowering, among others. Read on for more information if you're seeking for herbal cures for yourself or your kids.

Citrus balm

A perennial herb, lemon balm (Melissa officinalis) can reach a height of one metre. The blooms are tiny, white, and fragrant, while the leaves are split into oblong or elliptical leaflets. Since lemon balm has been used in folk medicine for so long, it is widely known as a treatment for anxiety and stress.

The potential of lemon balm to induce oxytocin release, which is known to lower stress levels and promote relaxation, is one of the herb's most significant qualities. Additionally, menthol and other essential oils with anti-inflammatory qualities may be found in lemon balm. In fact, research has shown that lemon balm can assist patients receiving radiation treatment need less pain medication.

Chamomile

Anxiety, sleeplessness, and digestive issues can all be effectively treated with chamomile, a widely recognised medicinal plant. Additionally, it has been used to enhance sleep and encourage relaxation. You may make chamomile tea or use it in supplements.

Rose

For millennia, people have used rose as a traditional remedy to cure a variety of illnesses. Rose oil is well recognised for its therapeutic abilities, which include the ability to cure skin disorders and speed up the healing of wounds.

Rose oil also helps with mood enhancement and anxiety reduction. Additionally, it can lower inflammation, support weight reduction, and enhance circulation in general. Rose oil is said to be effective in treating eczema and psoriasis.

Spearmint

The perennial plant spearmint is indigenous to Asia and Europe. It may reach a height of two feet and has tiny, elongated leaves that are pointed at the points and pale green in colour. Small, white flowers that bloom in clusters on long stalks are present.

Spearmint is well recognised for its strong aroma, which has been linked to positive health effects. Spearmint oil has anti-inflammatory properties and can aid with anxiety and stress reduction as well as cognitive performance. Additionally, spearmint might help you breathe easier since it can relieve congestion and respiratory illnesses.

Spearmint supplements may cause adverse effects include diarrhoea, flatulence, nausea, and vomiting. Therefore, if you are expecting or nursing, it's crucial to consult your doctor before consuming this herb.

Marshmallow

Since ancient times, marshmallow has been used as a traditional Chinese herbal remedy to cure a range of ailments. The use of marshmallow as a natural treatment for children's health issues has grown in popularity in recent years. The following are five advantages of giving marshmallows to kids:

1. Marshmallows can soothe agitated kids.

2. For kids with ADHD, marshmallows can assist increase focus and attention span.

3. Children's anxiety and sadness symptoms can be helped by marshmallows.

4. Marshmallow helps children with respiratory conditions including bronchitis and pneumonia.

5. Lastly, indigestion and diarrhoea in children are also successfully treated with marshmallow.

Lavender

Popular aromatherapy uses of lavender include the relief of pain, headaches, tension, and anxiety. In addition, it helps ease cramps, allergies, and sleeplessness. Eczema and psoriasis are two more skin disorders that lavender oil treats.

Violets

The plant violet is well known for boosting mood and calming anxiety. Along with controlling blood pressure and heart rate, it has also been used to treat depression and sleeplessness. Violet is also thought to help children's cognitive development.

Anise

An evergreen bush produces anise, a spice. Licorice and anise oil, which are used in food and medicinal, are made from the dried fruits of the anise plant. Additionally, anise is used as a flavouring in foods, beverages, and medicines.

Anise can help with gas and flatulence as well as digestion and inflammation, among other health advantages. In addition, it can lessen menstruation cramps, decrease cholesterol levels, as well as soothe cough and cold symptoms.

Cinnamon

Strong antioxidants like cinnamon have been demonstrated to aid diabetics' blood sugar levels. Additionally, it can aid in reducing inflammation and heart protection. Asthma, Crohn's disease, and ulcerative colitis are just a few of the ailments that cinnamon may help cure due to its anti-inflammatory and antibacterial characteristics.

Popular herbal remedy elder elder is used to treat respiratory conditions including bronchitis and pneumonia. Additionally, it helps to treat fevers, infections, and inflammation. Elderberry refers to the fruit of the elder tree. The berries can be consumed raw or used to produce jam, wine, or syrup.

Elder tree leaves and blooms are also used medicinally. For those who are allergic to other flowers, the blooms can be used as an alternative to tea while the leaves can be brewed to treat cold and flu symptoms. It has been demonstrated that elderflower tea helps elderly persons with their cognitive function.

Chapter 3:
Homemade Herbs Recipes for Kid's Health

Herbal Ginger Brew

This is a great brew for stomach cramps, indigestion, and nausea. It is an energy stimulant used to cure sore throats and coughs.

Ingredients:

- Syrup
- 1/2 cup peeled sliced ginger
- 1 cup water
- 1/4 cup pure maple syrup
- 1 cup carbonated water
- One tablespoon of lemon juice
- Grated lemon, rind

Directions:

1. For the syrup, combine water and ginger in a saucepan, and simmer for 30
1. minutes.
2. Cool slightly and strain.
3. Add maple syrup, and stir to mix.

Ginger Honey Lemon Tonic

This tonic is perfect for your youngster's flu, upset stomach, or sore throat. It's also great for chilly winter days. This tonic is soothing and healing, and it can be taken in advance when you or your child feel like you're about to come down with something.

Ingredients:

- 1 cup water
- One piece of 1-inch fresh ginger (or more depending on taste), peeled and chopped
- *1/2* medium lemon
- One teaspoon honey

Directions:

1. Place the water, ginger, lemon juice, and honey in a small saucepan over medium heat until heated.
2. Strain the mixture into a cup using a fine-mesh strainer.

Ginger Cough Syrup

This is a homemade cough syrup made of ginger and other ingredients. It's great for sore throats and coughs. It will greatly soothe your youngster's tickly, itchy throat and allow them to be comfortable enough to rest and sleep. Adults are advised to take 2-3 spoonfuls every few hours or as needed, so you should determine the recommended dosage for your child.

Ingredients:

- One teaspoon fresh grated ginger OR ¥4 teaspoon ground ginger V4 teaspoon cayenne pepper
- One clove of garlic, grated (optional)
- Two tablespoons of raw honey
- One tablespoon apple cider vinegar Two tablespoons water (optional)

Directions:

1. Cover the ingredients in a jar with a tight-fitting cover and shake well.
2. Shake to combine or whisk vigorously in a medium bowl.

Ginger Milk

For many years, ginger has been used to treat nausea and stomach issues. It relieves stomach ache pain and has several other health benefits. It's an anti-inflammatory that can help with a variety of stomach problems. This dish is great for youngsters and can be administered before bedtime to get the best results.

Ingredients:

- 1 cup milk
- One tablespoon of palm sugar
- 1/4 teaspoon dry ginger powder
- 1/4 teaspoon black pepper powder

Directions:

1. In a saucepan, heat 1 cup of milk until it is foamy. When the water boils, add the palm sugar and ginger powder.
2. Mix thoroughly for 2 to 3 minutes. Serve the milk after straining it.

Great Taste Tea Blend

This herbal tea blend not only tastes great but also smells great! It's perfect for kids who are picky about what they drink. It also includes peppermint, a great herb that kids recognize and is considered a children's favorite.

Ingredients:

- One teaspoon of Lemon Balm
- One teaspoon Peppermint
- One teaspoon Oatstraw
- One teaspoon of Lycii (Goji) Berries
- One teaspoon of Red Clover

Directions:

1. Tea infuser, tea bag, or tea nest filled with herbs; 3-4 cups boiling water over the herbs.
2. Let steep for 3-5 minutes and enjoy.
3. Add a little lemon, milk, or Honey.

Book 12:
Native Americans Do It Yourself

Chapter 1:
Infusions

Sore Throat Infusion

Preparation:

- Pour two cups of water into a pot, add one teaspoon of fresh ginger and bring it to a boil.
- Turn off the stove and let it steep for 10 minutes.
- Use 1-2 teaspoons of the mixture as often as needed for sore throat pain relief.

People who regularly take this infusion have fewer cases of sore throat every year because they have strong bacterial resistance.

Infusion of Sage

Preparation:

- Pour two cups of water into a pot, add one ounce of sage leaves, and bring it to a boil.
- Turn off the stove and let it steep for 10 minutes.
- Use 2-4 teaspoons of the mixture as often as needed for chest colds.

People who regularly take this infusion have fewer cases of sore throat every year because they have strong bacterial resistance.

Infusion of Fennel

Preparation:

- Pour two cups of water into a pot, add one teaspoon of fennel leaves, and bring it to a boil.
- Turn off the stove and let it steep for 10 minutes.
- Use 1-2 teaspoons of the mixture as often as needed for cold, cough, and respiratory disorders.
- People who regularly take this infusion have fewer cases of constipation yearly because they have strong bacterial resistance.

Infusion of Valerian

Preparation:

- Pour two cups of water in a pot, add one teaspoon of fresh parsley flowers and bring it to a boil.
- Turn off the stove and let it steep for 10 minutes.
- Use 2-4 teaspoons with 1/2 teaspoon of valerian root as needed for insomnia, anxiety, and nervousness.

People who regularly take this infusion have fewer cases of insomnia yearly because they have strong bacterial resistance.

Chapter 2:
Tea

Raspberry Tea

Serving Size: 1

Brewing Time: 10 minutes

Ingredients:

- . 1 c. water
- . 1/4 c. dried raspberry leaves
- . 1/4 c. dried lemongrass
- . 1/2 c. dried chamomile flowers
- . 1/2 c. dried orange peel

Directions:

1. Mix all the dried herbs listed above.
2. Boil water.
3. Add 1 tsp of tea mixture to a cup.
4. Pour hot water over it. Cover and steep for 5-10 minutes. The longer the time, the more tannin is extracted.
5. Consume hot, cold, or iced.

Hibiscus-Ginger Tea

Serving Size: 4 cups

Brewing Time: 15 minutes

Ingredients:

- 4 c. water
- 1 tbsp, hibiscus leaves
- 1 tbsp grated fresh ginger
- 3-5 mint leaves

Directions:

1. Boil water in a pot.
2. Take hibiscus and ginger and blend them in another pot.
3. Pour hot water over the tea mixture, cover, and steep for 10-12 minutes.
4. The color of the tea will turn ruby red, then add mint leaves for fresh flavor.
5. Serve hot or cold.

Chapter 3:
Decoction

Basil Decoction

Method:

- Boil 2-3 tbsp of Basil leaves in a cup of water.

- Steep for 10-15 minutes with a lid.

- To make the decoction more concentrated, add more Basil leaves.

- Take your hot decoction and strain it using a strainer or cheesecloth into an empty cup.

- Thoroughly clean up the filter if used before storing it for later use.

- Drink this hot herbal tea twice daily for best results.

- Other components for your decoction include mint, rosemary, and lavender.

- Also, Rosemary can be used instead of Basil for a more robust decoction.

German Chamomile Decoction

Method:

- Boil 1-2 tbsp of Chamomile flowers in a cup of water.

- Steep for 10-15 minutes with a lid.

- Take your Hot Chamomile decoction and strain it using a strainer or cheesecloth into an empty cup.

- Thoroughly clean up the filter if used before storing it for later use.

- Drink this hot herbal tea twice daily for best results.
- Other ingredients you may want to include in your decoction are mint leaves, rosemary, or lavender.
- Also, Rosemary can be used instead of Chamomile for a more robust decoction.

Chicory Decoction

Method:

- Boil 1-2 tbsp of Chicory roots in a cup of water.
- Steep for 5-10 minutes with a lid.
- Take your hot decoction and strain it using a strainer or cheesecloth into an empty cup.
- Thoroughly clean up the filter if used before storing it for later use.
- Drink this hot herbal tea twice daily for best results.
- Other ingredients you may want to include in your decoction are mint leaves, rosemary, or lavender.
- Chicory can be used instead of Chamomile for a more robust decoction.

Ginger Decoction

Method:

- Boil 1-2 tbsp of Ginger in a cup of water.
- Steep for 10-15 minutes with a lid.
- Take your hot decoction and strain it using a strainer or cheesecloth into an empty cup.
- Thoroughly clean up the filter if used before storing it for later use.
- Drink this hot herbal tea twice daily for best results.
- Other ingredients you may want to include in your decoction are mint leaves, rosemary, or lavender.

Chapter 4:
Popsicles

Ginger Mint Popsicles

- 1 cup of coconut water or any fruit juice of your choice (if you are on a low-calorie diet, you can replace it with water)
- 2-inch ginger root, peeled, sliced into 1/4 pieces
- 4 to 6 fresh mint leaves

Process: Add freshly sliced ginger and mint leaves to the blender. Pour in the fruit juice or coconut water. Blend until smooth. Pour into popsicle molds and freeze overnight.

Cucumber and Herb Popsicles

- 1 cup of fruit juice or coconut water
- 2 cucumbers, peeled, sliced into 1 /4 pieces
- 3-5 fresh mint leaves

Process: Place the jars in the blender. Add in mint leaves and make sure that they are completely blended. Pour in fruit juice or coconut water. Blend until smooth. Pour into popsicle molds and freeze overnight.

Fruit and Herb Popsicles

- 1 cup of fruit juice or coconut water
- a 2-inch piece of fresh ginger, peeled, sliced into 1/4 pieces

- 5 to 6 fresh mint leaves

Process: Place the jars in the blender. Add in mint leaves and ginger. Make sure that all the pieces are completely blended. Pour in fruit juice or coconut water. Blend until smooth. Pour into popsicle molds and freeze overnight.

Herbal Popsicles

- 1 cup of fruit juice or coconut water
- 5 to 7 fresh mint leaves

Process: Place the jars in the blender. Add mint leaves and make sure that they are completely blended. Pour in fruit juice or coconut water. Blend until smooth. Pour into popsicle molds and freeze overnight.

Chapter 5:
Baths

Lavender Bath

Preparation:

- Add 1 to 2 cups of dried lavender flower to your bathtub.
- Boil a pot of water and add 1/2 cup of Epsom salt.
- Pour the mixture into the bathtub, and then get into the tub after you've added water.
- Soak for 5 to 10 minutes.
- Use with caution because the Epsom salt may irritate those who are sensitive to it.

Sage Bath

Preparation:

- Place 1 /4 cup of dried sage in your bathtub and add hot water.
- Steep for 5 to 10 minutes before getting into the tub.
- For extra effect, you can leave the herbs in the tub after your bath.
- It is recommended not to use this herbal treatment if you are pregnant or breastfeeding because sage has properties that can make you feel like you're on an intense trip.

Rose Petal Bath

Preparation:

- Place 8 to 10 organic rose petals into your bathtub.
- Vitamin C in rose petals brightens and softens skin.
- Steep the rose petals in hot water for 3 to 5 minutes before getting into the tub.
- Rose glyceride is a substance in rose petals that can soothe irritations and inflammation caused by eczema and acne.

Ginger Bath

Ginger is an essential element in improving your skin's health.

The best ginger is fresh ginger, which can be added to your bath as a decoction or powder.

If you make the decoction, use two parts water for one part ginger root.

Preparation:

- For each bather, add 1/2 cup Epsom salt and 1 cup fresh ginger root.
- Use 3 to 4 cups of hot water for each person taking a bath.
- Steep in a pot for 5-10 minutes.
- When ready to take a bath, use 1/2 cup of the mixture with the Epsom salt and add it to your bathwater.
- Soak for 5-10 minutes before rinsing.

Precautions: do not use this herbal treatment if you have high blood pressure because ginger can increase blood pressure levels. Also, do not take this herbal bath if you are pregnant.

Chapter 6:
Washcloths

Eyewash

Preparation:

- Add a few drops of water to the eye spray bottle.
- Fill the rest of the bottle with peppermint essential oil.
- Use these eye drops to clean the eye area.

This is very good for people who suffer from dry eyes, as they can treat them with one quick and simple treatment. Refrigerate in an airtight container after each use to ensure potency.

The eyewash can also be used for other purposes, such as treating conjunctivitis, blepharitis, and other eye issues.

Tongue wash

Preparation:

- Fill the tongue spray bottle with water.
- Fill the rest of the bottle with Thyme essential oil.
- Use this tongue spray to clean the area around the mouth, and in its presence, you will feel a soothing sensation on your tongue.

This is a very good treatment if your mouth is filled with bad breath and a cleansing of the inside of your mouth. After usage, keep it in an airtight container for two weeks.

Tongue wash can be used on other body parts such as the inner thigh area, groin area, armpit, and any other areas that may need light cleaning and soothing.

Armpit wash

Preparation:

- Add a few drops of water to the armpit spray bottle.
- Add Lavender essential oil to the bottle.
- Use this armpit spray to clean your armpits, and you will feel a soothing sensation on your skin.

This is very good for people who work in the construction field, as it will help remove odors from the body and develop an antibacterial treatment for skin infections. In an airtight container, it lasts two weeks.

The armpit wash can also be used on other body areas such as the groin area, inner thigh area, and back of the neck to get a good cleaning.

Inner thigh wash

Preparation:

- Fill the inner thigh spray container with water.
- Add Lavender essential oil to the bottle.
- Use this inner thigh spray to clean the area around your groin, making you feel a soothing sensation.

This is very good for sports people, as it will help remove sweat and bacteria that may cause infections. It can create an antibacterial treatment for skin infections. After usage, keep it in an airtight container for two weeks.

The inner thigh wash can be used on other areas such as the armpit, groin, inner wrist, and other not-to-be-replaced areas.

Inner wrist wash

Preparation:

- Fill the inside wrist spray bottle with water.
- Add Lavender essential oil to the bottle.
- Use this inner wrist spray to clean the area around your hand, making you feel a soothing sensation.

This is very good for people who work in the construction field, as it will help remove odors from the body and develop an antibacterial treatment for skin infections. After usage, keep it in an airtight container for two weeks.

The inner wrist wash can also be used on other body areas, such as the groin area, armpit, inner thigh area, or other not-to-be-replaced areas.

Book 13:
Native American Dispensatory

Chapter 1:
Native American Medicine

Overview

Experts claim that "Native American medicine" includes more than 500 medical tenets and practises. Despite the fact that each tribe had its own rituals, they all shared the fundamental belief that man and nature are intimately linked and that maintaining a healthy balance is essential to good health. Imagine if everyone contributes to maintaining and protecting the environment. If so, we may use it to motivate society and motivate those who reside in and work near its bounds.

Even if nature cannot be seen with the naked eye and is untouched by technological advancement, humans may still perceive it via their senses. People and natural systems are both intricate beings that require cooperation to be in equilibrium. More than 40,000 years after its origin, traditional Native American medicine is still extensively used around the world, notably in the United States. But this is a far cry from how things were done only a few years ago, when documentation was based primarily on observations. It doesn't only emphasise creativity in general; it also goes beyond memorization of course material or honing just one gift. It seems sense that the majority of Native American elders are apprehensive about outsiders exploiting it. Herbs and other natural remedies are the mainstays of traditional Indian medicine, which aims to rebalance the internal and external environments of the body. This evaluation takes into account a person's physical makeup, mental health, emotional state, social circle, and way of life. To obtain peace of mind, it is important to be aware of the patient's interests and preferences.

The manner that Native Americans are treated is different from how everyone else on earth is addressed. There are alternatives for botanical and nutritional therapy, midwife-assisted bone setting, naturopathy (including hydrotherapy), and other specialised therapeutic approaches. The chapter on ceremonial and ritual medicine in this book. Because of the efforts of survivalists, many aspects of this unrecorded history have been successfully preserved. Native American medicine has been flexible for hundreds of years because Native Americans were increasingly concerned with maintaining their culture.

Modern Applications of Native American Medicine

This weekend marks the beginning of National American Indian Heritage Month, which recognises the significant role that early Americans had in the creation and development of the United States of America. Like many other indigenous influences, November and Remembrance Day are commemorated every year but occasionally ignored in our daily lives. Immigrants, for instance, popularised lacrosse while bringing with them a unique set of cultural values and traditions that have influenced how we live today.

The supply of medications and preventive measures are components of the global health ecosystem. Numerous indigenous peoples' and healers' customs and inventions have been used for thousands of years.

Many of the medical and public health advancements made by Native Americans are still in use today. However, the majority of people don't think twice about them. Most of the time, they would be unable to function well without them right now.

Injectors

Alexander Wood, a Scot, is credited with creating hypodermic needles in 1853, contrary to popular belief. Nevertheless, the device has been in use for a while. Native Americans in North America created a method of delivering fluids to the body using hollowed-out bird bones and an animal bladder before Europeans arrived in the area. The function of these early syringes ranged from administering medication to irrigating wounds. According to reports, these tools may also be used to give enemas and clean ears.

Tylenol, Aspirin, And Other Analgesics

Native American healers were early adopters of pain management. Willow bark (tree bark) has been used in traditional Chinese medicine as an anti-inflammatory and pain reliever for thousands of years. Salicin, an ingredient in this extract that has been shown to have anti-inflammatory actions, is present in high concentrations in this extract. Salicin, a chemical, is used to make salicylic acid, the active component in aspirin tablets. Topical creams, pain relievers taken orally, and anti-inflammatory medications can all be used to treat cuts, bruises, and wounds. There are several options available for painkillers. These include Jimson weed, a long-used topical pain treatment, and capsaicin, a substance generated by peppers that is still used today.

Sunscreen

The region's surviving traditions now reflect that Native Americans believed that some 2,500 plant species in North America had therapeutic value. For hundreds of years, many traditional civilizations have used a similar method to treat skin, mixing water and powdered herbs to make sun-protective therapies. Studies have shown that sunflower oil, wallflower extract, and aloe plant sap may all shield the skin from the sun's rays. Sunscreen has occasionally been used as animal fat or fish oil.

Instructions for using mouthwash and brushing your teeth

Americans are believed to have had better dental habits than later Europeans, despite the fact that tribes all across the continent used a variety of medications and procedures to clean their teeth. In certain cultures, the plant known as goldthread is used to make mouthwash. In addition to its medicinal uses, it was also rubbed on the gums to treat dental infections and to relieve discomfort in teething infants.

Suppositories

Haemorrhoids have caused doctors anxiety for a long time. Not only are blood vessels in the groyne area unsightly, but they can also be unpleasant. The ancient peoples of the Americas used dogwood trees to make medications thousands of years before contemporary therapies and dietary modifications. Dogwood is still applied topically to treat wounds, but less frequently than in the past. Haemorrhoids were once treated with little plugs made of compressed, wet dogwood wood, but this method is no longer practised.

We should all pause for a moment to consider how frequently we take public health and medicine for granted in keeping us healthy and safe. It is simple to overlook the contributions of individuals who made these discoveries and innovations possible, and it is even easier to assume they will always be there. There is a very high degree of sterility, refinement, and perfection in many modern procedures. In contrast, there are other sectors where we have not made as much progress as our ancestors. He has a great advantage since he can use the resources of the earth to make components and shapes that are useful for curing illnesses.

A Look at the Therapeutic Effects of Herbs

Both contemporary and historical societies place a high value on medicinal plants. Herbs, which have historically been used as medicines, can also be utilised as healthy supplements. The most popular therapeutic plants include dandelion, ginger, licorice, and turmeric. We'll look at some of these herbs' therapeutic benefits and how you might utilise them to enhance your health in this section. ### Subject: 5 Social Media Tips to Improve Your Brand's Visibility Intro: One of the most effective resources accessible to every organisation is social media. When used properly, it may increase website traffic and assist you in connecting with your target market. Social media's influence comes from both its wide audience as well as its capacity to attract loyal followers. Here are five suggestions for maximising the use of social media to raise awareness of and interest in your company.

They Could Aid In Blood Purification

Humans have long been aware of the therapeutic benefits of plants. Herbs have been utilised as a treatment for many illnesses since ancient times. Even today, people still employ herbal treatments to enhance their health and treat illnesses.

Herbs can aid with blood purification. Herbs not only help lower your chance of developing heart disease and other illnesses, but they may also help your blood become more healthy. By promoting circulation and eliminating toxins from your bloodstream, herbs can aid in the cleansing and detoxification of your body.

Dandelion, burdock, juniper, rosemary, sage, and thyme are some typical herbs that assist enhance blood quality. You might think about utilising these herbs as part of a healthy lifestyle plan to enhance your general health as the majority of them are thought to be safe for usage in big amounts.

They Possess Analgesic Qualities

Many botanicals have pain-relieving qualities. Aspirin, ibuprofen, and codeine are the most widely used and well-known. These herbs function by preventing the brain from sending pain signals. They may occasionally aid in reducing edoema or inflammation.

For millennia, people have utilised some plants to relieve pain. A such illustration is aspirin. Early in the 20th century, it was created as a non-steroidal anti-inflammatory medication (NSAID). It is one of the most often prescribed painkillers in use today.

Ibuprofen is another well-liked natural pain reliever. It functions by stopping the brain from sending pain signals and by reducing swelling or inflammation in the body. People with arthritis or other forms of joint discomfort are frequently administered it.

Another well-known natural analgesic is codeine. It functions by stopping the brain from sending pain signals and by reducing swelling or inflammation in the body. People with chronic pain issues including back pain, muscular pains, and headaches are frequently administered it.

They Are Effective as Antacids

Herbs are utilised for healing by many individuals, and a wide variety of herbs can be used for this. Ginger, garlic, turmeric, fennel, dandelion, and comfrey are a few of the most often utilised herbs for medical purposes.

These plants have long been utilised as antacids due to their well-known medicinal benefits. Some of these herbs not only have antacid characteristics but also have additional advantages including lowering inflammation and battling infection.

They're Effective Antihistamines.

Because they are unaware of what the ramifications of using herbs for medicine could be, some people may be reluctant to do so. The reality is that many of these herbs have been utilised for treating various health issues for a very long time, and many people still rely on them today to stay healthy. Birch, chamomile, lavender, and nettle are some of the most well-known and successful herbs for the treatment of allergies. These plants are all antihistamines and prevent allergy symptoms by preventing histamine from doing so.

Many people discover that these herbs are effective independent therapies or in conjunction with other medications, such as prescription meds or over-the-counter allergy medications. Given that every person's body reacts differently to various therapeutic treatments, it is crucial to speak with a healthcare practitioner about which herb could best fit your requirements.

They Possess Good Anti-Biotic Properties

For millennia, people have utilised some plants to successfully cure a variety of illnesses. Oregano is one such herb. Oregano is a fantastic choice for treating both minor and major health issues because to its anti-biotic and anti-inflammatory effects.

Antioxidants found in abundance in oregano can aid in the battle against the inflammatory cells. Additionally, the plant lowers bacterial levels in the body, which may help fend off diseases.

Oregano may work well as a therapy for a number of conditions when taken as directed by a healthcare professional, such as:

- Gingivitis
- intestinal inflammation
- expansion of Candida

- vulgarised acne
- infections brought on by fungus, bacteria, and viruses
- Ankylosing spondylitis
- Joint pain and psoriasis

They Have Sanitation

Any organic or synthetic substance that inhibits the development of bacteria or fungus is considered an antiseptic. Antiseptics are used to clean and disinfect tools, surfaces, and body tissues in pharmacies.

Traditional uses for several plants have antibacterial properties. Lavender oil, for instance, has antibacterial properties naturally and may be used to treat skin lesions. Additionally discovered to be a powerful antiseptic is oregano oil. Phenol and chlorhexidine gluconate are two examples of synthetic antiseptics.

They Are Spasmolytics

Traditional medicine has made use of a wide variety of plants. Several of these plants have antispasmodic properties that can help lessen the frequency and length of spasms or contractions.

Ginger, skullcap, lavender, and chamomile are some of the most popular antispasmodics. You can apply these herbs directly on the skin or consume them orally. They function by calming the muscles and lowering inflammation.

The frequency and intensity of spasms or contractions may be lessened for some people by taking an antispasmodic medication on a regular basis. Some antispasmodics may also contribute to a better overall state of health by reducing inflammation and reducing discomfort.

They're Useful as Diuretics

Some herbs are more effective than others when used as diuretics. Dandelion, parsley, and goldenseal are a few plants that are frequently used as diuretics. Because it contains anti-inflammatory effects, fenugreek is also a wonderful plant to use as a diuretic. The body's general eliminative system can also be strengthened with the use of herbs.

Some Herbs Work Well as Diuretics

Constipation may often be effectively treated with herbs. Dandelion, cascara sagrada, senna, fennel, and aloe vera are some of the most often used laxative plants. Each plant differs from the others in how it works as a laxative.

It is well known that dandelion may unclog blocked arteries and cleanse the intestines. Natural laxative cascara sagrada relieves constipation and improves digestion. Senna is an intestinal stimulant that aids in the movement of waste. Fennel has anti-inflammatory properties that ease constipation and enhance gut health in general. An plant that might calm the digestive tract and relieve constipation is aloe vera.

Several Herbs Possess Effective Antiparasitic Qualities

Some plants have powerful antiparasitic effects. The body's parasite population can be decreased with the use of these plants. They may even be able to fully recover from parasite infestations. Wormwood (Artemisia annua), garlic (Allium sativum), and feverfew (Feverfew Officinalis) are a few of the more popular treatments that contain these plants. Finding the proper herb for you is crucial since each of these plants offers various advantages against parasite illness.

Herb known as wormwood has anti-parasitic effects. It is frequently used to treat infections, especially those brought on by hookworms and roundworms. Wormwood also assists in stopping the onset of various infections.

Another herb with potent parasite-fighting abilities is garlic. It functions to disintegrate and eradicate parasite cells. Additional bacterial, viral, and infection-causing illnesses can be successfully treated with garlic.

When it comes to treating parasite illnesses, feverfew is a very potent treatment. It includes substances that can directly kill parasites and stop them from spreading deeper within the body. Fever and tiredness are other parasite infection symptoms that feverfew can treat.

A Few Herbs Make Effective Stimulants

Herbs have the potential to be potent stimulants, according to research on their therapeutic effects. Some plants, like ginger, have been utilised for pain relief and circulation enhancement for millennia. Other plants, including lavender and rosemary, are well recognised for their relaxing properties.

Anxiety and despair may both be effectively treated with herbs. Many people discover that taking herbal supplements before night promotes easier and deeper sleep. Additionally, herbal stimulants are effective when used in conjunction with other types of therapy, such cognitive behavioural therapy (CBT).

A Few Herbs Make Effective Sedatives

Some herbs could be the answer if you're trying to unwind. The following five plants have historically been used as sedatives:

Since ancient times, valerian (Valeriana officinalis), a plant related to the valerian family, has been used as a sedative. According to studies, it can aid in enhancing sleep quality and lowering anxiety and tension.

Another plant in the valerian family that has been used as a sedative for ages is hops (Humulus lupulus). It is believed to function by reducing central nervous system activity.

To calm the digestive system, chamomile (Matricaria chamomilla) is frequently used as a tea or extract. However, it can also be beneficial for reducing stress and anxiety. According to certain research, chamomile may even aid to enhance general cognitive performance.

Due to its capacity to increase serotonin levels in the brain, passionflower (Passiflora incarnata) has long been regarded as a potent relaxant. It is frequently used as a tincture or infusion to calm the mind and relax the muscles.

Due in part to its powerful perfume, lavender (Lavandula angustifolia) has been linked to calm since ancient times. To reduce the signs of stress and anxiety, lavender oil can be ingested or used topically.

Making Equipment for Herbal Medicines

If you're just getting started in the bizarre world of herbalism, selecting the right tools could be challenging. To make things simple, this list was created. Although it's far from complete, we hope it will help you get started. Over time, both your stock of herbs and your base of instruments will increase.

(Mason jars)

The best kitchen storage option is a mason jar. You may store everything and anything in them. Tea blends, dried herbs, herb vinegar, tinctures, tea leaves, and infused oils can all be kept inside of them. They are quite flexible. Maintain a range of sizes on hand.

- Scissors and baskets

You will need scissors to pick up the herbs and a basket to transport them in first. Any basket with a handle will do. A decent set of scissors are also necessary because some plant stems are rather thick. The pair is fairly sturdy and comfortable, and the blades may be sharpened as needed.

- Fine-mesh sieves in a range of sizes

For pressing out tinctures and filtering tea, you'll need strainers of various sizes. Start by using two single-mug strainers for individual tea cups and a larger, bowl-size strainer for larger quantities of liquids infused with herbs.

- Cheddar cloth

Herbs that have been infused into liquid can be squeezed, strained, and wrapped in a poultice using this.

- Measurement spoons and cups

When measuring, a quarter-ounce graduated measuring cup with a pour spout, along with cup, teaspoon, and tablespoon measures, are all helpful.

- Channels

When placing tinctures or other liquids into bottles with tiny holes, a little funnel is helpful.

- Containers

Medicines can be stored for a long time in blue or amber glass bottles. For tinctures and several other liquid therapies, the Boston round type is favoured, however any shape will work. Make it a habit to conserve and recycle any eye-catching glass bottles you come across. For instance, amber glass is a popular choice for kombucha products.

Storage bottles should be four to twelve ounces, whereas dose bottles should be one to two fluid ounces. For storing bottles, use standard bottle tops; however, dosing bottles must have dropper tips.

- Labelling

As soon as a cure is created, make sure to name it. In most cases, address labels will do; in an emergency, masking tape will do.

Use a blender

To combine lotions, cut up large pieces of fresh plant material, and do other duties, a standard kitchen blender will suffice.

- Tea Press The most practical way to make large quantities of tea is with a tea press. I like to use mine to create a healthy herbal infusion. The press does a great job of straining out all the plant matter! Making tea and my regular infusion mixture is a breeze with it. You may use a coffee press in its place if you don't have a tea press! To prevent your tea from tasting like coffee, keep your coffee maker and tea press separate.
- An herb mill

For many years, a simple, compact coffee grinder worked well for us. However, you might want to make a larger, more specialised equipment investment if you want to manufacture a lot of herb powders.

- · Thermos A good thermos is excellent for transporting tea to work or for usage when travelling. There are types that have a filter built straight into the lid, enabling you to fill the thermos with water and herbs right away.

Chapter 2:
Process of Extraction

Simple Extracts

Both fresh and dried extracts can be produced, or even both. While some of them may be produced using alcohol as a basis, the majority are safe to consume without it.

Herbs are extracted in water

These extracts are created from plants containing a lot of water. For instance, fresh ginger and mint leaves can be used for this, but fresh parsley or other herbs with a lower water content won't work as well since they won't infuse effectively in boiling water.

Make manageable chunks out of the herb.

Put the herbs in a jar with boiling water, then completely cover the container.

If you want to produce a stronger extract, soak it for at least 10 minutes; up to overnight is OK.

Use a cheesecloth or other type of sieve to remove the herbs' seeds.

Pour the liquid into a clean bottle that has a tight-fitting cover after allowing it to cool.

If you wish to lessen the strong flavour of strong herbs like ginger or mint and afterwards add them to your tinctures or teas, add distilled water (optional).

Store in a dim location.

Alcohol Herb Extraction

Although dried herbs are more readily available, they may also be used to make these extracts, which are typically produced with whole, fresh herbs. These extracts taste fantastic when consumed on their own or added to tinctures and teas.

Put the herb in a jar with the alcohol after chopping it into manageable bits.

Let it soak for at least three days; overnight is wonderful, but any longer may start to affect how the final result tastes.

Use a cheesecloth or other kind of sieve to remove the herbs.

Pour the liquid into a clean bottle that has a tight-fitting cover after allowing it to cool.

If you wish to lessen the strong flavour of strong herbs like ginger or mint and afterwards add them to your tinctures or teas, add distilled water (optional).

Store in a dim location.

Herb Extraction in Glycerin

Although dried herbs are more easily accessible, they can also be used to make these extracts, which are typically created with fresh herbs. These extracts taste fantastic when consumed on their own or added to tinctures and teas.

Make manageable chunks out of the herb.

Using a spoon, hand blender, or another mixing tool, thoroughly incorporate the herbs with the glycerin.

Allow it to soak for at least one day; overnight is OK, but longer is preferable.

Use a cheesecloth or other kind of sieve to remove the herbs.

Pour the liquid into a clean bottle that has a tight-fitting cover after allowing it to cool.

If you wish to lessen the strong flavour of strong herbs like ginger or mint and afterwards add them to your tinctures or teas, add distilled water (optional).

Store in a dim location.

Herb extraction in honey

These extracts are created by soaking and straining dry herbs before combining them with honey. These taste fantastic when added to tinctures and teas, but they may also be consumed on their own if appropriately diluted.

In a jar or other container, cover dry herbs with boiling water (or distilled water).

If you wish to create a stronger extract, leave the mixture covered for longer.

Use a sieve, cheesecloth, or another means of straining to remove the herbs.

The herbs should be completely mixed with the honey before being added.

Allow it sit for many days; overnight is OK, but longer time is preferable.

Pour into a clean glass container with a tight-fitting cap after filtering the herbs with a colander, cheesecloth, or another technique.

If you wish to lessen the strong flavour of strong herbs like ginger or mint and afterwards add them to your tinctures or teas, add distilled water (optional).

Store in a dim location.

Homemade Infusions/Tinctures

These extracts are created from dry herbs that have been heavily distilled, often to 80 proof. They may be used for infusions, tinctures, baths, etc. since they have a robust, strong flavour that is not too sweet as a result.

Put the dried herb in a container, then pour alcohol over it.

If you want an even stronger extraction, let rest for two weeks to an hour before utilising.

The herbs should be strained out and kept in a dark location in a glass jar with a tight-fitting cover.

Herb Extraction in Vinegar

These extracts are created by soaking and straining dry herbs before adding them to the vinegar. These taste fantastic either consumed on their own or added to tinctures and drinks.

Make manageable chunks out of the herb.

Leave at least an inch of space between the herb and the vinegar so that it may fully infuse and not be lost when you strain the herbs. Add vinegar to your jar, bottle, or other container.

Allow to sit for at least an hour; overnight is preferable, but less time works just as well.

Pour the herbs into a clean glass jar with a tight-fitting cover and store in a dark area after straining them using a colander, cheesecloth, or another means of straining.

If you wish to lessen the strong flavour of strong herbs like ginger or mint and afterwards add them to your tinctures or teas, add distilled water (optional).

Store in a dim location.

Modern Extraction Methods

Do you want to create extracts that are robust and strong but don't necessary taste like candy? See what happens if you use these strategies!

Extracts from percolation

For this extract, you'll need to use a lot of alcohol—usually 80 proof. Don't allow your herbs dry out; instead, soak them in the alcohol. Then, drain the herbs through a sieve, cheesecloth, or other means, and store them in a dark location in a clean glass jar with a tight-fitting cover.

Allow it to sit for a few days; overnight is OK, but longer is preferable.

Pour the herbs into a clean glass jar with a tight-fitting cover and store it somewhere dark after straining them using a sieve, cheesecloth, or another means of straining.

These extracts can be applied in a variety of ways. However, the fundamental concept is to let them rest for a few weeks until they gain enough potency to be added to tinctures, teas, or infusions.

Extracts of fluids

An herbal extract is considerably different from this kind of extract. It's a technique for boosting the power of your tinctures and teas without causing the herbs to oxidise, go bad, or gradually lose flavour. Usually, the alcohol is less than 80 percent and includes vodka and absinthe.

For this procedure, you'll need a glass jar with a wide opening. A blender that can be dipped a few inches into the mixture, such as an immersion blender or a stick blender, is also required.

After adding herbs, alcohol, water, or vinegar, the glass jar should have a cover. Use your immersion blender at a low speed so that it doesn't splash out as you continue to add liquid until it is about an inch from the top of the container (allowing room for shaking).

Vodka or absinthe, water, and vinegar, to taste, go into your jar with the herbs. Blend on low speed until thoroughly blended and no liquid escapes the container.

Extracts from Soxhlet

The Soxhlet technique, named after Friedrich Soxhlet, who created it in 1879, is another approach to manufacture tinctures. Plant material, either fresh or dried, should be added to an extraction chamber with water and ethanol as the solvent. To effortlessly remove all liquids from this container by gravity feed without having to worry about syphoning any solid components back up into your mixture, attach an extractor tube that reaches below the liquid level. Attach a collecting device below the condenser to collect liquid byproducts. Connect a condenser tube at the top of this apparatus to capture and re-condense alcohol vaporised during distillation.

Heat distilled water and plant material in an extraction chamber until it boils for about 20 minutes in a double boiler or boiling water bath. In order to prevent steam pressure loss during the distillation process under reduced atmospheric pressure, remove the pot from the heat while it is still hot, add more boiled water (to maintain that level), and cover with a lid or another sealable device. Next, wait 30 to 60 hours at room temperature before returning to the pot and removing the contents by gravity feed without syphoning any solid components back into your mixture. Finally, attach some sort of collection device below the condenser tub.

Chapter 3:
Different Methods for Preparing And Using Your Herbs

Plants can be used as medicines in four different ways: as water infusions or decoctions; as tinctures from prolonged immersion in an alcohol and water mixture; as salves from transferring the herb's power to an oil base; and as whole plants by chewing or eating the root; or grinding the plant and taking it directly; or as capsules.

The healer prayed at each stage of transforming the plant into another form to be used as medicine. They thought the plant would come to life and become effective medicine if they sat with it and invoked its spirit through ritual and prayer.

Feel free to express gratitude to Mother Nature and recognise the symbiotic relationship between people and nature. Even if you don't believe it, over time you'll be able to increase the effectiveness of your therapies by forging a more profound, meaningful connection with the plants. After all, when you give your task your whole attention and care, you are less likely to make mistakes and, to put it in more "scientific terms," you are more likely to use the gifts you were given with a clear focus.

Making Decoctions and Infusions

To prepare infusions, herbs are soaked in cold or warm (but not boiling) water. Use the purest water you can find instead of tap water. The best options are distilled water, well-maintained wells or springs, or precipitation.

Herbs having significant volatile oil content have to be steeped in cold water. Warm water is ideal for another type of plant. For instance, a yarrow cooks in boiling water without becoming slightly bitter. This is because only the aromatic components of yarrow are soluble in cold water, not the bitter ones.

To allow the water to absorb the plant's therapeutic qualities, they should be left for anywhere between fifteen minutes and overnight, depending on the herb. For infusions and decoctions, glass or earthenware jars are the best options. A quart or pint canning jar's screw lid guards against heat-induced fracturing and nutrients floating away in the steam.

An Illustration Of A Hot Infusion

The nutritional benefits of this infusion are typically employed, especially for menopausal women.

1 pound of dried, sliced and sifted nettles, oat straw, red clover, alfalfa, horsetail and spearmint should all be combined in a large mixing dish.

Pour boiling water into a quart jar halfway, then top with one cup of the mixture. The evening should be set aside.

Over two days, infusions should not be kept in storage since they will go bad. For a person weighing 130 to 160 pounds, the usual recommendation is to consume 16 ounces of infusion each day.

When creating infusions with hot water, remember to follow these general guidelines:

Leaves: 1 ounce in 1 quart of boiling water, carefully covered, for 4 hours. Longer steeping times are required for leaves that are more rigid.

Flowers: Boil 1 ounce of flowers in 1 quart of water for 2 hours. Blooms that are more delicate need less time.

One ounce of seeds per pint of water, steeped in hot water for 30 minutes. Rose hips mature more slowly than other, more aromatic seeds like fennel.

– Root and bark: Boil one pint of water for eight hours with one ounce of bark and roots. Some barks, like slippery elm, need less upkeep. Cool infusions are preferred since herbs react differently in cold and hot water. The same process is used to make cold infusions as hot infusions. Herbs must be steeped for a long time; this is a skill that can only be acquired through practise. Infusions are less efficient than decoctions, which are created using boiling water. One ounce of herb, three cups of water, and a continual boil until the liquid is reduced by half are the usual ingredients.

Tip: Opt for stainless steel or glass containers rather than aluminium ones. Depending on the plant, doses might range from a tablespoon to a cup.

Decoctions and infusions should be kept in the refrigerator for no more than two days.

Infusions that are hot are frequently used to treat stomach issues and reduce gastric discomfort. Additionally, it helps to avoid nausea and vomiting.

Blend of Herbs

A fresh or dried plant is steeped in either straight alcohol or an alcohol and water solution to create a tincture for internal use.

When a plant is young, it has a certain quantity of water. One fresh plant is added to 190-proof alcohol for every two parts of alcohol. For instance, three ounces of fresh yarrow and six ounces of 190-proof alcohol might be placed in a jar.

Mason jars are the best choice for this use. The tincture is sealed with a tight-fitting lid and kept out of direct sunlight for two weeks. The herb is then crushed in a cloth to absorb as much liquid as possible before being decanted. Alcohol is used only to extract water from plants.

Alcohol and water will be combined to create the final tincture. I don't chop or slice fresh herbs into tiny pieces, as many herbalists do. They contend that the surface area exposed to the alcohol increases with the tincture's potency. It's best to leave the herbs whole.

While certain plants, like myrrh gum, don't need much water, others, like mint, need. As a consequence, you add the same quantity of water the plant had when it was fresh to the mixture while producing a tincture from a dried plant.

Dry plant tinctures are commonly prepared in a five-to-one ratio, meaning that there should be five parts liquid to every one component dried herb. For instance, 30% of the weight of osha root is made up of water. Add fifty ounces of liquid, 35 ounces of 95% alcohol, and 15 ounces of water to ten ounces of powdered Osha root.

In a blender, normally, dried herbs are ground as finely as possible. It's best to keep them whole until you're ready to utilise them. The tincture is decanted and the liquid is extracted from the plant material after a further two weeks.

Fresh plants often produce about the same amount as you put in. Similar to this, you get the most out of roots and other dried materials. Amber jars are ideal for tincture storage because they shield the consistency of the tincture from sunlight-caused chemical deterioration. The tinctures are so well-protected that they can survive for years.

Then, herbal tinctures can be blended and administered. Because of their convenient usage and lengthy shelf life, tinctures are preferred by herbalists.

The tincture is frequently used to alleviate restlessness, regulate hormones, heal skin issues, and boost the immune system.

Combination Tincture Recipe for a Stomach Ailment - Ten millilitres of each of the following: yarrow, betony, and poleo mint.

- Use a dropper to combine the contents in an ounce amber container. - Use a third to a half of a dropper. This combination typically works to calm an upset stomach or nausea within a few seconds.

Salves

Application examples for salves: Skin conditions are routinely treated and relieved with salves. Additionally, ischemia, bruising, and muscular soreness are all treated with it.

Utilising Oil Infusions to Create Salves

Extraction of the medicinal components from the plant and transfer to an oil basis are the initial steps in the creation of a salve. Beeswax is then added to the oil, thickening and hardening it.

preparation of the plant extract:

Dry herbs should be ground into a fine powder before using them to create an oil infusion.

The oil should be poured over the crushed herbs in a glass baking dish. A great option is olive oil.

Add some oil to the herbs. To make sure they are thoroughly submerged, add 1/2 to 1/4 inch of oil.

Bake for eight hours (overnight) at a low temperature in the oven. Some herbalists like to boil the herbs at 100 degrees for up to ten days.

When ready, press the herbs to extract the oil in a thick, tightly woven cloth.

Fresh herbs may be used to create an oil infusion by putting them in a mason jar and adding just enough oil to thoroughly cover them.

Before pressing with a towel, let the herbs dry in the sun for two weeks. Give the decanted oil some time to settle. The natural water in the herbs will settle to the bottom after a day. Remove the oil, then throw away the water. After that, they apply the oil and wait two weeks. After the oil has been drained, the water and alcohol are still present.

Making Beeswax Salve: A How-To

Half-fill a glass or stainless steel frying pan with the oil infusion. Heat the burner's top slowly. For each cup of heated oil, add 2 ounces of chopped beeswax. Many people like beeswax that has been grated, but I just break it up and mix it in. It correctly melts in this manner.

A few melted beeswax drips should be placed on a tiny dish to cool.

Use the equation shown below:

Cast iron and aluminium should not be used. It is better to utilise transparent glass or unblemished stainless steel.

All of the herbs should be ground into a fine powder, or as close to one as you can achieve.

Combine the oil and herbs.

Bake for 24 hours at low heat.

The herbs should be taken out and allowed to cool before being pressed through a cloth to get all the oil.

Reintroduce the oil after cleaning the pan and gently reheating it on the burner.

Beeswax should be around four ounces in weight.

Add one-fourth of a teaspoon of vitamin E.

Place labels on the salve containers after spooning the substance inside.

If you'd like your salve to smell good, add some essential oil.

Salve or wet therapy may not work on all wounds. In such scenario, I applied the dried herbs to the wound immediately. The herbs in the wound-salve combination, when finely powdered, halt bleeding, hasten healing while avoiding infection. Wound salve helps the wound heal after it has started to do so. The comfrey root reduces the possibility of scarring by hastening cellular repair and wound closure. The antibacterial, antifungal, and antiviral properties of echinacea, usnea, chaparral, and OSHA are all similar. Burdock is a great skin treatment, while cranesbill aids in stopping bleeding.

Making Pills and Capsules

There is no reason why you couldn't produce your own meds if you are accustomed to consuming over-the-counter medications. Anyone who has worked with modelling clay may create plant medicines. While making them, keep in mind the dose recommendations for the herbs you're using. To keep them supple, season them with spices and keep them in the refrigerator. To live organically, we don't have to step outside of our comfort zones.

Simple capsules and pills Preparation

Start with a small quantity of finely powdered herbs and gradually add more until the mixture resembles hard bread dough. 10 teaspoons of ground herbs and just enough water to make a ball that retains its shape when formed into a ball are the standard ingredients for a pill preparation.

The pill dough should be formed into a thin rope, divided into smaller pieces, and formed into pea-sized balls.

Take the pills right away, or bake them at a low temperature to gently harden them so you can store them. Only enough of these pills are produced for a 3–4 week supply due to their limited shelf life.

How to Use Capsules and Pills: For any issue brought on by the herbs used, take one dosage with water.

The following are typical uses for pills and capsules: according to the herbs used.

How to Make a Poultice

A poultice, also known as a cataplasm, is a paste produced from therapeutic plants, herbs, and other ingredients. To lessen inflammation and boost healing, the paste is rubbed to the body using a warm, moist cloth. For years, people have used this well-known home medicine to cure inflammation, insect bites, and other illnesses.

Calendula poultice ingredients include: six ounces boiling water; two tablespoons powdered clay; ten drops lavender essential oil; one heaping handful each of fresh violet leaves and calendula flowers; and one heaping handful each of fresh plantain leaves.

Instructions

The remaining ingredients should be processed or blended with four ounces of boiling water until the mixture resembles pesto.

1. To reach the proper consistency, you might need to add additional clay, water, or herbs.
2. Up to three days should pass before utilising.

3. If using dried herbs, replace one handful of fresh herbs with 14 cups of dry herbs.
4. Make sure the poultice is thick and consistent in order to have the desired result.
5. Poultices are frequently applied to bruises, small wounds, arthritic discomfort, and minor traumas.
6. washing and taking a bath

Regularly taking hot baths not only promotes relaxation but also helps prevent a number of illnesses.

Even while taking a hot bath may be a peaceful experience and reduce anxiety, adding herbs greatly increases the therapeutic potential. One of the easiest ways to relax after a long day is to take a hot bath for at least 20 minutes.

Your anxiety can be reduced by the warmth of the water, and taking a bath with herbs will have extra benefits. It will occur.

your body with energy, your mind with peace, and give you a beautiful experience.

The medicinal benefits of the herbs also help to calm the skin, release the muscles and joints, and stimulate the circulatory system. Not only that, but the herbs also have a lovely fragrance that keeps you fresh all day.

How to Prepare Herbal Body Washes and Baths

One cup of spring water, one tablespoon of grated soap, three tablespoons of fresh or dried herbs or flowers, three drops of essential oil, and a drizzle of almond oil infused with herbs.

Instructions

1. Use a mortar and pestle to pound the flowers and herbs into a paste or powder.
2. In a small saucepan, combine the herbs and water. Bring to a boil, then lower the heat to a simmer.
3. Turn off the heat under the pan.
4. In a saucepan, bring the herbal water back to a simmer.

5. Use a wire whisk to thoroughly combine the almond oil and grated soap until the oil has completely dissolved. A few seconds are all that are needed for the liquid to turn into foam.

6. Prior to adding the essential oil and thoroughly blending, let the herbal bath soap cool fully.

The aroma will last for around a month. It is not required to be chilled.

Washes and baths are frequently used to unwind and relieve discomfort.

Deodorant production

Let's say you gave up the artificially flavour to increase the diversity of your pit microbiota. You could then be curious as to what a natural product is. In addition to synthetic and artificial chemicals, deodorants frequently contain the following three ingredients:

An aromatic scent can be obtained using lavender, sandalwood, or bergamot essential oils.

To deal with moisture, use natural absorbent items like baking soda, arrowroot, or cornflour.

Natural deodorants don't block sweat glands the way antiperspirants do, but they also don't contain the potentially harmful aluminium.

What's in Arrowroot Deodorant?

- 1/3 cup coconut oil
- 1 cup arrowroot starch Baking soda,
- one cup
- six drops of essential oils, if preferred.

Instructions:

1. Combine arrowroot powder and baking soda.
2. Add the essential oils that you choose.
3. Fill a glass jar with the mixture.
4. Warm it between your fingers until it becomes liquid before applying.
5. To your pits, apply it.

Try experimenting with various powders, bases, and oils. As bases, cocoa butter, shea butter, and coconut oil work well.

The following are typical uses for herbal deodorants: It helps to make body odour better.

Production of essential oils

Essential oils are produced by cold pressing or distillation. To make the finished product, the aromatic components are first removed, and then carrier oil is added. Since chemically derived essential oils are not regarded as genuine essential oils, the method of production is crucial.

a quarter-teaspoon of rosemary oil extract, two little glass bottles with lids, and chamomile oil

- 1 tablespoon vitamin E and 1 tablespoon a little plastic funnel
- a strainer
- a chopping block
- 2 500 litres virgin olive oil and 2 cups of chamomile flowers.

Instructions

- The glass container may be sterilised by soaking it in hot water for a few minutes and then letting it dry.
- Then add some olive oil, about 3A full.
- Once thoroughly coated and steeped in the oil, gently mix the dried chamomile flowers into the olive oil.
- When you're done, firmly fasten the cover.
- A site that receives at least six hours of direct sunshine each day should be chosen for the glass bottle.
- Once a day, carefully remove the lid from the bottle to check its condition and wipe any moisture with a paper towel.
- Put the cover back on and give it a good shake. Give the mixture fifteen days to settle.
- Transfer the chamomile oil to a fresh, sterilised glass container after two weeks.

- The chamomile oil should then be combined with the rosemary oil extract and vitamin E.

Our suggestion is to get dried chamomile flowers from a health food store. You should pick your chamomile flowers early if you plan to use them yourself so they have time to dry before you use them.

The following uses for essential oils are frequent: It assists in easing stress and anxiety. It is suitable for proper skincare as well.

Utilising herbs in their unprocessed form

When put on a wound directly, the same herbs and salve work wonders. They are blended, ground as finely as possible, and then sparingly sprinkled on the wound. By adding the fine powder to socks and shoes, athlete's foot can be treated by reducing friction on the wound that coarser grinding causes.

You can consume various herbs as needed. Osha is a wonderful illustration since it may be used to treat upper respiratory infections and sore throats caused by bacteria and viruses. Because of its potency, a little amount usually suffices. In some circumstances, using both whole and tinctured herbs can be beneficial.

Chapter 4:
The Method for Storing Your Herbs in

Herbs lose their characteristics fast if improperly prepared or kept, even when they are dry.

The majority of herbalists dry their fresh herbs for preservation since they lose their potency in just a few days. Herbs should be separated from their stems and laid out in loose, single layers on a smooth, clean surface to dry.

Large plants can be hung on a line in a dry location, like an attic or warm basement. Herbs should be covered with cheesecloth since they draw flies and other insects.

Herbs lose their potency rapidly, thus the faster they can dry, the better. It takes around a week on average.

When a plant has lost its aroma but is still dry enough to break, it is said to be sufficiently dry. If it entirely collapses after treatment, it has been too dried.

Roots take about three weeks longer to dry than leaves and blooms, and they should be well cleaned before drying.

Until fully dried, they should be kept in glazed ceramic, dark glass, or metal containers with tight-fitting lids. Essential oils can be absorbed by plastic bags or food storage containers, so maintain the potency of your herbs.

Your preserved herbs can be harmed by the sun, air, heat, moisture, and reactive metals like aluminium, tin, and copper.

They progressively weaken the strength and efficacy of the herbs. Herbs should be kept in a cool, quiet, well-ventilated space, such a pantry, basement, or kitchen cabinet.

We all understand the distinction between vine-ripened and gas-ripened tomatoes since we've eaten and contrasted them. Always use the highest-quality herb you can find when creating medications for long-term preservation, such as tinctures, oils, and salves. Start off slowly and increase your dosage as you get a feel for the medicine.

The thought of having a five-year supply of ineffective tinctures irritates me more than anything. Your time, the resources of the plant, and your money are all wasted. potentially worse, if you're producing a medicinal tincture, it can potentially be fatal.

Herb Cabinet

As soon as you can after selecting your herbs, get them ready for storage. Even a few hours of exposure to the elements might cause herbs to degrade.

Scrub the dirt off.

Remove any garbage or dead leaves. Sort the seeds, stalks, and leaves from the waste material. Roots should be cleaned and dried off before spreading out to dry. While leaves and blooms should ideally be kept entire, roots should be chopped into 1-inch-thick pieces.

The Benefits of Crystal Clear Glass Tars

To keep an eye on your herbs, store them in transparent glass jars. The colours will then start to alter, which is a sign of corruption. Simply keep the jars in the dark and behind a curtain or door.

Different Storage Techniques

Herbs can be preserved using a variety of techniques.

Drying

The simplest and best method to keep your vegetables is to dry it. It doesn't need any specialised tools or supplies. All you need is a place that is adequately ventilated and out of the wind and sun. To enable air to travel through the drying plants, gather the herbs into 1-inch-diameter bundles and tie them with rubber bands or threads.

Then, hang them in a cool, dry location with adequate airflow.

The essential oils are drawn into the leaves when they are hung upside down. Keep several bunches evenly spaced apart when drying herbs on a line.

Smaller quantities of herbs can also be stored in paper bags.

The bags effectively absorb moisture while shielding the plants from light. Up until they are dry, shake or stir the herbs every day. When drying seeds, this is extremely advantageous. Make a drainage hole at the top of the bag if the plant has a lot of moisture.

Sheer curtains may be stapled to a frame to create simple screens. To dry, spread out the herbs on a thin sheet.

For greenery and loose blossoms, this screen works fantastically. Transfer the herbs to sealed containers like glass jars after they are crisp-dry.

A birch-bark box might be made if you're a purist. Chemicals from the paper birch's bark that prevent mould growth make storage simpler.

Freezing

Another strategy for keeping and preserving the food is freezing. For one minute, blanch the herb in boiling water. The herb should then be quickly drained and chilled in cold water. Drain once again.

Spread the herb out thinly on a tray and store it in the freezer to quickly freeze to avoid a quart-sized lump of frozen herb. Put it in freezer-safe containers and just remove what you require at a time.

Extracting or Tincturing

An easy and traditional way to preserve herbs for use in medicine is through tincturing. When made properly, a tincture, which is a liquid herbal extract, may keep your herbs fresh for months or even years. Alcohol and apple cider vinegar are the two most often used components in tinctures.

If you're going to consume alcohol, make sure the ABV is at least 40%. You can use raw, organic apple cider vinegar if you don't want to drink alcohol or have liver issues.

The shelf life of tinctures made from vinegar is less than that of tinctures made from alcohol. You should be careful while selecting your solvent if you're looking for a certain effect or part of the plant.

Herbal Liqueurs

One of my favourite pharmaceutical approaches is the use of herb-infused oils. Most of them may be used in the kitchen to improve the flavour of food. Others, however, are ideal for use in herbal skincare products.

Canning

To increase the shelf life of some herbs, they can be made into syrups, jellies, or preserves and preserved. Think of the healing and practical elderberry preserves, hawthorn berry jam, and violet flower syrup.

Herbal Cream Another time-honored way of preserving herbs for cooking is by making herbal butter. Before freezing your herbs later, chop them into little bits and fold them into the butter.

The herb butter should be spread out on parchment paper or a freezer sheet, shaped into a cylinder, and frozen for later use.

Book 14:
Native American Medicinal Plants

Chapter 1:
Plants for Beauty

Wisteria

If not maintained in control, wisteria is prone to become lanky and straggly, but the effort is well worth it. With its big, glossy, and sometimes variegated leaves, this hardy perennial may grow to a height of ten feet or higher. Some cultivars even have a scent! Wisteria tolerates minor soil neglect and does best in full sun or partial shade. Plant hardwood cuttings collected in the autumn or propagate by division in the spring.

NATIVE AREA: North Iran, China, Korea, Japan, Southern Canada, Eastern United States.

SEEDS AS MEDICINAL PART

USES IN MEDICINE: Used as a diuretic and to treat heart conditions.

Wisteria Sinensis is its scientific name.

Passionflower

The Passifloraceae family includes the passionflower (Passiflora incarnata), which is indigenous to Brazil, Paraguay, and Argentina. Passionflower has a long history of use as a natural treatment for ailments ranging from anxiety to heart disorders. Due to its high content of flavonoids and antioxidants, passionflower is utilised in skin care products in addition to its more conventional purposes.

ORIGINAL AREA: Central and South America as well as the Southeast United States.

THE ABOVE-GROUND PARTS ARE THE MEDICINAL PART.

Supplement for the diet to treat anxiety and sleep issues. used to treat symptoms of menopause, pain, irregular heartbeat, and attention deficit hyperactivity disorder.

Passiflora incarnata is its scientific name.

Lilac

The flower's solely therapeutic use are currently unclear. The berries and leaves of the lilac plant are what give it its medicinal qualities. It is said to have formerly been employed as a tea or infusion as an anti-periodic. Anti-periodic simply means that an illness, like malaria, is prevented from recurring. According to certain research, it may have a febrifuge effect, which might help lower fever.

Lilac blossoms have astringent, aromatic, and perhaps bitter qualities. Astringents are chemicals that pull, tighten, and dry tissues, including the skin. It would be wonderful to use a cold or warm infusion as a face toner.

Inflammation stimulates blood flow, which leads to healing when an aromatic effect is present (imagine the GI system). Eating raw flowers may help with digestive issues including flatulence and constipation. Making your own fragrance oil and capturing the aromatics in an oil that has been infused with herbs can be wonderful ways to capture the aromatics for therapeutic uses.

This plant, which has its origins in Africa, Europe, and Asia, grows well on any well-drained soil, although it does best in temperate climes.

African, European, and Asian native regions

Fruits, flowers, and leaves are medicinal components.

USES IN MEDICINE Anti-periodic implies it prevents the recurrence of disorders.

NAME IN SCIENCE: Syringa vulgaris.

Echinacea

About 30 blooming plants in the Lamiaceae family of mints belong to the genus Echinacea. Members are tiny trees or shrubs that are indigenous to Asia, Europe, and North America.

They are used as a medicinal plant to treat skin infections and other diseases, and are often dried and powdered.

NATIVE AREA: The region of the United States east of the Rocky Mountains

The root, flower, and leaf are medicinal parts.

MEDICAL PURPOSE: To reduce inflammation and strengthen the immune system of the body.

DESCRIPTION IN SCIENCE: Echinacea purpurea

Chapter 2:
Medicinal Plants

Peppermint

Because it has been used for many years to cure a wide range of diseases, peppermint is a well-known plant. Traditional uses of peppermint include easing headaches, lowering blood pressure, and enhancing digestion. Additionally, it works well for treating sadness and anxiety.

Peppermint oil is sometimes used to treat acne. Others use peppermint tea to aid with insomnia and enjoy it before bed.

EUROPE AND THE MIDDLE EAST: NATIVE AREA.

OIL IS A MEDICINALPART.

Digestive issues, sinus infections, headaches, the common cold, and other illnesses are treated with medicine.

Mentha Piperita is its scientific name.

'Ole Vera'

Aloe vera may be used to heal small burns from different causes as well as insect bites, despite being best recognised for treating sunburns. Aloe vera's anti-inflammatory qualities aid to relieve gout discomfort. But it can also aid in the treatment of eczema or dry skin. This plant is frequently used to treat skin disorders including acne as well as burns and scrapes. It includes toxins that can gradually support complete healing within the body.

Due to aloe vera's capacity to boost metabolism, burn fat, and aid in cell regeneration, it has been extensively researched for its efficacy in promoting good skin and weight reduction. This succulent plant offers several health advantages, including the ability to cure diabetes, psoriasis, burns, and more. It still remains true now as the basic treatment for many illnesses that was employed in antiquity. A word of warning, though: this plant contains poisons that can be dangerous to people. Use of aloe vera juice should be avoided. Never use this plant without a healthcare professional's approval.

Skin burns and wounds are treated with aloe vera to speed up healing. Additionally, it supports good reproductive function in postpartum women.

NATIVE AREA: The Arabian Peninsula, Madagascar, and Africa.

Leaf is a medicinal part.

MEDICAL USE: Reduce blood sugar levels, cure sunburns, relieve heartburn, and prevent dental plaque.

Blackberry

The eastern and midwestern regions of the United States are home to the blackberry bush. Berries with a deep purple hue are utilised as food, medicinal, and dye. For millennia, blackberry extracts have been utilised as medicines. Blackberry extracts are frequently used to treat inflammation, the flu, chest congestion, and colds.

North temperate areas are my native land.

The fruit, root, and leaf are medicinal parts.

DIARRAHEA, DIABETES, GOUT, FLUID RETENTION, PAIN AND Swelling (INFLAMMATION), AS WELL AS TO PREVENT CANCER AND HEART DISEASE.

Rubus, a scientific name.

Almond Leaf

An excellent plant for healing is olive leaf. In addition to being rich in antioxidants, it also possesses anti-inflammatory qualities. This implies that it may aid in lowering bodily inflammation, which may aid in easing discomfort and symptoms. Olive leaf is a benign plant that is secure for the majority of people.

Africa, Asia, and the Mediterranean are its native continents.

Leaf is a medicinal part.

Greater Immune System Strength: Medical Uses.

NAME IN SCIENCE: Olea europaea.

Plants for Fertility, Chapter 3

Woman's Mantle

A blooming plant called lady's mantle (Alchemilla Mollis) has historically been used to boost female fertility. Because it can increase cervical mucus quality and encourage ovulation, lady's mantle is a successful therapy for infertility. A lady's mantle can also support greater fertility and sperm production.

It's crucial to speak with a physician or naturopath before using lady's mantle to get its advantages. Additionally, you shouldn't use this herb without first talking to your doctor because it may cause negative effects including nausea and vomiting.

Turkey and the Carpathian Mountains are the native regions.

Leaves and roots are medicinal parts.

MEDICINAL USES: As a diuretic, an anti-anemic, and an anti-diabetic, as well as for wounds and ulcers, hernias, and muscular atrophy.

Benevolent Thistles

Alchemilla is its scientific name.

The tannins in blessed thistles may help with edoema, coughing, and diarrhoea. There is no scientific evidence to support the use of blessed thistle for dyspepsia, infections, wounds, or other conditions.

ORIGINAL AREA: The Mediterranean area.

Leaves and roots are medicinal parts.

MEDICAL USES Wounds, infections, and indigestion.

Cnicus Benedictus is his scientific name.

Red Cohosh

Unquestionably, one of the most well-liked herbal treatments for female fertility is black cohosh. Numerous studies have demonstrated that it can support ovulation and enhance uterine function.

Black cohosh also lessens menopausal symptoms, eases menstrual cramps, and boosts libido, among other advantages. Other disorders including PMS, anxiety, depression, and joint pain are also successfully treated by it.

Take black cohosh frequently on an empty stomach before eating anything else to receive the maximum reproductive benefits from it. Additionally, as it might dry out the body, drink a lot of water when taking it.

ORIGINAL PLACE: North America.

Rhizomes and roots are medicinal parts.

MEDICAL USE: Strengthening brittle bones.

Actaea racemose is the formal name.

Acai

Fruits like acai have anti-inflammatory and circulatory-improving properties. When there are additional factors, such as endometriosis, fibroids, or scar tissue from prior surgical operations, it can be beneficial for implantation problems. Berry Acai. The palm tree known as the acai (Euterpe oleracea Mart.) is native to South America. It is a common plant in Brazil, Colombia, Surinam, and the floodplains of the Amazon.

NATIVE AREA: Suriname, Brazil, and Colombia

Berries are an edible part.

MEDICINAL USE Arthritis, erectile dysfunction, skin quality, shedding pounds, lowering cholesterol, and general wellness.

NAME IN SCIENCE: Euterpe oleracea.

Chapter 4:
Plants for Wealth

Cinnamon

Cinnamon is a spice that is frequently used to flavour cakes and pastries made in the European tradition. Additionally, it serves as an intensifier in savoury meals like curry and chilli. Cinnamon can improve general health by assisting with blood sugar regulation. Cinnamon also contains antimicrobial qualities that are helpful for maintaining healthy dental hygiene.

Pakistan, Southern Asia, Papua New Guinea, and Indonesia are the native regions.

Fruit is a medicinal part.

MEDICINAL USE Carminative (gas), laxative (antispasmodic), stimulant (circulatory effects), antimicrobial (bactericidal, fungicidal, etc.).

Basil

One of the most widely grown plants worldwide is basil. This herb provides a lot of advantages for your physical and mental well-being. Numerous essential oils in basil have medicinal effects. Additionally, basil works to develop a cheerful outlook, shield against evil energy, and improve riches and success.

Basil is a potent natural treatment for a number of illnesses, including respiratory issues, sinus infections, the flu, and colds. Additionally, it might increase circulation and lessen inflammation. Constipation, diarrhoea, and other digestive issues can benefit from the use of basil. Additionally, basil works well to promote relaxation and lower stress levels.

NATIVE AREA: Southeast Asia, central Africa, and India

Medical parts are those that grow on the plant's surface.

Medical uses for stomach issues include intestinal gas, spasms, diarrhoea, constipation, and lack of appetite.

Ocimum basilicum: the scientific name.

Rosemary

for plenty, wealth, and financial prosperity. For matters pertaining to money, it serves as a natural cleanser.

Rosemary is also known as "The Herb of Remembrance" and has been used in commemorative ceremonies throughout history. This herb is frequently used to treat headaches, suppress coughs, get rid of gas buildup, and improve digestion. It can also be used as an antibacterial for wounds, cuts, scrapes, or other skin conditions. When applied to the scalp, it increases blood circulation, which may encourage the growth of hair follicles.

Hills in Portugal, northwest Spain, and the Mediterranean are native habitats.

Leaf and oil are the medicinal component.

MEDICAL PURPOSE: Reduces the danger of infection and aids in the immune system's defence against existing illnesses.

Salvia Rosmarinus is its scientific name.

Sage

Salvia officinalis, the common sage or just sage, is a herb that is commonly used to help with many things, including sore throats, coughs, and respiratory ailments. It can also be boiled with other herbs for treating digestive issues such as gas, nausea, diarrhoea, and cramps. Sage directly affects your psychic senses, making you aware of information that is being withheld from you. It is also used to aid in meditation and allows greater access to the subconscious mind.

ORIGINAL AREA: The Mediterranean

The leaf is a medical part.

USAGES IN MEDICINE: For digestive issues, to lessen excessive sweat and saliva production, for depression, memory loss, and Alzheimer's disease.

Salvia officinalis is its scientific name.

Chapter 5:
Plants for Good Luck

Mistletoe

The berries that mistletoe produces are said to be sacred to the Norse gods and were used as a sign of peace in times of war. Mistletoe is an evergreen shrub that is associated with luck. It can also be used as an ornamental plant and is found growing in many different parts of the world.

ORIGINAL PLACE: Mexico.

Flower, fruit, leaf, and stem are medicinal parts.

Seizures, headaches, and signs of menopause are all medical uses.

NAME IN SCIENCE: Viscum album.

Cane toad

Because of its form and the fact that it makes a good broom when ground up, this plant was frequently employed by ancient Egyptians as a fertility charm. The seeds were frequently used as a laxative and purgative, which is why the plant was also regarded to be a potent aphrodisiac.

Castor oil is used on the skin to soften it and remove cysts, growths, and warts. Some individuals use castor seed paste to the skin as a poultice for boils, carbuncles, pockets of infection (abscesses), inflammatory skin disorders, inflammation of the middle ear, and migraine headaches.

India and China are the NATIVE AREA.

SEED IS A MEDICINAL PART.

MEDICAL USES Skin conditions that cause inflammation.

MEDIUM: Ricinus communis, scientific name.

Anise star

The star-shaped fruit of the star anise, which is a member of the magnolia family and is grown in parts of Asia, Europe, and North America, was once considered a good luck charm in China but is now primarily used to flavour foods and beverages. It has a strong licorice flavour, which makes it an ideal ingredient in some herbal teas.

Anise seed possesses antifungal, antibacterial, and anti-inflammatory properties, which may assist with stomach ulcers, blood sugar management, depression, and menopausal symptoms when used in conjunction with a wholesome diet and active lifestyle.

NATIVE AREA: North America, Europe, and Asia.

Oil is a medical part.

Respiratory tract infections, cough, bronchitis, the flu, lung swelling (inflammation), swine flu, and avian flu are among the conditions for which it is used medically.

Illicium verum is its scientific name.

Holly

Holly is a popular choice because it is regarded as a symbol of protection; other plants frequently connected with luck include roses; daffodils; chrysanthemums; and forget-me-nots. If you're unsure which plants might be lucky, consult a local gardener or consult online plant guides.

Eastern and central United States are the region's native land.

FRUITS: THE MEDICINAL PART.

Coughs, fevers, gastrointestinal issues, heart disease, and other illnesses are treated with medicine.

Ilex, a scientific name.

Chapter 6:
Plants for Protection

Grape

This control charm may aid an agitated or furious person's life by bringing calm by allowing them to let go of any anger or frustrations they may be experiencing. The grape is a tranquil plant, and its juice can help them acquire emotional balance and conquer emotional obstacles. It is also excellent in healing charms.

The fruit, skin, leaves, and seeds of grapes are used as medicine. Grapes are rich in flavonoids, which have antioxidant properties and may lower the risk of heart disease as well as provide other health benefits. Red grape varieties have higher levels of antioxidants than white or blush grape varieties.

AREA OF ORIGIN: The Middle East.

Fruit, peel, leaves, and seed are medicinal components.

Mandrake

There are many different species of mandrake, all of which are toxic to varying degrees, with the Indian mandrake being the deadliest. Other species include the European mandrake and the American mandrake. Mandrake is a highly poisonous plant that can cause severe harm if ingested. It has long been used as a herbal remedy for treating various ailments, but its use today is primarily ceremonial.

If you are fortunate enough to survive exposure to this plant, seek medical attention as soon as you can. The root of the mandrake contains a number of toxins, including atropine, hyoscyamine, and scopolamine. All of these substances block nerve impulses and can cause paralysis or death if ingested. Symptoms of exposure to mandrake root include dilated pupils, difficulty breathing, and a fast heart rate.

This plant is utilised for defence as well since it has a poisonous quality.

The areas around the Mediterranean Sea are native areas.

Leaves and roots are medicinal parts.

MEDICINAL USES Whooping cough, asthma, hay fever, convulsions, stomach ulcers, colic, and constipation.

Mandragora oflicinarum is its scientific name.

Lemon

Lemons can be used in curses and hexes to ensure that the people you want to ruin will experience the worst of their bad luck. Be careful when handling lemons, as they can cause blindness if ingested. Lemons attract the good in your life and can help them attract money and positive energy in your life.

The mountainous regions of southern Europe and northern Africa are where this perennial member of the mint family originally originated, but it has since naturalised in practically every warm or temperate region on the planet.

ASIA AND INDIA ARE NATIVE AREA.

Fruit, juice, and peel are its medicinal components.

MEDICAL USE: For treating kidney stones, the common cold, the flu, ringing in the ears, and Meniere's disease.

Citrus limon is its scientific name.

Marigold

There are several plants that may be used for protection, such as marigolds, which have historically been used to ward off evil, defend against spells, and cure mental and physical wounds.

Marigolds may be grown in the garden to help ward off pests and protect plants from pesticides and other pollutants. A few ounces of dried marigold petals create a small teapot or add to bathwater.

NATIVE AREA: Tropical America, South America, and the southwest of North America.

Flowers are a medical component.

Book 15:
Herbalism and Natural Medicine

Chapter 1:
Introduction to Herbalism

Welcome to the captivating realm of herbalism, a world where the healing power of nature meets the art of natural medicine. In this chapter, we embark on an enlightening journey to explore the wonders of herbalism and its profound impact on health and well-being.

Herbalism, also known as herbal medicine or herbology, is an ancient practice that harnesses the therapeutic potential of plants to support the body's innate ability to heal. This age-old wisdom has been cherished by civilizations throughout history, passed down through generations and refined by diverse cultures around the globe.

As we delve into the essence of herbalism, we unveil a profound philosophy rooted in the belief that true wellness encompasses the harmony of mind, body, and spirit. Herbalism recognizes the interconnectedness of these aspects, acknowledging that vibrant health emerges from nurturing the whole being, rather than solely addressing symptoms or ailments.

Tracing the roots of herbalism takes us on a captivating journey through time and across continents. From the ancient Egyptians' reverence for botanical remedies to the wisdom of traditional Chinese medicine, each culture has contributed its unique insights and herbal knowledge. Indigenous healers, intimately connected to the land, have cultivated their understanding of local plants, passing down traditional practices and remedies that continue to enrich the world of herbalism.

At the heart of herbalism lies a profound respect for the wisdom of nature. Through centuries of observation and experimentation, herbalists have identified the diverse properties and therapeutic benefits of an array of medicinal plants. From soothing chamomile and revitalizing ginseng to calming lavender and immune-boosting echinacea, nature's pharmacy provides a vast array of botanical allies to support our well-being.

In the pages that follow, we will delve deeper into the fascinating world of herbalism, exploring the art of preparing herbal remedies, understanding the various methods of administration, and uncovering the specific applications for common ailments. By embracing the knowledge and practices of herbalism, we open ourselves to a world of gentle yet potent healing, where the gifts of nature contribute to our vitality and flourishing.

Join us as we embark on this extraordinary journey into the realm of herbalism, where ancient wisdom and modern science converge to illuminate the path toward vibrant health and natural well-being.

Chapter 2:
History and Philosophy of Herbalism

In this chapter, we delve into the captivating history and profound philosophy of herbalism. We explore how herbalism has evolved throughout the ages, drawing inspiration from diverse cultures and embracing unique perspectives on health and healing.

The roots of herbalism stretch back to ancient civilizations, where plants were regarded as invaluable sources of healing. From the ancient Egyptians, who meticulously recorded their botanical knowledge on papyrus scrolls, to the Chinese, who developed a sophisticated system of herbal medicine, herbalism has flourished across the globe.

In Europe, herbalism took shape during the Middle Ages when knowledge of medicinal plants was preserved by monks and herbalists. The Renaissance period witnessed a resurgence of interest in herbal medicine, as scholars like Paracelsus explored the medicinal properties of plants and emphasized the importance of individualized treatments.

Indigenous cultures worldwide have also developed their unique herbal traditions, drawing upon their deep connection to the land and ancestral wisdom. Native American herbalism, for example, honors the sacred bond between humans and nature, emphasizing the spiritual aspects of healing and the significance of herbal remedies in maintaining harmony within the community.

The philosophy of herbalism is rooted in a holistic approach to health and well-being. It recognizes that the body is a complex ecosystem, interconnected with the mind and spirit. Herbalists embrace the belief that by restoring balance and addressing the underlying causes of illness, true healing can be achieved.

Herbalism also acknowledges the importance of individualization in treatment. Each person is viewed as a unique entity, with specific constitutional factors and needs. Herbalists carefully select plants and create personalized formulations to restore harmony within the individual, taking into account factors such as temperament, physical constitution, and the specific symptoms or imbalances presented.

Throughout history, herbalism has adapted to changing times and incorporated scientific advancements. Modern herbalists combine traditional wisdom with scientific research, exploring the active constituents of plants and their mechanisms of action. This integration of ancient knowledge and contemporary science enhances the understanding and application of herbal medicine in the present day.

As we embark on this journey through the history and philosophy of herbalism, we gain a deeper appreciation for the diverse cultural perspectives and the profound wisdom that has shaped this field. Join us as we explore the fascinating interplay between tradition, science, and the human quest for healing and well-being.

Chapter 3:
Basics of Natural Medicine

In this chapter, we embark on a journey to explore the fundamental principles and practices that form the bedrock of natural medicine. As we delve into the essence of this holistic approach to health and well-being, we discover the core elements that guide its philosophy.

At the heart of natural medicine lies a profound recognition of the intricate interplay between the various aspects of our being. Rather than viewing health as a collection of isolated symptoms, natural medicine embraces the concept of the whole person – body, mind, and spirit – as an interconnected system. It acknowledges that true wellness emerges from the harmonious balance and integration of these aspects.

A cornerstone of natural medicine is its emphasis on prevention and proactive health management. It recognizes the importance of cultivating a healthy lifestyle, nourishing our bodies with wholesome nutrition, engaging in regular physical activity, managing stress, and allowing ample time for rest and rejuvenation. By adopting these lifestyle practices, we lay a strong foundation for well-being and work to prevent the onset of disease.

One of the key principles of natural medicine is its commitment to individualized care. Recognizing that each person is unique, with their own constitution, genetic makeup, and life experiences, natural medicine tailors treatment to address the specific needs of the individual. This personalized approach ensures that interventions are tailored to each person's unique circumstances, fostering a deeper level of healing and restoration.

Natural medicine integrates a diverse array of therapeutic modalities and approaches. From herbal medicine and nutritional interventions to physical therapies, mind-body practices, and energy-based modalities, it draws upon a wide spectrum of tools to support healing. This integration allows for a comprehensive and multifaceted approach to addressing the complexities of health and well-being.

Central to the philosophy of natural medicine is the promotion of self-care. Natural medicine empowers individuals to become active participants in their own healing journey. By encouraging self-awareness, self-education, and self-responsibility, it fosters a deep sense of empowerment and autonomy. Through self-care practices such as conscious eating, regular exercise, stress reduction techniques, and mindful living, individuals can cultivate their own well-being and play an active role in maintaining their health.

As we navigate the terrain of natural medicine, we uncover the beauty and wisdom of a holistic approach to health. By embracing the principles of integration, prevention, individualized care, and self-empowerment, we embark on a path that honors the inherent healing potential within us, supporting us in achieving optimal well-being and a vibrant, balanced life.

Chapter 4:
Mind-Body Connection in Natural Healing

In this chapter, we embark on a fascinating exploration of the intricate relationship between the mind and body in the realm of natural healing. We delve into the profound understanding that our mental and emotional well-being can significantly impact our physical health, and vice versa. Through this exploration, we gain a deeper appreciation for the power of the mind-body connection in promoting holistic well-being.

Across cultures and throughout history, healing traditions have recognized the inherent link between our thoughts, emotions, and physical well-being. Natural healing approaches, such as herbal medicine and other holistic modalities, embrace the understanding that our mental and emotional states can profoundly influence our physical health.

At the heart of natural healing lies the recognition that the mind and body are not separate entities, but interconnected aspects of our being. They exist in a dynamic relationship, with each exerting an influence on the other. This unity invites us to explore the deeper layers of our consciousness and recognize the immense potential for healing that lies within ourselves.

Within the realm of natural healing, the power of the mind takes center stage. Practices such as mindfulness, meditation, visualization, and positive affirmations are integral to nurturing the mind-body connection. These techniques enable us to cultivate a state of inner balance, peace, and clarity, creating a harmonious environment for healing to unfold.

Mindfulness practices invite us to be fully present in the moment, embracing a non-judgmental awareness of our thoughts, emotions, and bodily sensations. By cultivating this heightened state of awareness, we can develop a deeper understanding of the impact our thoughts and emotions have on our physical well-being.

Meditation offers a pathway to stillness and inner peace. Through regular meditation practice, we can quiet the mind, release stress, and tap into a profound sense of calm. This state of inner tranquility provides fertile ground for the body's innate healing mechanisms to operate optimally.

Visualization techniques harness the power of the imagination. By creating vivid mental images of health, vitality, and healing, we can stimulate the body's natural healing responses. Visualizing ourselves in a state of wellness and picturing the restoration of balance and harmony can have a transformative impact on our overall well-being.

Positive affirmations serve as powerful tools to reprogram our subconscious mind. By consciously choosing and repeating positive statements, we can override negative thought patterns and beliefs that may hinder our healing process. Affirmations help us cultivate a positive mindset, shifting our focus towards health, vitality, and well-being.

Through the cultivation of the mind-body connection, we tap into the remarkable potential for healing and well-being that lies within us. By embracing practices that nurture this connection, we empower ourselves to take an active role in our own healing journey. The mind-body connection becomes a gateway to harmonious integration, supporting us in achieving optimal health and vibrant living.

Book 16:
Native American Tinctures

Chapter 1:
Introduction to Herbal Tinctures

In this chapter, we embark on an exploration of the captivating world of herbal tinctures. These concentrated extracts, celebrated for their healing properties, have been cherished for centuries. As we delve into their rich history, preparation methods, and therapeutic benefits, we gain a deeper appreciation for the power of these potent herbal remedies.

Herbal tinctures are a remarkable embodiment of nature's healing potential. Through a process called maceration, medicinal plants are immersed in a solvent, typically alcohol or a mixture of alcohol and water. This allows for the extraction of the plant's active constituents, creating a concentrated liquid that captures the essence of the herb. By harnessing the power of these herbal extracts, tinctures offer a convenient and effective means of utilizing the healing properties of plants.

The use of tinctures can be traced back to ancient times, where they held a prominent place in various healing traditions. Across cultures and continents, from traditional Chinese medicine to European herbalism, tinctures were revered for their therapeutic benefits. The art of tincture-making has been passed down through generations, preserving the wisdom of our ancestors and contributing to the vast wealth of herbal knowledge.

Preparing herbal tinctures is a process that combines scientific principles with the artistry of herbal medicine. It begins with selecting the appropriate plant material, considering factors such as its botanical identity, quality, and medicinal properties. Proper sterilization techniques are employed to ensure the integrity and safety of the tincture. The choice of solvent, whether it be alcohol or a mixture of alcohol and water, influences the extraction process and the resulting concentration of active compounds. The duration of extraction is carefully determined to optimize the extraction of the plant's beneficial constituents.

The therapeutic potential of herbal tinctures is vast and diverse. By concentrating the medicinal compounds of the plant, tinctures offer a potent and convenient means of delivering their healing benefits. The concentrated form allows for better absorption and assimilation in the body, promoting rapid and targeted effects. Tinctures can be used for a wide range of health concerns, from supporting immune function and enhancing digestion to promoting relaxation and relieving discomfort.

As we dive deeper into the world of herbal tinctures, we open ourselves to the wealth of knowledge and healing potential that these extracts offer. Through their long history of use and continued relevance in modern herbal medicine, tinctures provide us with a powerful tool to support our well-being and embrace the wisdom of nature's remedies.

Chapter 2:
Preparation of Tinctures

In this chapter, we explore the art and science behind the preparation of herbal tinctures. We dive into the step-by-step process, from selecting the appropriate plant material to creating a high-quality tincture that captures the essence of the medicinal herb.

Selecting the Right Plant Material:

The first step in tincture preparation is choosing the right plant material. Quality is key, as the effectiveness of the tincture depends on the potency and integrity of the herbs used. We explore considerations such as plant species, part of the plant to be used (leaves, flowers, roots, etc.), and the ideal time for harvest to ensure optimal medicinal properties.

Proper Cleaning and Drying:

Once the plant material is collected, it is important to clean it thoroughly to remove any dirt or debris. Proper drying techniques are then employed to preserve the potency of the herbs. We discuss various drying methods, such as air drying or using a dehydrator, and the importance of maintaining optimal temperature and airflow during the process.

Choosing the Solvent:

The choice of solvent is a crucial decision in tincture preparation. Alcohol, typically high-proof grain alcohol, is commonly used due to its ability to effectively extract the medicinal constituents of the plant. We also explore alternative solvents, such as glycerin or vinegar, which can be used for alcohol-free tinctures.

Maceration and Extraction:

Maceration is the process of steeping the dried plant material in the chosen solvent. We discuss the proper ratios of plant material to solvent and the importance of using non-reactive glass or ceramic containers for the maceration process. The duration of maceration depends on the herb being used and can vary from weeks to several months, allowing for a thorough extraction of the plant's beneficial compounds.

Straining and Filtering:

After the maceration period, the liquid extract is strained to separate the plant material from the tincture. We explore different straining methods, such as using cheesecloth or a fine mesh strainer, to ensure a clear and pure tincture. Filtration may also be employed to further refine the tincture and remove any sediment or particulate matter.

Storage and Dosage:

Finally, we discuss the proper storage of tinctures in dark glass bottles, away from direct sunlight and excessive heat. Proper labeling with the plant name, date of preparation, and dosage instructions is essential. We also delve into determining the appropriate dosage for tinctures, considering factors such as the herb's potency, individual needs, and guidance from experienced herbalists or healthcare professionals.

By mastering the art of tincture preparation, we unlock the potential of medicinal plants to support our well-being. The careful selection of plant material, the proper extraction methods, and the understanding of dosage and storage ensure that we can create high-quality tinctures that harness the healing properties of nature's remedies.

Chapter 3:
Utilizing Tinctures for Health and Well-being

In this chapter, we explore the diverse ways in which herbal tinctures can be utilized to support health and well-being. As we delve into the wide range of applications for tinctures, we uncover their versatility and effectiveness in promoting optimal wellness.

Internal Use:

Tinctures are commonly taken internally for their medicinal benefits. We discuss various methods of administration, such as taking tinctures directly under the tongue or diluting them in water, tea, or juice. We explore how tinctures can be used to support digestive health, promote immune function, enhance cardiovascular wellness, and address specific health concerns.

External Applications:

Tinctures also have a place in external applications for topical use. We explore how tinctures can be used in the form of compresses, liniments, or added to skincare products. From soothing skin irritations and relieving muscle tension to supporting wound healing and promoting healthy hair and scalp, tinctures offer a natural and versatile option for external wellness applications.

Customized Formulations:

One of the advantages of tinctures is their ability to be combined and customized to create unique formulations. We discuss the art of herbal formulation, where different tinctures can be blended together to address specific health concerns or individual needs. This flexibility allows for a personalized approach to herbal medicine, tailoring treatments to each person's unique requirements.

Supporting Holistic Well-being:

Tinctures are not only used to address specific health issues but also to promote overall holistic well-being. We explore how incorporating tinctures into daily self-care routines can enhance vitality, support emotional balance, and foster a deeper connection with nature. Tinctures can be incorporated into rituals, meditation practices, or simply enjoyed as part of a mindful wellness routine.

Safety and Considerations:

While tinctures are generally safe, it is important to consider individual sensitivities, allergies, and possible herb-drug interactions. We discuss the importance of consulting with a qualified healthcare professional or herbalist before using tinctures, especially if pregnant, breastfeeding, or taking prescription medications. We also emphasize the significance of using high-quality, properly labeled tinctures from reputable sources.

By harnessing the potential of herbal tinctures, we open ourselves to a world of natural remedies that support our health and well-being. Whether taken internally, used topically, or incorporated into personalized formulations, tinctures offer a versatile and effective means of harnessing the healing power of plants. By embracing their use with knowledge and care, we can enhance our vitality and cultivate a deeper sense of balance and harmony in our lives.

Book 17:
Native American Infusions

Chapter 1:
Herbal Infusions: Basic Concepts

I n this chapter, we embark on a journey into the realm of herbal infusions, exploring the basic concepts and techniques that unlock the medicinal potential of herbs through the art of infusion. We delve into the fascinating world of herbal teas and discover how these aromatic brews can nurture our well-being.

Unveiling Herbal Infusions:

Herbal infusions, also known as herbal teas or tisanes, are delightful beverages created by steeping aromatic plant material in hot water. Unlike true teas derived from the Camellia sinensis plant, herbal infusions are caffeine-free and can be crafted from a wide range of herbs, flowers, leaves, and even roots. We explore the versatility and diversity of herbs used in infusions, each offering unique flavors and therapeutic properties.

The Art of Steeping:

Steeping is the process that allows the herbs to release their beneficial compounds into the water, creating a flavorful and aromatic infusion. We discuss the proper techniques for steeping herbal infusions, including water temperature, infusion time, and the importance of using high-quality, filtered water to enhance the taste and maximize the extraction of medicinal properties.

Customizing Your Infusions:

One of the joys of herbal infusions is the ability to create personalized blends tailored to individual preferences and wellness needs. We explore the art of blending herbs, discussing flavor profiles, and combining herbs to create balanced and harmonious infusions. Whether seeking relaxation, invigoration, immune support, or digestive aid, customizing herbal infusions allows us to craft beverages that align with our unique tastes and well-being goals.

Unleashing the Healing Power:

Herbal infusions offer more than just delightful flavors; they also possess a wealth of medicinal benefits. We delve into the therapeutic properties of various herbs commonly used in infusions, such as calming chamomile, uplifting peppermint, soothing lavender, and revitalizing nettle. By understanding the properties of different herbs, we can intentionally select those that support our specific health needs and promote overall wellness.

Ritual and Mindfulness:

Beyond their medicinal properties, herbal infusions invite us to embrace moments of ritual and mindfulness. We explore the art of creating a mindful tea-drinking practice, savoring each sip and cultivating an awareness of the present moment. Infusions can be enjoyed as a form of self-care, providing an opportunity to pause, reconnect with nature, and nurture our well-being.

As we journey into the realm of herbal infusions, we discover the enchantment and healing potential of these aromatic brews. By exploring the art of steeping, customizing blends, understanding the medicinal properties of herbs, and embracing mindful tea-drinking rituals, we unlock a world of sensory delight and holistic wellness. Join us as we sip and savor the magic of herbal infusions, immersing ourselves in the gentle embrace of nature's remedies.

Chapter 2:
Preparation and Usage of Infusions

In this chapter, we delve into the art of preparing and using herbal infusions. We explore the step-by-step process of creating flavorful and therapeutic infusions, as well as the various ways they can be incorporated into our daily lives for maximum well-being.

Gathering and Preparing Herbs:

The first step in preparing herbal infusions is gathering high-quality herbs. Whether using fresh or dried herbs, we discuss the importance of sourcing herbs from reputable suppliers or growing them in your own garden. We also explore the proper handling and storage of herbs to preserve their freshness and potency.

Infusion Techniques:

We delve into the different methods of infusion, from the traditional steeping in hot water to the more advanced techniques like cold infusions and sun teas. We discuss the optimal water temperature and steeping times for different herbs, ensuring the extraction of their aromatic flavors and medicinal properties.

Straining and Filtering:

Once the infusion is complete, it is essential to strain and filter the liquid to remove any plant material. We explore various straining methods, such as using a fine-mesh sieve or cheesecloth, to achieve a clear and smooth infusion. Proper straining and filtration contribute to the overall enjoyment of the infusion.

Enhancing Flavor and Benefits:

Herbal infusions can be customized to enhance their flavor and therapeutic benefits. We explore ways to enhance the taste of infusions, such as adding a touch of honey, lemon, or other natural sweeteners and flavorings. Additionally, we discuss the potential benefits of combining different herbs in a single infusion to create synergistic effects.

Serving and Enjoyment:

The serving and enjoyment of herbal infusions are just as important as their preparation. We discuss different serving vessels, such as teapots or individual cups, and the importance of using heat-resistant materials. We also explore the art of mindful tea-drinking, encouraging a moment of pause and presence to fully savor the flavors and embrace the therapeutic experience.

Incorporating Infusions into Daily Life:

Herbal infusions offer a versatile way to incorporate the benefits of herbs into our daily lives. We discuss various ways to enjoy infusions, from sipping them as standalone beverages to incorporating them into recipes for soups, smoothies, or herbal popsicles. Infusions can also be used topically for skincare or hair rinses, expanding their usefulness beyond internal consumption.

By mastering the art of herbal infusion preparation and usage, we unlock a world of sensory delight and well-being. From the gathering of herbs to the thoughtful steeping and enjoyment of flavorful infusions, we can embrace the therapeutic benefits of these natural brews in our daily lives. Join us as we savor the aromatic pleasures and holistic nourishment that herbal infusions offer, inviting nature's healing touch into every cup.

Chapter 3:
Infusions for Health and Treatment of Specific Disorders

In this chapter, we delve into the therapeutic potential of herbal infusions and explore their application in promoting health and addressing specific health concerns. We uncover the healing properties of various herbs and discover how infusions can be used as natural remedies for a wide range of disorders.

Promoting Digestive Health:

Herbal infusions can provide gentle and effective support for digestive health. We discuss herbs like peppermint, chamomile, ginger, and fennel, which are known for their digestive properties. These infusions can help alleviate symptoms such as indigestion, bloating, nausea, and digestive discomfort.

Supporting Immune Function:

Certain herbs possess immune-boosting properties that can help fortify our body's defense mechanisms. We explore infusions made from herbs like echinacea, elderberry, astragalus, and rosehip, which are renowned for their immune-supportive qualities. These infusions can be used to strengthen the immune system and promote overall well-being.

Calming the Nervous System:

Stress and anxiety can take a toll on our overall well-being. Herbal infusions offer a natural and soothing way to calm the nervous system and promote relaxation. We discuss infusions made from herbs such as lavender, lemon balm, passionflower, and chamomile, known for their calming and anxiety-reducing properties.

Supporting Sleep and Relaxation:

Restful sleep is essential for our overall health and vitality. We explore the soothing properties of herbs like valerian root, chamomile, passionflower, and lavender, which can be used to create infusions that promote relaxation and support a good night's sleep.

Addressing Respiratory Conditions:

Herbal infusions can be used to alleviate respiratory symptoms and support respiratory health. We discuss infusions made from herbs such as thyme, eucalyptus, peppermint, and licorice, which possess expectorant, decongestant, and soothing properties. These infusions can provide relief from coughs, congestion, and other respiratory discomforts.

Supporting Women's Health:

Women's health can be supported by specific herbal infusions. We explore the benefits of infusions made from herbs like red raspberry leaf, nettle, dong quai, and chasteberry, which can help regulate menstrual cycles, alleviate menstrual cramps, support hormonal balance, and promote overall reproductive health.

Enhancing Skin Health:

Herbal infusions can be used topically or consumed to support healthy skin. We discuss the benefits of infusions made from herbs like calendula, chamomile, green tea, and burdock root, which possess anti-inflammatory, antioxidant, and skin-soothing properties. These infusions can be used as facial steams, compresses, or consumed to promote radiant and healthy skin.

By harnessing the healing properties of specific herbs in the form of infusions, we unlock a natural and gentle way to address specific health concerns. As we explore the therapeutic potential of various herbal infusions, we can tailor our brews to support our unique health needs and promote overall well-being. Join us as we discover the power of herbal infusions in promoting health and finding natural remedies for specific disorders.

Book 18:
Native American Remedies for Common Ailments

Chapter 1:
Headaches and Migraines

Headaches and migraines can be incredibly disruptive, causing discomfort and hindering our ability to carry out daily activities. In this chapter, we embark on a journey to explore natural remedies and holistic approaches that offer relief from these common ailments. By delving into the causes and triggers of headaches and migraines, we can adopt a comprehensive approach to managing and preventing them.

First and foremost, it is essential to understand the nature of headaches and migraines. These conditions are characterized by throbbing or pulsating pain in the head, often accompanied by additional symptoms such as sensitivity to light and sound, nausea, and even visual disturbances. By recognizing the different types of headaches, including tension headaches, cluster headaches, and migraines, we can gain insight into their distinct characteristics and potential triggers.

Identifying triggers is a crucial step in managing headaches and migraines effectively. Triggers can vary significantly from person to person, and it is important to pay attention to individual experiences and patterns. Some common triggers include stress, certain foods and beverages (such as caffeine, chocolate, and alcohol), hormonal changes, environmental factors (like bright lights and strong odors), and physical factors (such as poor posture or lack of sleep). By becoming aware of these triggers, individuals can take proactive measures to minimize their exposure and reduce the frequency or intensity of their headaches and migraines.

Natural remedies and holistic approaches play a significant role in relieving the symptoms associated with headaches and migraines. Herbal infusions can be particularly helpful, offering soothing and calming effects. Peppermint, known for its cooling properties, may help relieve tension and promote relaxation. Lavender, with its calming and stress-reducing qualities, can provide a sense of tranquility. Chamomile, renowned for its calming effects, may help alleviate headaches caused by stress and anxiety. These herbal infusions not only offer potential relief but also create a serene and comforting experience.

Additionally, lifestyle modifications can make a substantial difference in managing headaches and migraines. Regular exercise, adequate hydration, and sufficient sleep are foundational pillars of good health and can contribute to the prevention of headaches. Mindfulness techniques, such as meditation and deep breathing exercises, can help reduce stress levels and promote overall well-being. It is also crucial to establish consistent routines and prioritize self-care, allowing time for relaxation, hobbies, and activities that bring joy and foster a sense of balance.

Chapter 2:
Insomnia and Sleep Disorders

Achieving restful and rejuvenating sleep is crucial for our overall well-being. However, many individuals face challenges with insomnia and other sleep disorders that disrupt their ability to attain quality rest. In this chapter, we embark on a journey to explore natural remedies and holistic approaches that can help promote a deep and restorative sleep. By understanding the causes and triggers of insomnia and sleep disorders, we can adopt strategies to improve sleep quality and foster optimal rest.

Insomnia, a common sleep disorder, manifests as difficulty falling asleep, staying asleep, or experiencing non-restorative sleep. It can be caused by various factors, including stress, anxiety, certain medications, medical conditions, and lifestyle choices. By delving into the intricacies of insomnia, we gain insight into the underlying causes and triggers that contribute to sleep disturbances.

Other sleep disorders, such as sleep apnea, restless legs syndrome, and narcolepsy, can also significantly impact the quality of sleep. Understanding the nature of these disorders and their associated symptoms helps us recognize the specific challenges individuals face in achieving restful sleep.

Natural remedies and holistic approaches play a vital role in promoting healthy sleep patterns and addressing sleep disorders. Herbal infusions can be particularly beneficial in promoting relaxation and preparing the body for sleep. Chamomile, with its soothing and calming properties, is often recommended to aid in sleep initiation. Passionflower and valerian root are known for their sedative effects and may help improve sleep quality. Incorporating these herbs into a bedtime routine, through gentle infusion or aromatherapy, can create a peaceful and conducive environment for sleep.

In addition to herbal remedies, creating a conducive sleep environment is crucial for promoting restful sleep. This includes establishing a consistent sleep schedule, creating a comfortable and clutter-free sleep environment, and minimizing exposure to stimulating activities and screens before bedtime. Creating a soothing pre-sleep routine, such as practicing relaxation techniques or engaging in a calming activity like reading, can help signal the body and mind to unwind and prepare for sleep.

It is also important to consider lifestyle factors that may affect sleep quality. Regular exercise, especially earlier in the day, promotes overall physical and mental well-being and can contribute to better sleep. Managing stress through practices like mindfulness meditation, deep breathing exercises, or journaling can help calm the mind and promote relaxation before bedtime. Additionally, adopting a balanced diet, limiting caffeine and alcohol consumption, and avoiding heavy meals close to bedtime can support better sleep patterns.

For individuals experiencing chronic or persistent sleep disorders, seeking guidance from a healthcare professional or sleep specialist may be beneficial. They can provide further evaluation, diagnosis, and personalized recommendations to address specific sleep challenges.

Chapter 3:
Digestive Disorders

Maintaining a healthy digestive system is crucial for overall well-being, yet many individuals struggle with digestive disorders that disrupt their daily lives. In this chapter, we embark on a journey to explore natural remedies and holistic approaches that promote digestive health and address common digestive disorders. By understanding the causes and triggers of these conditions, we can implement strategies to support optimal digestive function and alleviate discomfort.

Digestive disorders encompass a wide range of conditions affecting the gastrointestinal tract, including indigestion, bloating, acid reflux, and irritable bowel syndrome (IBS). These conditions can manifest with symptoms such as abdominal pain, gas, diarrhea, constipation, or a combination of these. By delving into the intricacies of digestive disorders, we gain insight into their multifaceted nature and the potential factors contributing to their development.

Natural remedies and holistic approaches offer effective strategies for managing and alleviating digestive disorders. Herbal infusions can play a significant role in promoting digestive health. For example, chamomile has long been used to soothe digestive discomfort, reduce inflammation, and aid in digestion. Peppermint has been shown to relax the muscles of the gastrointestinal tract, easing symptoms of indigestion and bloating. Ginger is known for its anti-inflammatory and digestive properties, helping to relieve nausea, improve digestion, and reduce intestinal spasms. By incorporating these herbs into infusions, individuals can benefit from their therapeutic effects and support digestive well-being.

Dietary modifications also play a crucial role in managing digestive disorders. Implementing a balanced and fiber-rich diet, avoiding trigger foods that exacerbate symptoms (such as fatty or spicy foods), and practicing mindful eating can help support optimal digestion. Additionally, staying hydrated, consuming probiotic-rich foods (such as yogurt and fermented vegetables), and incorporating gut-friendly foods like ginger, turmeric, and fennel into meals can contribute to a healthy digestive system.

Lifestyle factors can significantly impact digestive health. Stress reduction techniques, such as meditation, deep breathing exercises, or engaging in calming activities like yoga or tai chi, can help manage stress-related digestive symptoms. Regular physical activity can also support healthy digestion by promoting movement in the gastrointestinal tract and reducing constipation.

In some cases, seeking guidance from a healthcare professional or gastroenterologist may be necessary, especially for individuals with chronic or severe digestive disorders. They can provide further evaluation, diagnosis, and personalized recommendations to address specific digestive challenges

Chapter 4:
Skin Conditions

Our skin is not only the largest organ in our body but also a reflection of our overall health and well-being. Skin conditions, such as acne, eczema, psoriasis, and dermatitis, can have a significant impact on our physical and emotional well-being. In this chapter, we embark on a journey to explore natural remedies and holistic approaches that promote skin health and address common skin conditions. By understanding the underlying causes and triggers of these conditions, we can implement strategies to nurture and maintain healthy, radiant skin.

Skin conditions can manifest in various ways and have different underlying causes. Acne, for example, occurs when hair follicles become clogged with oil and dead skin cells, leading to the formation of pimples, blackheads, and whiteheads. Eczema and dermatitis are characterized by red, itchy, and inflamed patches on the skin, often triggered by allergens or irritants. Psoriasis involves an overactive immune system, resulting in the rapid buildup of skin cells, causing thick, silvery scales and red patches on the skin. Understanding the distinct characteristics and triggers of these conditions is crucial in developing an effective approach to managing and treating them.

Holistic approaches to skin health involve addressing not only the symptoms but also the underlying factors contributing to skin conditions. One important aspect is maintaining a balanced and nutritious diet. Consuming a variety of fruits, vegetables, whole grains, and healthy fats provides the body with essential nutrients and antioxidants that support skin health. Additionally, staying hydrated by drinking an adequate amount of water each day helps keep the skin hydrated and promotes its elasticity.

Managing stress is another vital component of holistic skin care. Stress can trigger or exacerbate skin conditions, so implementing stress reduction techniques such as meditation, deep breathing exercises, or engaging in activities that promote relaxation can have a positive impact on the skin. Adequate sleep is also crucial for skin health, as it allows the body to repair and regenerate the skin cells during the night.

Incorporating herbal remedies into a skincare routine can provide natural support for various skin conditions. Calendula, with its anti-inflammatory properties, can soothe irritated skin and promote healing. Aloe vera has moisturizing and cooling effects, making it beneficial for soothing sunburns and dry skin. Tea tree oil possesses antibacterial properties and can be useful in managing acne. These herbal remedies can be used topically as creams, ointments, or infused into carrier oils for gentle application.

In some cases, seeking guidance from a dermatologist or skincare professional may be necessary, especially for chronic or severe skin conditions. They can provide further evaluation, diagnosis, and personalized recommendations tailored to the individual's specific needs.

Book 19:
Native American Antibiotics

Chapter 1:
Key Concepts of
Natural Antibiotics

Antibiotics have played a critical role in modern medicine, helping us combat bacterial infections and safeguard our health. However, the widespread use and misuse of synthetic antibiotics have raised concerns about antibiotic resistance. In this chapter, we embark on a journey to explore the key concepts of natural antibiotics, presenting alternative approaches that can support our immune system and effectively fight bacterial infections.

Natural antibiotics encompass a wide range of substances derived from plants, fungi, and other natural sources. These compounds possess inherent antimicrobial properties and have been used for centuries in traditional medicine to treat infections and promote healing. What sets natural antibiotics apart is their ability to inhibit the growth or destroy harmful bacteria, providing a holistic and less disruptive approach to combating bacterial infections.

When considering natural antibiotics, we can categorize them as broad-spectrum or narrow-spectrum. Broad-spectrum natural antibiotics, such as garlic, oregano oil, and grapefruit seed extract, exhibit activity against a wide range of bacterial strains. On the other hand, narrow-spectrum natural antibiotics, like tea tree oil or manuka honey, are more specific in their action, targeting certain types of bacteria. This diversity allows for a tailored approach in addressing specific bacterial infections.

In addition to their direct antimicrobial effects, natural antibiotics also play a crucial role in supporting and strengthening our immune system. They can stimulate immune responses, enhance the activity of immune cells, and promote overall immune health. By boosting our immune system, we empower our bodies to better defend against bacterial infections, reducing the need for synthetic antibiotics.

One significant advantage of natural antibiotics is their potential to minimize the risk of antibiotic resistance. Antibiotic resistance arises when bacteria adapt and develop mechanisms to withstand the effects of synthetic antibiotics. Natural antibiotics, with their complex composition of various bioactive compounds, offer a unique advantage. Bacteria may find it more challenging to develop resistance against the diverse array of compounds present in natural antibiotics. By judiciously utilizing natural antibiotics, we can help preserve the effectiveness of these valuable medicines and mitigate the risk of antibiotic resistance.

Incorporating natural antibiotics into our everyday lives is both practical and accessible. We can embrace them as part of a healthy and balanced diet, incorporating ingredients such as garlic, ginger, and turmeric into our meals. Herbal infusions made from antimicrobial herbs like thyme, echinacea, or sage can be enjoyed as flavorful and immune-boosting beverages. Additionally, topical applications of natural antibiotics, such as tea tree oil or aloe vera gel, can be utilized for skin infections or wound healing.

Chapter 2:
Herbs with Antibacterial Properties

Nature has bestowed upon us a rich abundance of plants and herbs, many of which possess extraordinary antibacterial properties. In this chapter, we embark on a journey to explore a selection of herbs celebrated for their remarkable ability to combat bacterial infections and promote healing. By delving into the antibacterial properties of these herbs, we can unlock their therapeutic potential and embrace them as valuable tools in our natural medicine arsenal.

Among the standout herbs with potent antibacterial properties is garlic (Allium sativum). Garlic has long been hailed for its culinary and medicinal uses. Its active compound, allicin, exudes antimicrobial effects that span a broad spectrum, targeting various bacteria responsible for respiratory and digestive tract infections. Whether consumed raw or cooked, integrated into our meals or taken in supplement form, garlic serves as a powerful ally in supporting immune health and combating bacterial infections.

Another notable herb renowned for its immune-enhancing and antibacterial properties is echinacea (Echinacea purpurea). Echinacea has been cherished for centuries as a natural remedy for colds, flu, and other infections. Its bioactive compounds stimulate the immune system, promoting the production of white blood cells that help fend off bacteria. With its broad-spectrum antimicrobial effects, echinacea can be utilized to support overall immune function and aid in the prevention and treatment of bacterial infections.

Tea tree oil (Melaleuca alternifolia) is a versatile and potent herbal extract with notable antibacterial properties. Originating from the leaves of the tea tree, this essential oil has long been used in traditional medicine for its antimicrobial effects. It exhibits activity against a wide range of bacteria, including those responsible for skin infections and respiratory conditions. Tea tree oil can be applied topically, either directly or diluted, to treat skin infections or used in inhalation therapy to alleviate respiratory symptoms.

Goldenseal (Hydrastis canadensis) is an herb indigenous to North America and has a history of traditional use as an antibacterial agent. The key compound in goldenseal, berberine, possesses antimicrobial properties and can inhibit the growth of various bacteria. This herb has been used topically for wound healing and internally for digestive infections. However, due to its popularity, it is important to ensure that goldenseal is sustainably sourced to avoid depleting wild populations.

The herb thyme (Thymus vulgaris) not only adds flavor to our culinary creations but also harbors impressive antibacterial properties. Thyme contains thymol, a potent antimicrobial compound known for its ability to inhibit the growth of bacteria. It has been utilized as a natural remedy for respiratory infections, such as bronchitis and sore throat, as well as for oral hygiene purposes. Incorporating thyme into our cooking or enjoying it as an herbal infusion can provide us with its beneficial antibacterial effects.

As we explore the remarkable world of herbs with antibacterial properties, we uncover a treasure trove of natural remedies that support our immune system and combat bacterial infections. From garlic's culinary versatility to echinacea's immune-boosting prowess, tea tree oil's topical application, goldenseal's historical significance, and thyme's culinary and medicinal uses, these herbs offer an arsenal of antibacterial support. By incorporating these herbs into our holistic approach to wellness, we can tap into the power of nature and embrace the bounty it offers in promoting our health and well-being.

Chapter 3:
Using Natural Antibiotics for Infections and Diseases

In this chapter, we embark on a practical exploration of how natural antibiotics can be effectively used to address infections and diseases. We delve into the diverse ways in which these powerful remedies can be harnessed to combat bacterial infections, bolster immune health, and promote overall well-being. By understanding the practical application of natural antibiotics, we can embrace a holistic approach to healing and unlock our body's innate potential to fight infections.

One effective way to utilize natural antibiotics is through topical application. When it comes to skin infections, tea tree oil stands out as a powerful natural remedy. Diluted tea tree oil can be directly applied to the affected area, harnessing its potent antimicrobial properties to combat bacterial growth and promote healing. Aloe vera gel, renowned for its soothing and restorative effects, can also be used topically to alleviate skin irritations and facilitate wound healing. These topical applications provide targeted antibacterial effects while nourishing and protecting the skin.

Incorporating natural antibiotics into our oral consumption practices can be highly beneficial in combating internal bacterial infections and supporting immune health. Garlic, with its broad-spectrum antimicrobial properties, can be easily incorporated into our meals or taken as a supplement. Whether raw, cooked, or in capsule form, garlic's bioactive compounds enter our system, aiding in the fight against bacterial infections. Echinacea, known for its immune-enhancing effects, can be consumed as a tea infusion or in the form of capsules.

By ingesting natural antibiotics, we allow their bioactive compounds to circulate throughout our bloodstream, strengthening our immune response and aiding in the elimination of harmful bacteria.

Another method of using natural antibiotics is through herbal infusions or teas. Infusing antimicrobial herbs such as thyme, sage, or chamomile allows us to extract their beneficial compounds and enjoy them in a warm and soothing beverage. These herbal infusions can support immune health, soothe respiratory infections, and provide a comforting experience.

It is important to note that while natural antibiotics offer significant therapeutic potential, they should not be seen as a replacement for professional medical advice. For severe or persistent infections, it is essential to consult with a healthcare professional who can provide an accurate diagnosis and prescribe the appropriate treatment.

By embracing the practical application of natural antibiotics, we tap into the innate wisdom of nature and unlock powerful tools to support our health. Whether through topical application, oral consumption, or herbal infusions, natural antibiotics offer us a holistic and empowering approach to combating bacterial infections and promoting overall well-being. Let us embrace the synergy between nature and our bodies as we embark on this journey of healing and vitality.

Book 20:
Native American Medicinal Herbs and Natural Remedies

Chapter 1:
Introduction to Medicinal Herbs

Nature has long been a source of healing and well-being, providing us with a vast array of medicinal herbs. In this chapter, we embark on a journey to explore the world of medicinal herbs, uncovering their fascinating properties and potential for promoting health and healing. By understanding the principles of medicinal herbs, we can tap into the bountiful offerings of nature and embrace their therapeutic benefits.

The Power of Medicinal Herbs:

Medicinal herbs have been used for centuries in various traditional healing systems, such as Ayurveda, Traditional Chinese Medicine, and Indigenous practices. These herbs contain bioactive compounds that interact with our bodies to promote health and healing. From enhancing immune function to reducing inflammation and supporting organ systems, medicinal herbs offer a holistic approach to well-being.

The Diversity of Medicinal Herbs:

The world of medicinal herbs is incredibly diverse, with a multitude of plants offering unique healing properties. Some well-known examples include chamomile, known for its calming and digestive benefits, and lavender, cherished for its relaxing and soothing effects. Other notable herbs include echinacea, turmeric, ginseng, and ginger, each with its own set of therapeutic properties and applications.

Methods of Preparation:

Medicinal herbs can be prepared in various forms to optimize their healing potential. Herbal infusions, also known as herbal teas, involve steeping dried herbs in hot water to extract their beneficial compounds. Tinctures are concentrated herbal extracts typically made by macerating herbs in alcohol or glycerin. Other preparations include capsules, powders, oils, and salves, offering flexibility in incorporating medicinal herbs into our daily lives.

Holistic Approach to Healing:

Medicinal herbs embrace a holistic approach to healing, addressing the underlying causes of imbalances and supporting the body's natural healing processes. Rather than targeting specific symptoms, they aim to restore harmony and promote overall well-being. This holistic perspective acknowledges the interconnectedness of our physical, mental, and emotional health.

Safety and Precautions:

While medicinal herbs are generally considered safe, it is important to exercise caution and consult with a healthcare professional, especially if you have underlying health conditions or are taking medications. Some herbs may interact with certain medications or have contraindications for specific individuals. Understanding proper dosages and potential side effects is crucial for safe and effective use.

As we delve into the world of medicinal herbs, we open ourselves to a treasure trove of natural remedies and healing potential. By embracing their therapeutic benefits, we can incorporate medicinal herbs into our daily routines, promoting health, balance, and vitality. Let us journey together into the realm of medicinal herbs and discover the transformative power of nature's pharmacy.

Chapter 2:
Preparation and Usage of Medicinal Herbs

In this chapter, we explore the various methods of preparing and utilizing medicinal herbs to harness their healing potential. From herbal infusions to tinctures and other preparations, understanding the different techniques allows us to unlock the full benefits of these remarkable plants. By mastering the art of preparation and usage, we can effectively incorporate medicinal herbs into our wellness routines and experience their transformative effects.

Herbal Infusions:

Herbal infusions, commonly known as herbal teas, are a popular and accessible way to prepare medicinal herbs. To create an infusion, dried herbs are steeped in hot water, allowing their beneficial compounds to infuse into the liquid. This gentle extraction method retains the herb's volatile oils and delicate properties. Herbal infusions can be enjoyed on their own or combined with other herbs for a customized blend.

Decoctions:

Decoctions are another method of preparing medicinal herbs, particularly for tougher plant materials like roots, barks, and seeds. In this process, the herbs are simmered in water over low heat for an extended period, extracting their beneficial components. Decoctions tend to be more concentrated than infusions and are often used for herbs with stronger medicinal properties.

Tinctures:

Tinctures are concentrated herbal extracts typically made by macerating herbs in alcohol or glycerin. This method extracts the herb's active constituents, resulting in a potent and shelf-stable liquid. Tinctures offer convenience and versatility in dosage and can be taken orally or applied topically. They are especially useful for herbs that require a higher concentration or have a longer shelf life.

Powders and Capsules:

Medicinal herbs can also be prepared in powdered form for ease of consumption. Dried herbs are ground into a fine powder, which can be encapsulated or added to food and beverages. Powders and capsules offer a convenient way to incorporate herbs into daily routines, especially when precise dosages are desired or when the taste of certain herbs is less desirable.

Oils and Salves:

Some medicinal herbs lend themselves well to external applications. Herbal oils can be created by infusing herbs in carrier oils, such as olive oil or coconut oil, to extract their therapeutic properties. These oils can be used for massage, topical applications, or added to bathwater. Herbal salves, made by combining infused oils with beeswax, provide a semi-solid preparation suitable for topical use on skin conditions, wounds, or muscle aches.

As we explore the various methods of preparing and using medicinal herbs, it is important to remember that each herb may require different preparation techniques and dosages. It is advisable to consult reliable sources, herbalists, or healthcare professionals to ensure proper usage and to understand any potential interactions or contraindications.

By mastering the art of preparation and understanding the diverse applications of medicinal herbs, we unlock their full potential for healing and well-being. Whether through herbal infusions, tinctures, powders, oils, or salves, these preparations offer us a gateway to the transformative power of nature's medicine. Let us embrace the wisdom of traditional practices and modern knowledge as we incorporate the preparation and usage of medicinal herbs into our holistic wellness journey.

Chapter 3:
Natural Remedies for Specific Health Issues

In this chapter, we delve into the world of natural remedies for specific health issues. We explore how medicinal herbs and holistic approaches can be utilized to address common ailments and promote well-being. By understanding the targeted applications of natural remedies, we can embrace personalized approaches to support our health and find relief from specific health concerns.

Headaches and Migraines:

Headaches and migraines can be debilitating, affecting our daily lives. Natural remedies offer a range of solutions to alleviate the pain and discomfort. Peppermint oil, applied topically or inhaled, can provide a cooling effect and relieve tension headaches. Feverfew, an herb known for its anti-inflammatory properties, may help reduce the frequency and severity of migraines. Relaxation techniques, such as deep breathing exercises or meditation, can also complement natural remedies for headache relief.

Insomnia and Sleep Disorders:

Restful sleep is essential for our overall well-being. Natural remedies can promote better sleep and address insomnia and sleep disorders. Herbal infusions, such as chamomile or valerian root, have calming properties that can help relax the mind and induce sleep. Lavender oil, used in aromatherapy or as a topical application, can promote relaxation and improve sleep quality. Establishing a consistent bedtime routine and creating a conducive sleep environment are also important factors in achieving restful sleep.

Digestive Disorders:

Digestive disorders, such as indigestion, bloating, and acid reflux, can significantly impact our quality of life. Natural remedies offer gentle yet effective solutions to support digestive health. Ginger, known for its anti-inflammatory properties, can help soothe digestive discomfort and improve digestion. Peppermint tea can alleviate symptoms of indigestion and bloating. Probiotic-rich foods, such as yogurt and fermented vegetables, promote a healthy gut microbiome, aiding digestion. Additionally, mindful eating practices, such as chewing food thoroughly and eating in a relaxed environment, can support optimal digestion.

Skin Conditions:

Skin conditions like acne, eczema, and psoriasis can affect our confidence and well-being. Natural remedies offer holistic approaches to promote healthy skin. Tea tree oil possesses antimicrobial properties that can help combat acne-causing bacteria. Aloe vera gel, with its soothing and moisturizing effects, can alleviate skin irritations and promote healing. Calendula, known for its anti-inflammatory properties, can provide relief for various skin conditions. Maintaining a balanced and nutrient-rich diet, along with proper skincare routines, also plays a crucial role in managing skin health.

By exploring natural remedies for specific health issues, we can embrace personalized approaches to well-being. It is important to note that these remedies are intended as complementary approaches and may not replace professional medical advice. Consulting with healthcare professionals, herbalists, or naturopaths can provide further guidance and ensure the integration of natural remedies within a comprehensive healthcare plan.

With the wealth of natural remedies available, we can nurture our health and find relief from specific health concerns. By incorporating targeted herbs, lifestyle adjustments, and holistic practices, we empower ourselves to support our well-being and embark on a journey of natural healing. Let us embrace the wisdom of nature and the transformative power of natural remedies as we navigate the path to better health and vitality.

Conclusion

One of the most distinctive cultures in the world is that of the Native Americans. It is rife with tradition and has a long history. This is reflected in the medication they utilise, which is focused on natural cures and treatments. Native Americans and their cultural practises in medicine are among the many contributions they may provide to the world. Here is a summary of Native American culture and medicine.

Herbalism is one of the primary forms of Native American medicine. Herbalism is the practise of treating or preventing disease with herbs. Herbs can be used topically or internally. They can be consumed as dietary supplements or used in conventional therapeutic rituals. Native Americans employ more than 1,000 plants, many of which have medicinal characteristics, to treat everything from cancer to simple colds.

Sagebrush, cedar tree bark, catnip, wild oregano, chamomile, calendula flowers, lavender flowers, and raspberry leaves are a few common plants utilised by Native Americans. Sagebrush is one illustration; it eases the symptoms of asthma, nausea, and migraines. Additionally helpful for reducing pain and relaxing your nerves is cedar tree bark. Both animals and people frequently use catnip as a sedative, and studies have shown that it can also aid with anxiety reduction and memory enhancement. Wild oregano contains anti-inflammatory qualities and may be used to treat a variety of conditions, such as diarrhoea, colds, and flu symptoms. In addition to being a potent sedative, chamomile has been found to assist persons with dementia or Alzheimer's disease feel less anxious. Calendula flowers are used to treat a variety of skin conditions and can lessen the visibility of scars. It is common practise to use lavender flowers to alleviate sleeplessness and anxiety. In contrast, raspberry leaves are a safe and effective natural remedy for inflammation, fever, and diarrhoea.

Native American healing practises are frequently regarded as some of the most efficient and comprehensive types of medicine. These medications frequently have a long history of usage by indigenous people and were generally created using conventional techniques and materials. A number of factors can make Native American remedies substantially distinct from modern medicine. For instance, plants or herbs are frequently the key components of traditional American remedies. Modern medications, on the other hand, frequently employ more synthetic materials.

Native American remedies are frequently created to cure particular ailments as well. Modern medications, in contrast, aim to either prevent or treat illnesses. Despite these variations, both types of medication have benefits and drawbacks.

The fact that native American remedies are frequently more successful than modern drugs in treating specific illnesses is one of their major benefits. Since Native American treatments focus on the root causes of these issues rather than merely treating the symptoms, they are frequently effective for curing ailments including diabetes, asthma, and arthritis. Additionally, native American cures are frequently more successful than contemporary drugs at treating chronic ailments since they are based on conventional techniques and components.

Native American remedies can often be less safe for long-term usage than contemporary drugs, which is a significant drawback. If used improperly or in excessive dosages, some native American treatments can have strong, harmful consequences. Additionally, some indigenous people may be forced to utilise inferior substitutes since they don't always have access to high-quality native American remedies.

Overall, compared to modern drugs, native American remedies offer both numerous benefits and drawbacks. They can be less safe and more challenging to operate, even if they sometimes may be more effective.

Some of the oldest living cultures in the world are those of the Native Americans. They have a lengthy history, and their traditions and rituals are distinctive. Native Americans are a culturally varied group, with each tribe having its own traditions and worldview. They hunt and do subsistence farming as a way of life.

Tribes who live on the ground, like the Apache and Navajo, must be able to swiftly adjust to shifting climatic conditions since they live in arid environments. On the Great Plains, where they must be able to travel great distances for the game, the nomadic Lakota Sioux people dwell.

Based on their religious convictions, each tribe has its own traditional medical practises. For instance, the Cherokee cure themselves with botanical medicines. The Apache, on the other hand, employ medicinal plants and animal parts to heal illnesses.

The culture of the Native Americans is extensive, complicated, and full of deeply held beliefs and customs. Spirituality, community, regard for the environment, and faith in the force of nature are some of the most essential values for Native Americans.

Native American worldviews serve as the foundation for their spiritual beliefs. They think that everything, including plants, animals, and common occurrences like thunder and lightning, has a spirit. Native Americans get protection and guidance from these spirits as they go through life.

Community is yet another essential trait for Native Americans. In their eyes, all living creatures are a part of a bigger system. Native Americans hold that in order to be happy and content, one must be connected to both the spiritual and the ground of their society. Many traditional Native American rites and ceremonies are built on this link.

The medical tradition of Native Americans is one of their most well-known cultural aspects. For thousands of years, aboriginal people have used traditional remedies to heal both physical and mental disorders. Many of these medications are being utilised in conventional therapeutic rituals today.

Native American culture is rich in customs and principles that have moulded the peoples' present-day identities.

Made in United States
Troutdale, OR
04/27/2024

19476208R00190